MONOGRAPHS OF THE
SOCIETY FOR RESEARCH IN
CHILD DEVELOPMENT

Serial No. 259, Vol. 64, No. 4, 1999

ADOLESCENT SIBLINGS IN STEPFAMILIES: FAMILY FUNCTIONING AND ADOLESCENT ADJUSTMENT

E. Mavis Hetherington,
Sandra H. Henderson, and David Reiss

IN COLLABORATION WITH
Edward R. Anderson
Margaret Bridges
Raymond W. Chan
Glendessa M. Insabella
Kathleen M. Jodl
Jungmeen E. Kim
Anne S. Mitchell
Thomas G. O'Connor
Monica J. Skaggs
Lorraine C. Taylor

WITH COMMENTARY BY
James H. Bray

MONOGRAPHS OF THE SOCIETY FOR RESEARCH IN CHILD DEVELOPMENT
Serial No. 259, Vol. 64, No. 4, 1999

CONTENTS

ABSTRACT

HETHERINGTON, E. MAVIS, HENDERSON, SANDRA H., and REISS, DAVID, in collaboration with ANDERSON, EDWARD R.; BRIDGES, MARGARET; CHAN, RAYMOND W.; INSABELLA, GLENDESSA M.; JODL, KATHLEEN M.; KIM, JUNGMEEN E.; MITCHELL, ANNE S.; O'CONNOR, THOMAS G.; SKAGGS, MONICA J.; and TAYLOR, LORRAINE C.; Adolescent Siblings in Stepfamilies: Family Functioning and Adolescent Adjustment. With commentary by James H. Bray. *Monographs of the Society for Research in Child Development*, 1999, **64**(4, Serial No. 259).

This longitudinal study examined family relationships and the adjustment of two adolescent siblings, varying in the degree of biological relatedness, in nonstepfamilies and in stabilized simple and complex stepfamilies. All couples in stepfamilies had been remarried for a minimum of 5 years and an average of 9 years. Families were seen twice, 3 years apart. Family relationships and children's adjustment were assessed using interview and questionnaire measures obtained from mothers, fathers/stepfathers, and the two siblings and from observational measures of family interactions in the home. Family type and gender differences in marital relationships, parent-child relationships, and sibling relationships as well as in adolescent adjustment were examined.

The results suggest that, even in these long-established stepfamilies, there are some differences in family relationships and in adolescent adjustment from those in nonstepfamilies. Few differences, however, between nonstepfamilies and simple stepfamilies, in which all children were fully biologically related siblings from the mothers' previous marriage, were found. Results obtained were associated with differences in biological relatedness between family members and with living in a complex stepfamily household in which residential siblings had different relationships to the biological parents. Mothers were higher than fathers in all aspects of parenting, however, including amount of time spent in child care, warmth, negativity, control, and monitoring. Greater caretaking involvement and warmth were found for parents with their own biologically related children than with step-children. Biologically related siblings showed both more positivity and negativity in their relationships than did stepsiblings. Being in a complex stepfamily, in contrast to a nonstepfamily, was associated with more problems in family relationships such as parent-child conflict, and in adolescent adjustment such as lower social responsibility and cognitive agency, and higher externalizing in adolescents. There was no evidence that girls were more adversely affected than boys by being in a stepfamily, as has been found with younger children. Moreover, it was found that the associations among family process variables and adolescent adjustment were fairly similar for boys and girls and among different types of families.

Finally, there was evidence that adolescence is a time of considerable change in family relations and adolescent adjustment. A decrease in marital quality, decreases in parental warmth, monitoring and control, and mother-adolescent conflict, and decreases in sibling positivity and negativity were found over time. These patterns did not differ for the different family groups. Similarly, the declines in cognitive agency and self-worth and increases in sociability and autonomy over the course of the study were found in adolescents in all family types.

I. FAMILY FUNCTIONING AND THE ADJUSTMENT OF ADOLESCENT SIBLINGS IN DIVERSE TYPES OF FAMILIES

E. Mavis Hetherington

As marriage has become a more optional, less permanent institution there has been a decline in the proportion of two-parent households in first marriages and an increase in the number of single-parent households and stepfamilies in the United States. The percentage of children under age 18 living with both biological parents has decreased from 90% in 1970 to 69% in 1994 (U.S. Bureau of the Census, 1995). This change is, in large part, due to the increase since the early 1960s in both the divorce rate and birth rate to single mothers. Although there has been a modest decline in the divorce rate over the last 15 years, it still is estimated that 50% of marriages will end in divorce and about 60% of children born in the 1990s will live for some time in a single-parent household (Bumpass & Raley, 1995; Bumpass & Sweet, 1989; Furstenberg & Cherlin, 1991). Although the number of households headed by a single father has tripled since 1974, making them the fastest growing family type in the United States, over 80% of single-parent households are headed by mothers (Meyer & Garasky, 1993).

Living in a single-parent household is a temporary situation for most parents and children, as 75% of men and 66% of women eventually will remarry (Booth & Edwards, 1992; Bumpass & Raley, 1995; Bumpass, Sweet, & Castro-Martin, 1990; Cherlin & Furstenberg, 1994). Thirty percent of divorced people remarry within a year (Wilson & Clarke, 1992), and within 4 years of parental separation, half of all children whose parents divorced will have a stepfather enter the family (Furstenberg, 1988). The amount of repartnering of single and divorced parents has often been underestimated.

1

Cohabitation, which has increased dramatically, often occurs before or as an alternative to remarriage (Bumpass & Raley, 1995; Cherlin & Furstenberg, 1994; Ganong & Coleman, 1994).

Among remarriages, divorce occurs more rapidly and at a higher rate than in first marriages. Sixty percent of remarriages end in divorce and about one quarter of remarriages terminate within 5 years of the remarriage (Cherlin & Furstenberg, 1994; Tzeng & Mare, 1995). The presence of stepchildren increases the risk of marital dissolution in a remarriage by 50%, which may explain, in part, why couples with remarried wives, who are more likely to have custody of children, are twice as likely to divorce as those with remarried husbands (Tzeng & Mare, 1995). It is estimated that the time for restabilization of the family following remarriage is about 5 years, over twice as long as that for divorce, or restabilization may not occur at all because of the frequently altering composition, changes, and early divorce in stepfamilies. Hence many parents and children are experiencing additional family disruptions before stabilization in a stepfamily has occurred (Cherlin & Furstenberg, 1994; Hetherington, Bridges, & Insabella, 1998; Hetherington & Jodl, 1994; Visher & Visher, 1990).

PERSPECTIVES ON STEPFAMILIES

Although research on remarriage and stepfamilies has accelerated rapidly since 1980, it is only recently that substantial efforts to build and test alternative theories regarding remarriage and stepfamilies have arisen (Ganong & Coleman, 1994). No single theory is preeminent in guiding stepfamily research, although family systems theory dominates clinical conceptualizations and practice. Most researchers combine perspectives and test hypotheses based on multiple theories in their work and many theories are interrelated. A brief overview of four theoretical perspectives on family relations and child adjustment in stepfamilies will be provided as a background for the conceptual framework utilized in this *Monograph*.

Family Systems Perspective

Family systems theorists view each family member as part of an interdependent, interactional system in which the behavior of each individual or subsystem, such as the marital, parent-child, or sibling subsystem, modifies that of other subsystems. The whole family system, as well as the relationships and functioning of subsystems and individuals within the family, are altered in stepfamily formation. The greater complexity found in stepfamilies requires redefinitions of external boundaries involving who is or is not a

2

member of the stepfamily, and also of internal boundaries involving rules, roles, alliances, and membership within the stepfamily (Anderson et al., 1999; Bray, 1999; Bray & Berger, 1993; Crosbie-Burnett, 1989; Ganong & Coleman, 1994; McGoldrick & Carter, 1989; O'Connor, Hetherington, & Reiss, 1998). When families go through a transition, such as a remarriage, that involves multiple changes, stresses, and reorganization, there is a period of disruption and destabilizing in family relationships and functioning. This period often is followed by the gradual emergence of a new homeostasis, which may differ from that found among nuclear families in first marriages with biological children, and different patterns and processes may be salutary in nondivorced and remarried families (Bray & Berger, 1993; Hetherington & Jodl, 1994).

Risk and Resiliency Perspective

Remarriage and stepfamily formation involve notable life changes and an increase in both positive and negative life events (Hetherington, Cox, & Cox, 1985). It can present an escape from poverty for single mothers and an opportunity for forming new gratifying and supportive relationships that can promote the well-being of children and adults. It can offer a ready-made family for stepparents who want and enjoy children. It also can lead, however, to increased stress, problems in family relationships, and anger and acrimony that undermine the happiness, health, and adjustment of family members (Bray & Berger, 1993; Hetherington, 1989; Hetherington & Jodl, 1994). There is great diversity in the response to remarriage and to life in a stepfamily that depends on the balance between individual, familial, and extrafamilial vulnerability and protective factors (Hetherington, 1989, 1991a; Werner, 1993). In spite of the many changes and stresses encountered in stepfamily formation, most stepchildren in the long run emerge as reasonably competent, well-functioning individuals. They are resilient in the face of challenges to adjustment or development associated with living in a stepfamily. A minority of children, however, also manifest developmental delays and psychological and social problems associated with their parent's remarriage (Amato & Keith, 1991a; Bray & Berger, 1993; Hetherington, 1993; Hetherington & Clingempeel, 1992; Hetherington & Jodl, 1994). One of the major goals of this study is to examine some of the risk and protective factors that contribute to these variations in adjustment.

Evolutionary and Attachment Perspectives

Both evolutionary theory and attachment theory would predict that the formation of strong bonds of affection and involvement between stepparents

3

and stepchildren would be difficult (Glenn, 1994). Evolutionary theory emphasizes that human beings use reproductive strategies that increase the chances of survival of their genes into the next generation and hence are more invested in nurturing and protecting biological offspring than stepchildren (Daly & Wilson, 1987). Attachment theory, which also is based on evolutionary theory, would suggest that when behaviors in parents and infants that have evolved to promote bonding and survival of the young do not occur at the time of formation of specific attachments in the first year, secure attachments and close parent child relationships will be less likely to develop (Bowlby, 1969). Neither evolutionary theory nor attachment theory would propose that warm, caring relationships cannot develop with step-parents and stepchildren, but would suggest that such relationships will be more difficult to attain than with biological parents and children. The great diversity, however, in parent-child relations in stepfamilies, with many step-parents and stepchildren forming close relationships (Hetherington, 1994; Hetherington & Clingempeel, 1992), and the finding that some stepfathers invest more resources in residential stepchildren than in nonresidential biological children (Furstenberg & Cherlin, 1991), suggest that although biological relatedness and early attachment may be important, their influence can be modified or overridden by later experiences and family relationships.

Evolutionary theory also would suggest that differential parental treatment of siblings in the same family would be based more on differences in biological relatedness than on the type of family. Thus, greater differences in parental treatment would be expected with stepchildren and biological children, than with two siblings who were both biologically related to the parent in either a stepfamily or nonstepfamily. Within family differences in parental treatment of siblings or nonshared environment have been related to diverse aspects of children's social competence, various forms of externalizing such as antisocial behavior, delinquency, and oppositional behavior, and to internalizing including depression and suicidal ideation (e.g., Daniels et al., 1985; Dunn et al., 1990; Dunn & McGuire, 1994; Henderson, Hetherington, Mekos, & Reiss, 1996; Mekos, Hetherington, & Reiss, 1996; Reiss et al., 1995; Stocker, 1995; Tejerina-Allen et al., 1994).

Developmental Perspective

Families and children must cope with challenges associated with both normative and nonnormative life transitions. Different stages of development and different kinds of family transitions present families and their members with varied developmental challenges. The unique adaptive tasks confronted in adolescence and in stepfamilies are examined in this study.

Adaptive tasks in adolescence. This study focuses on family relationships and the adjustment of pairs of adolescent siblings assessed twice, 3 years apart, as the siblings move further into adolescence. Adolescence is a time of notable physical, social, emotional, cognitive, and behavioral changes. Some of the normative developmental tasks encountered in adolescence that will be examined in this study include becoming more independent and autonomous while maintaining bonds of attachment with family members, achieving in school and acquiring the learning skills needed for higher education or work, developing socially responsible behavior, forming close relationships within and across gender, and developing a coherent sense of identity involving positive self-worth (Masten & Coatsworth, 1998). Adolescence also is a time of the emergence of or increase in psychological disorders such as depression (Cicchetti & Toth, 1998) or antisocial behavior (Loeber & Stouthamer-Loeber, 1998), which also will be explored in this study.

It has been proposed that the first decade of life may be more difficult for boys and the second decade for girls as they cope with emerging sexuality and conflicting messages and standards about gender roles and achievement (Werner, 1993). Certainly depression increases (Cicchetti & Toth, 1998) and self-worth diminishes over the course of adolescence in girls (Block & Rubins, 1993; Masten & Coatsworth, 1998), although antisocial behavior is found to remain higher in boys (Loeber & Stouthamer-Loeber, 1998). In addition, it has been suggested that the adolescent transition may be particularly difficult for children in divorced or remarried families and that adolescence may trigger problems in children whose parents earlier have gone through marital transitions (Bray, 1999; Bray & Berger, 1993; Hetherington, 1993; Hetherington & Clingempeel, 1992; Hetherington & Jodl, 1994).

Adaptive tasks in stepfamilies. Each family transition and family form involves unique challenges, risks, and resources that may influence the adjustment and well-being of family members. Remarriage is the fastest route out of poverty for divorced single women and their children, and the addition of a stepparent may provide not only economic resources, but also emotional and instrumental support for custodial parents and children (Zill, Morrison, & Coiro, 1993). Higher rates, however, of marital dissolution in stepfamilies are found and most studies report no consistent benefits in emotional and social development, externalizing problems, or achievement for children in stepfamilies over those in single-parent households (Anderson et al., 1999; Cherlin & Furstenberg, 1994; Hetherington & Clingempeel, 1992; Hetherington & Jodl, 1994; Zill, 1988; Zill, Morrison, & Coiro, 1993). This suggests that other stresses and risk factors may be countering the potential advantages of a remarriage, or that the adverse consequences of divorce and life in a single-parent family may be difficult to overcome. To some extent, stepfamilies' success in coping with the adaptive

5

challenges they face depends on their past family history, expectations, and beliefs (Kurdek, 1994). When remarried families use traditional nuclear family functioning, roles, and relationships as their comparative ideal, clinicians suggest that dissatisfaction and problems within the stepfamily are inevitable (Bray & Berger, 1993; Visher & Visher, 1990).

Stepfamilies differ from other family forms not only in their structure, biological relationships, diversity, and complexity, but also in their roles and functioning. An overarching challenge that confronts all families is in constructing and agreeing on acceptable, fulfilling family roles and developing salutary relationships that promote the well-being of family members (Cherlin & Furstenberg, 1994; Ganong & Coleman, 1994; Hetherington & Jodl, 1994). This task may be more difficult in stepfamilies because of diverse marital and family histories, more complex family structure, and because of less social and legal consensus on stepparent roles and responsibilities (Cherlin & Furstenberg, 1994; Fine & Kurdek, 1994b).

Building a stepfamily consists of a set of unique challenges and adaptive tasks. The first adaptive task confronted by stepfamilies is to develop and sustain a strong marital bond in the presence of children. There is considerable evidence that, for many biological parents in first marriages, the birth of a child or presence of children is associated with declines in marital satisfaction and problems in marital relationships (Cowan & Cowan, 1990). In stepfamilies, the presence of children may present even greater risks for the conjugal relationship (Tzeng & Mare, 1995). The second task is the maintenance of a supportive relationship of biological parents with their children as the children are confronted with changes and concerns associated with the entry of stepkin. The third task involves developing and delineating constructive, agreed upon, and acceptable stepparent roles, relationships, and responsibilities. The fourth task is the child's adjustment to the parents' conjugal relationship, to possible alterations in the relationship with the biological custodial parent and to the formation of a relationship with a new stepparent. The fifth task is the development or maintenance by children of relationships with biological siblings, half siblings, and stepsiblings within and outside of the household.

The final task involves family members coping with relationships with kin and stepkin outside of the household, such as the noncustodial parent, nonresidential stepparent, grandparents, and stepgrandparents. When there have been multiple marriages of biological parents and stepparents and births to these various unions, such relationships can be diverse, labile, and complex (Bohannon, 1984; Clingempeel, Brand, & Segal, 1987; Ganong & Coleman, 1994). Children's membership in two or more households has become increasingly common and this membership often shifts over time (Ahrons & Wallisch, 1987; Jacobson, 1987; Maccoby & Mnookin, 1992), thus children's living arrangements have become increasingly complex and fluid.

GOALS OF THE STUDY

The views taken in this *Monograph* are taken from all of the above per-spectives. Family functioning, relationships among family subsystems, and the adjustment of two adolescent siblings in nonstepfamily and in simple and complex stepfamily households are examined. In this study, nonstepfamilies are families in which all of the children are the result of the couple's current marriage. Simple stepfamilies are those in which all children present in the home are from the mother's previous marriage. Complex stepfamilies in-clude households in which the siblings have different biological relationships with parents and thus may include both half siblings and stepsiblings. It should be noted that this definition of a complex stepfamily, which refers only to members of the household of primary residence, differs from that sometimes used, which also considers complexity of relationships with kin and stepkin outside the household (Bray, 1990a). The role of biological relat-edness in family relationships and the influence of differential parental treat-ment on the adjustment of adolescent siblings also are explored. Although it is recognized that relationships outside of the household are important and that many stepchildren spend time with noncustodial parents, it is relation-ships within the household of primary residence that are the focus of this presentation. Neither family relations external to the household of primary residence nor peer relations are systematically examined in this *Monograph*.

This study has some special features that are rare in studies of step-families, and these should be noted. First, it studies stabilized stepfamilies who have been married a minimum of 5 years and an average of almost 9 years. Thus, these families are more comparable to nonstepfamilies with marriages of longer duration. By this time the lifetime rates of marital dis-solution for first marriages and remarriages are fairly similar, although the risk for marital dissolution continues to be modestly greater in remarriages. According to women's reports, lifetime estimates of divorce are 19% in first marriages and 23% in second marriages at 5 years after marriage, and 30% and 37% at 10 years after marriage. According to men's reports, they are 16% in first marriages and 20% in second marriages at 5 years after marriage and 27% and 31% at 10 years (Sweet & Bumpass, 1987). Second, as noted above, it studies different kinds of stepfamilies and includes a large sample of blended families in which unrelated stepsiblings are present, one from the mother's previous marriage and one from the father's previous marriage. Since father custody occurs only in about 13% of divorces, studies involving a large sample of such families are relatively rare. Third, the study examines marital, parent-child, and sibling relationships and their associa-tion with the adjustment of two siblings in each family. Fourth, it explores the role of biological relatedness in family relationships in different types of families. Finally, since the relationships and adjustment of two same sex

7

adolescent siblings, no more than 4 years apart in age in each family is explored, it permits within family as well as more traditional between family analyses to be performed. It should be noted, however, that the controls in this study related to the duration of marriage, the use of adolescent same sex siblings and a large number of blended stepfamilies make generalizations to a randomly selected sample of stepfamilies inappropriate.

The literature review that follows is focused on research findings related to the issues examined in this study. A review of the research findings on family relations in stepfamilies will be followed by a discussion of the association of the marital relationship, parent-child relationship, and sibling relationship with the adjustment of children in stepfamilies and nonstepfamilies. Finally, a summary of research on the adjustment of children in different types of stepfamilies in comparison to nonstepfamilies will be presented.

FAMILY RELATIONSHIPS IN STEPFAMILIES

Papernow (1993) has remarked that family relationships in stepfamilies would be viewed as dysfunctional from a family systems perspective with new stepfamilies characterized by "a weak couple system, a tightly bonded parent-child alliance and potential interference in family functioning from an outsider" (p. 346). Other investigators have argued that there is nothing inherently problematic in stepfamilies (Coleman, 1994; Kurdek, 1994), and that diversity rather than deviance in structure, in family roles and relationships, and in the adjustment of family members in stepfamilies, should be emphasized (Ganong & Coleman, 1994; Hetherington, 1989; Hetherington and Jodl, 1994).

Many researchers have stated that the quality of family relationships and family processes are more important than family type or structure in shaping the adjustment of family members (Amato, 1994; Demo & Acock, 1996; Forgatch et al., 1995; Hetherington, 1993; Hetherington & Clingempeel, 1992; Simons et al., 1996, Zill, 1994). Although there are many similarities in the relationships among processes within and between family subsystems that contribute to adaptive functioning in nondivorced two-parent families and in stepfamilies, there also are some notable differences (Bray & Berger, 1993; Hetherington, 1989, 1991b, 1993). Researchers and clinicians report that stepfamilies, in comparison to nondivorced nuclear families, are less cohesive, have less clear role expectations, and are more flexible in response to change (Bray, 1988; Bray & Berger, 1993; Visher & Visher, 1988). It has been proposed that more open family boundaries that facilitate the multiple exits and entrances of children in binuclear families may be adaptive in stepfamilies. In addition, less close ties among family subsystems and decreased bonding and closeness in stepfamilies may promote adaptation to the unique challenges confronted by stepfamilies (Bray & Hetherington, 1993; Ganong & Coleman, 1994).

Adaptation in stepfamilies is a process that takes place over time and is influenced by preceding experiences in earlier marriages and cohabiting relationships in a divorced single-parent household. Following family transitions, there often are disruptions in family relationships and processes and in the adjustment of family members. These disruptions in family process, however, stabilize and moderate over time (Hetherington, 1989; Hetherington & Jodl, 1994). Most studies do not consider length of time in a family when comparing first married families and stepfamilies. Studies often compare long-established nondivorced families to stepfamilies in early stages of family formation, with detrimental conclusions drawn about stepfamilies (Hetherington & Clingempeel, 1992). Such research confounds the early stresses of family formation with characteristics and dynamics of stepfamily relationships. Few studies compare stabilized stepfamilies with stabilized families in first marriages as will be done in this study.

Marital Relationships in Stepfamilies

Many hypotheses have been advanced as to why marital relationships in first marriages and remarriages might differ and why marital dissolution occurs more rapidly and frequently in remarried families (Booth & Edwards, 1992; Bray, 1999; Ganong & Coleman, 1994). These hypotheses not only involve the incomplete institutionalization of stepfamilies, the difficulty in building a conjugal bond in the presence of children, and problems in coparenting, but also individual characteristics of spouses. Some of these characteristics are personality characteristics, others are attitudinal. Some divorce-prone individuals have characteristics such as unregulated behavior, depression, alcoholism, aggressiveness, or interpersonal insensitivity (Amato, 1993; Capaldi & Patterson, 1991; Forgatch, Patterson, & Ray, 1995; Gotlib & McCabe, 1990; McGue & Lykken, 1992) that increase their probability of having difficulties in social relationships, especially in intimate relationships, which will lead to multiple marital transitions.

In addition, some individuals are divorce-prone because of dysfunctional beliefs about relationships or a lack of commitment to marriage (Baucom & Epstein, 1990; Kelly & Conley, 1987, Kurdek, 1994). A previously married spouse, having survived one divorce, may have a lower tolerance or threshold for unsatisfying relationships and a higher threshold for gratifying ones, and may consider divorce a more acceptable option to an unsatisfying marriage (Booth & Edwards, 1992).

9

Researchers have been interested not only in differences and similarities in marital satisfaction, instability and the quality of the marital relationships in first marriages and in remarriages, but also in risk and protective factors associated with these marital outcomes and how they may vary in diverse family types.

Marital relations in diverse family forms. Differences in self-reports of marital satisfaction or of the quality of marital relationship of couples in first marriages and remarriages are found rarely and when obtained tend to be small in magnitude (Booth & Edwards, 1992; Ganong & Coleman, 1994). Marital satisfaction does decline more rapidly, however, in remarried than first married couples (Kurdek, 1991). Differences in the affective quality of the relationship are more likely to be found in observational than in self-report studies. Remarried couples have been observed to be more negative, coercive, and conflictual, less positive and supportive, and to have poorer problem-solving skills in their interactions (Bray, 1999; Bray & Berger, 1993; Hetherington, 1993; Hetherington & Clingempeel, 1992; Farrell & Markman, 1986; Larson & Allgold, 1987).

Research findings are more consistent in highlighting differences between spouses in stepfamilies and never divorced families on dimensions of the marital relationship other than marital satisfaction, such as coparenting roles and the division of household labor. Perhaps as a consequence of the different tasks of the remarriage, or because the processes of mate selection are different in first compared to second marriages (Spanier & Furstenberg, 1982), remarried couples view their relationships as comparatively more open and willing to confront conflict, more pragmatic and less romantic, and more egalitarian regarding both childrearing and household chores (Furstenberg, 1990; Giles-Sims, 1987; Hetherington et al., 1992). The contribution of coparenting roles, parent/child relationships and division of labor to marital satisfaction and functioning may be especially important in comparing nondivorced and remarried partners.

Marital quality and coparenting. Although remarried partners may report no differences from first married couples in marital satisfaction and general marital conflict, they do report that they have higher rates of conflict regarding childrearing (Schultz, Schultz, & Olson, 1991) and that childrearing issues are their most frequent source of dissension (Walker & Messinger, 1979). Complexity in stepfamily relations within the household with children differing in patterns of biological relatedness to the parents may increase conflict over childrearing, differential treatment, and differential involvement of parents with children (Henderson, Hetherington, Mekos, & Reiss, 1996; Hetherington & Jodl, 1994). It is well substantiated that parents are more involved and less disengaged with their own biologically related children than with stepchildren (Bray, 1999; Bray & Berger, 1993; Hetherington, 1993, 1999; Hetherington & Jodl, 1994), and mothers and fathers may be willing to assume more responsibility and do more work for their own children than a stepchild.

Associations among marital satisfaction, marital quality, and parent-child relationships. There is less consensus about the associations and direction of effects among marital satisfaction, marital quality, and parent-child relationships in stepfamilies compared to nondivorced families. Some of these inconsistencies may be related to child gender and age of the child at the time of remarriage and assessment, or to length of time in a remarriage.

In most first marriages, the marital relationship is viewed as the cornerstone of good family functioning. In stepfamilies, however, the centrality of the marital subsystem and the contribution of the functioning of the marital relationship to other subsystems and to the well-being of family members may differ from that in first marriages. It has been argued that subsystems are more encapsulated and independent in stepfamilies (Bray & Berger, 1993), and that the stepparent-stepchild relationship, rather than the marital relationship, is pivotal in stepfamilies (Crosbie-Burnett, 1984). Moreover, it has been suggested that to a greater extent in stepfamilies than in nondivorced families, marital functioning and instability is a product of the presence of children, the quality of the coparenting relationships, and of parent-child/stepchild relationships (Clingempeel, 1981; Hetherington & Clingempeel, 1992; Pasley & Ihinger-Tallman, 1988; White & Booth, 1985). Some studies have indicated that the associations among marital satisfaction, communication patterns, conflict resolution skills, and affect found in first marriages may not occur in remarriages (Farrell & Markman, 1986; Larson & Allgood, 1987).

In first marriages, a positive marital relationship provides emotional and instrumental support and promotes the psychological well-being and competent parenting of the spouse (Belsky, 1984; Cowan, Cowan, & Schulz, 1996). In first marriages, facilitative effects of a close marital relationship or negative effects of a conflictual, unsatisfying relationship are found more often in the parenting of fathers than mothers, especially fathers with daughters (Cowan et al., 1996). Although it has been speculated that the association between marital quality and the parent-child relationship may be less closely linked in stepfamilies, the results of research are inconsistent. Some studies have reported that early in a remarriage preadolescent children may be more resistant to the stepfather, if the marital relationship is close (Hetherington, 1991b; Hetherington & Jodl, 1994). Most studies, however, have found a harmonious, satisfying marital relationship is associated with competent parenting and more positive relations between children and parents not only in first marriages but also among children, parents, and stepparents in remarriages (Bray, 1999a, 1999b; Bray & Berger, 1993; Crosbie- Burnett, 1984; Fine & Kurdek, 1995; Hetherington, 1991b, 1993; Hetherington & Clingempeel, 1992; Hetherington & Jodl, 1994; Hobart, 1988). One study even reported that in stepfamilies the correlation between stepparents' perceptions of marital quality and their reports of the quality of their relationship with their stepchildren is higher than that found for biological parents and children (Fine & Kurdek, 1995).

When differences between first marriages and stepfamilies in the association between the marital relationship and parent-child relationship are found they are most likely to occur in the child's behavior toward the stepparent. This varies with age and gender. Preadolescent stepdaughters are more likely to show intense and sustained resistance to the entry of a stepfather and more conflict with the stepfather if the marital relationship is positive and satisfying, and if the daughter had been close to the biological custodial mother before the entry of the stepfather (Brand & Clingempeel, 1987; Hetherington, 1993). Although preadolescent boys also initially may resist the entry of a stepparent, they are more likely than girls eventually to accept and benefit from the presence of a stepfather. In addition, acceptance of the stepparent by boys is facilitated by a positive conjugal relationship (Amato & Keith, 1991a; Hetherington, 1993; Hetherington & Clingempeel, 1992; Hetherington & Jodl, 1994). In contrast to the gender differences found in association between the marital relationship and the child's behavior toward the stepparent in preadolescents, a satisfying, close marital relationship promotes more positive, harmonious stepfather-stepchild relationships with both adolescent daughters and sons (Bray & Berger, 1993; Hetherington, 1993; Hetherington & Jodl, 1994). It has been speculated that as girls go through the physical and social changes and heightened awareness and concern with sexuality that accompany adolescence, a close marital relationship may be perceived as a protective buffer against inappropriate intimacy between stepfather and stepdaughter (Hetherington, 1993).

Gender differences in childcare and the division of household labor in nondivorced and remarried families. Some of the most robust gender differences in the marital relationship have been found in participation in household tasks and in childcare (Perry-Jenkins & Folk, 1994; Thompson & Walker, 1989). Despite the increase in fathers' involvement in housework and childcare in the past 2 decades, husbands, in general, contribute much less time than do wives to the total amount of family work and they are more satisfied with the division of labor than are wives (Barnett & Baruch, 1987; Cowan, 1988; Hoffman, 1989; Crouter, Perry-Jenkins, Huston, & McHale, 1987). Remarried spouses report a more egalitarian relationship in dealing with household work and childrearing (Ganong & Coleman, 1989; Furstenberg, 1990; Giles-Sims, 1987), but couples in both types of families tend to divide these tasks along traditional gender roles, with the bulk of the childrearing responsibility falling on wives (Demo & Acock, 1993; Guisinger, Cowan, & Schuldberg, 1989). Although stepfathers may have the option to remain disengaged and participate less in childcare than do biological fathers, most divorced custodial fathers expect the new stepmother to participate actively in housework and in childcare and custodial fathers' concerns about child-care may be a major motivating factor for remarrying (Brand, Clingempeel, & Bowen-Woodward, 1988; Hetherington & Henderson, 1997).

Links among family role satisfaction, marital satisfaction, and personal well-being are stronger and more consistently obtained for wives than husbands (Ward, 1993). In fact, studies examining these links for husbands are so inconsistent that no firm conclusions can be drawn (Baruch & Barnett, 1987; Crouter, Perry-Jenkins, Huston, & McHale, 1987; Pleck, 1985; Ross, Mirowsky, & Hubor, 1983; Suitor, 1991). In wives, however, perceived fairness and satisfaction with household roles are associated with greater marital satisfaction and closeness (Greenberger & O'Neil, 1993), with less conflict and resentment in the marriage (Pina & Bengtson, 1993; Erickson, 1993), and with elevated personal well-being (Barnett & Baruch, 1987) and less depression (Ross, Mirowsky, & Huber, 1983).

Most of the research on gender differences in the associations among household roles, role satisfaction, and marital relationships has included only nondivorced families. Because remarried couples may have different expectations about their relationships and are more practical and equitable in household responsibilities than nondivorced couples, the above patterns of associations, based primarily on nondivorced couples, may not generalize to couples in remarried families.

Depressive symptoms and marital relations. This study will examine the role of parental depression in both marital relations and parent-child relation-ships. Depressive symptoms in parents frequently have been identified as a risk factor for marital problems and instability and for inept parenting, although depression in wives is more disruptive to family relations than depression in husbands (Gotlib & Whiffen, 1989; Johnson & Jacob, 1997). There is some evidence that elevated depression is found in people who experience multiple marital transitions (Capaldi & Patterson, 1991; O'Connor, Hawkins, Dunn, Thorpe, & Golding, 1998), and in the early stage of a remarriage as couples are coping with the changes and challenges in their new family situation (Hetherington & Clingempeel, 1992).

Numerous studies document the link of depressive symptoms with dis-tressed marital relations (Gotlib & Meltzer, 1987) and more negative marital interactions (Johnson & Jacob, 1997). O'Leary and his colleagues (1994) reported that the odds of depressive symptoms in a man or woman experi-encing marital discord are approximately 10 times greater than the odds of depressive symptomatology in an individual not experiencing marital discord. Marital and parent-child interactions involving a depressed partner or parent are characterized by poor communication, negative affect, tension, lack of responsiveness, and overt and covert hostility (Cicchetti & Toth, 1998; Gotlib & Hooley, 1988; McLeod & Eckberg, 1993). This is associated with poor marital quality and instability and with adverse consequences in the adjustment of children (Cicchetti & Toth, 1998). Although the association between the quality of marital relations and depressive symptomatology is robust, whether marital discord is a cause, a consequence, or a correlate of depressive symptoms is unclear.

Longitudinal change in marriage. Most studies of risk and protective factors associated with marital satisfaction and functioning have been cross-sectional studies. Longitudinal studies suggest that concurrent factors associated with marital satisfaction and the quality of the marital relationship may not be the same as those that predict later marital satisfaction and instability (Gottman, 1994; Kurdek, 1995a, 1995b). For example, parenting satisfaction and conflict regarding childrearing may be unrelated to concurrently assessed marital satisfaction (Kurdek, 1996), but nonetheless may lead to subsequent marital conflict and even divorce (Block, Block, & Morrison, 1981). In general, negative aspects of marital problem-solving behavior, such as wives' complaining, criticizing, contempt, and confrontational behavior, and husbands' stonewalling or withdrawal, are more salient in undermining long-term marital stability (Gottman, 1994; Hetherington, 1999) and marital satisfaction (Kurdek, 1995a, 1995b) than are positive aspects of the relationship in protecting against such deterioration in both first marriages and remarriages (Hetherington & Clingempeel, 1992). Positivity may be more important, however, in predicting marital outcomes in nondivorced than in remarried families (Hetherington & Clingempeel, 1992).

Many of the studies of longitudinal change in the quality of marriage have examined alterations in the early years of marriage when marital satisfaction shows a notable drop (Markman & Hahlweg, 1993) or changes associated with normative and nonnormative life events (Karney & Bradbury, 1995). Few of these studies have explored similarities and differences in the predictors of changes in marital relationships in more stable, longer established marriages in different types of families (Dindia & Cavary, 1993) as will be done in this study.

There is evidence that individual attributes of spouses, such as depression and antisocial behavior, satisfaction and participation in family roles, the quality of the conjugal relationship and of marital interactions, and behavior problems in children may contribute to marital satisfaction or dissatisfaction and marital instability. In this *Monograph*, differences between these factors in first married and remarried couples will be examined and their contribution over time to marital satisfaction and functioning will be explored.

Parent-Child Relations in Stepfamilies

The review of the literature to follow focuses on residential parents and stepparents, since this *Monograph* explores family relations within the primary residence in different kinds of stepfamilies and in nonstepfamilies. This focus is not meant to belittle the influence of family members outside of the household, but they are not the topic of this study.

Remarried custodial parents and their children. Both positive and negative life changes increase in the early stages of remarriage (Hetherington et al., 1985) as parents are coping with the many alterations in their life and family situation. It therefore is not surprising that some remarried parents are initially preoccupied, anxious, and depressed as they are attempting to establish a new marital relationship while simultaneously trying to be supportive and reassuring with their children and new spouse in the challenges they confront (Hetherington & Clingempeel, 1992). Although there are temporary perturbations in parenting following a remarriage with both extremes of greater permissiveness and lack of control (Hetherington & Jodl, 1994) and greater authoritarianism and punitiveness (Bray, Berger, Silverblatt, & Hollier, 1987), most remarried mothers and fathers with young children differ little in parenting their biological children from those in first marriages as the marriage stabilizes (Hetherington & Jodl, 1994). Over time, both remarried mothers and fathers reengage, regain control, become more authoritative in their parenting, and show few differences from parents in first marriages, except when the children are early adolescents (Bray & Berger, 1993; Hetherington, 1993; Hetherington & Clingempeel, 1992; Hetherington & Jodl, 1994). Problems in relations of the biological custodial parent and child not only are more common when the remarriage occurs when children are in adolescence (Hetherington, 1993; Hetherington & Clingempeel, 1992; Hetherington & Jodl, 1994), but adolescence also triggers problems in parent-child relationships that previously may have been relatively congenial and constructive (Bray & Berger, 1993; Hetherington & Jodl, 1994). The realignments in family relationships that occur in all families with adolescent children are more marked and turbulent in single-parent families and stepfamilies (Anderson et al., 1999; Bray & Berger, 1993; Hetherington, 1991b; Hetherington & Clingempeel, 1992; Hetherington & Jodl, 1994).

Although parental behavior becomes more responsive and authoritative over time, more negative and less positive behaviors in the child toward the custodial parent following remarriage are more sustained (Bray & Berger, 1993; Hetherington & Jodl, 1994). When gender differences are found, problems between children and parents are greater and more enduring for girls than for boys in both stepfather and stepmother families (Brand, Clingempeel, & Bowen-Woodward, 1988; Hetherington & Jodl, 1994).

Stepparents and stepchildren. Stepparents and stepchildren have little choice in their relationship, as they enter a family situation that is incidental to the mutual attraction of the adult couple. Many stepparents enter remarriage, however, with an unrealistic expectation of instant reciprocal love in their relationships with their stepchildren and are doomed to disappointment (Visher & Visher, 1988). Although this has not been tested empirically, it has been suggested that mutual attachment of the stepparent and stepchild will take as long as the child's age at the time of remarriage (Mills, 1984), a not very encouraging prognosis for remarriages that occur when offspring are adolescents. Both stepfathers and stepmothers want their new marriage to be successful and often initially attempt to ingratiate themselves with their stepchildren (Brand et al., 1988; Bray & Berger, 1993; Hetherington, 1993; Kurdek & Fine, 1993a). When stepparents persistently encounter resistance and aversive behavior, however, especially from stepdaughters, they may become more distant and disengaged, feel less rapport and closeness, and exhibit less warmth, control, and monitoring than is found in nondivorced families (Anderson et al., 1999; Brand et al., 1988; Bray & Berger, 1993; Hetherington, 1993; Hetherington & Clingempeel, 1992; Hetherington & Jodl, 1994; Kurdek & Fine, 1993b). Some studies have reported that, in the early stages of a remarriage, stepfathers are less involved, critical, and concerned than biological fathers in nondivorced families about minor issues such as homework, cleanliness, manners, dress, and chores (Hetherington, 1993). Most studies report, however, greater conflict and negativity between stepparents and children, especially with adolescent stepdaughters (Brand et al., 1988; Bray & Berger, 1993; Hetherington & Clingempeel, 1992; Hetherington & Jodl, 1994; Kurdek & Fine, 1993b). This finding is reflected in rates of physical abuse by stepfathers seven times higher than biological fathers (Wilson, Daly, & Weghorst, 1980), homicide rates with infants and young children 100 times higher (Daly & Wilson, 1996), and rates of incest over four times higher (Finkelhor, 1987; Russell, 1984).

Although children in nondivorced nuclear families and eventually in stepfamilies benefit from authoritative parents who are high in warmth, control, and monitoring, the role of disciplinarian must be undertaken with caution by stepparents. Stepparents who are most effective initially establish a warm supportive role with stepchildren and support the biological parent's discipline. Control attempts must be made gradually or may not be attained at all (Bray & Berger, 1993; Fine, Voydanoff, & Donnelly, 1993;

Hetherington, 1993; Hetherington & Clingempeel, 1992; Hetherington & Jodl, 1994; Kelly, 1992). Stepparents' discipline is most effective when the biological custodial parent and stepparent agree on childrearing, and the biological parent supports the stepparent's efforts without abdicating responsibilities as the primary parent (Clingempeel, Brand, & Segal, 1987).

Stepmothers have more problematic relations with their stepchildren than do stepfathers (Clingempeel, Brand, & Ievoli, 1984; Duberman, 1973; Furstenberg, 1987; Furstenberg & Nord, 1987; MacDonald & DeMaris, 1996; Santrock et al., 1988; Visher & Visher, 1978). Two factors may contribute to this. First, as noted earlier, many remarried fathers expect stepmothers to assume the primary role of caretaker and disciplinarian (Fine et al., 1993; Thomson, McLanahan, & Curtin, 1992; Waldren, 1986; Whitsett & Land, 1992) and this leads to children's resentment and conflict with both parents, especially by daughters. Second, noncustodial mothers remain much more actively involved with their children than do noncustodial fathers (Hetherington & Jodl, 1994; Seltzer & Bianchi, 1988), and stepmothers and biological mothers are more likely to get into competitive relationships that precipitate loyalty conflicts in children (Hetherington & Jodl, 1994).

Children's behavior toward stepparents. Although discussions of parent-child relationships in remarried families usually focus on the role of the parent and stepparent, children play an active role in shaping this relationship. Some research indicates that in the face of a resistant stepchild, even a well-intentioned stepparent may fail in building a close constructive relationship (Brown, Green, & Druckman, 1990). When a remarriage occurs when children are adolescents, the behavior of the stepchild may be more salient than that of the stepparent in influencing future parent-child relations (Hetherington & Clingempeel, 1992; Hetherington & Jodl, 1994). In the early stage of remarriage, children are more negative, and less warm and communicative toward both the custodial parent and stepparent (Bray & Berger, 1993; Clingempeel, Brand, & Ievoli, 1984; Hetherington, 1993; Hetherington & Clingempeel, 1992). Relations between younger stepsons and stepfathers improve over time and boys are more likely to form and benefit from a close relationship with a stepfather than are girls (Amato & Keith, 1991a; Hetherington, 1993; Zimiles & Lee, 1991). Younger girls in stepfamilies, in comparison to those in nondivorced nuclear families, exhibit more defiant, aggressive, and disruptive behavior toward both biological mothers and stepfathers, whereas withdrawn, sullen, avoidant, noncommunicative behavior is more common with adolescent stepdaughters and stepfathers (Hetherington, 1993). One observational study found that adolescent stepdaughters spoke to their stepfathers 30% less than did daughters with their biological nondivorced fathers (Vuchinich, Hetherington, Vuchinich, & Clingempeel, 1991). Adolescent stepsons and stepdaughters remain more coercive and less warm and responsive to step-parents (Anderson et al., 1999; Bray & Berger, 1993; Hetherington, 1993) even after 26 months in a remarried family (Hetherington & Clingempeel, 1992). These problems are more marked in stepmother than in stepfather families, and children view their relations with stepmothers as more stress-ful and nonsupportive than those with stepfathers (Clingempeel et al., 1984; Furstenberg, 1987).

About one third of adolescent boys and one quarter of adolescent girls in stepfamilies, in comparison to about 10% in nondivorced two-parent fam-ilies, disengage from their families and spend little time in family activities or at home (Hetherington, 1993; Hetherington & Jodl, 1994). If this disengage-ment is associated with lack of adult supervision and involvement with an antisocial low achieving peer group, it increases the risk for school dropout, substance abuse, sexual activity, and delinquency (Hetherington & Jodl, 1994). Disengagement also can be a constructive solution to a dysfunctional, conflictual, and difficult family situation if it involves a close relationship with a caring involved adult such as the parent of a friend, a grandparent, teacher, or coach.

Cherlin and Furstenberg (1994) reported that one of the few differences between offspring in single-parent families and stepfamilies is that stepchildren, especially stepdaughters, leave home earlier and they attribute the earlier home leaving to family conflict. In adulthood, relations between stepchildren and stepparents remain more distant with less contact and mutual support than is found in biologically related parents and children (Amato & Keith, 1991b; Hetherington, 1999; White, 1994).

Relationships between biological parents and children, and especially between stepparents and stepchildren, have been found to differ from those in nonstepfamilies. Parents are closer to and more actively involved in controlling and monitoring their own children's behavior than that of stepchildren. Greater difficulties have been reported in stepdaughter-stepparent relationships than stepson-stepparent relationships, although this is usually found with preadolescents. More difficulties may emerge in complex stepfamilies where multiple biological relationships may present a unique challenge. In this study, we will examine the parent/stepparent-child relationships of adolescent boys and girls in simple and complex stepfamilies. Gender differences, family type differences, and differences associated with biological relatedness of parents and children will be the focus in our examination of parent-child relationships.

Sibling Relationships

Establishing a relationship with a sibling is a challenge for all children who have them. When a sibling relationship is conflictual or distressing, children and adolescents do not have the option of terminating that relationship as can be done in friendships. Hence, although there is affection and positive interactions exhibited in both sibling and peer relations, greater negativity and conflict are found in sibling relationships (Buhrmester, 1992). It has been remarked that siblings show considerable pragmatic understanding of how to annoy and how to console each other (Dunn & Kendrick, 1982).

Coercive, acrimonious parent-child relationships often are found to be associated with conflictual, aggressive sibling relationships (Patterson, 1982, 1984; Patterson, Reid, & Dishion, 1992). Furthermore, under changing life circumstances and increased stresses, such as are found when confronting parents' divorces or remarriages, sibling relationships may alter, and either exacerbate problems in adjusting to the marital transition or protect siblings from adverse outcomes (Anderson et al., 1999; Anderson, Lindner, & Bennion, 1992; Hetherington, 1989, 1991a).

Sibling relationships play an important role in children's emotional, cognitive, and behavioral development (Bank & Kahn, 1982; Boer & Dunn, 1992). Little is known, however, about the role of the diverse sibling relationships found in stepfamilies. Children in remarried families may have to relate to a complex array of full-, half- and stepsiblings within and outside of their primary household (Ganong & Coleman, 1994; Ihinger-Tallman, 1987). Children from multiple remarriages and cohabiting relationships may experience added complexities in sibling relationships. In studies of sibling relationships in remarried families, investigators frequently have failed to distinguish among different types of sibling relationships, disregarding possible differences in quality, functioning, and contributions of these relationships.

Studies of full, biologically related siblings from a mother's previous marriage in stepfather families find less positive, more rivalrous or disengaged sibling relationships, especially in boys, in comparison to children in nondivorced families (Hetherington, 1989; Hetherington & Clingempeel, 1992; Hetherington & Jodl, 1994). Close, protective relationships are found in a subset of female full siblings in stepfamilies, but boys in stepfamilies rarely receive support from either male or female siblings (Hetherington, 1989; Hetherington & Clingempeel, 1992). As siblings move through adolescence and young adulthood, increasing disengagement from siblings occurs as they become more involved in relationships outside of the family (Anderson & Rice, 1992; Hetherington, 1999). This disengagement is more marked for siblings in stepfamilies (Hetherington & Clingempeel, 1992; Hetherington & Jodl, 1994; White & Reidmann, 1992) and, in young adulthood, it is greatest for nonbiologically related stepsiblings (Hetherington, 1999).

19

One third of children entering a stepfamily have a half sibling within 4 years, and two thirds of children in stepfamilies have either a half sibling or a full sibling (Bumpass, 1984b). Half siblings who live together most of the time regard themselves simply as siblings (Bernstein, 1989; Ganong & Coleman, 1988). Those who live apart make a greater distinction between full and half siblings (Bernstein, 1989). A qualitative study found that relationships between half siblings were more positive when half siblings lived together, were similar in temperament, farther apart in age, and when the remarried family had been together for a longer period of time (Bernstein, 1989).

When remarried parents combine their children from previous relationships in blended households, children experience many life changes. These include changes in family size and the child's position in the family, competition over scarce resources such as parental attention, space and privacy, relating to someone without a shared family history and with whom the child may have little in common, and possible sexual attraction (Rosenberg & Hajfal, 1985; Walsh, 1992). It may be easier, however, for children to justify differential treatment of siblings by parents in blended stepfamilies on the basis of biological relatedness, leading to reduced sibling rivalry. Full and half siblings may be especially sensitive to differential parenting by the residential biological parent. For children in blended families, either friendship formation or disengagement with stepsiblings may occur. Many residential stepsiblings, however, form successful satellite relationships that provide both support and companionship (Ihinger-Tallman, 1987), and conflict between stepsiblings does not appear to be excessive (Beer, 1992; Duberman, 1975; Ganong & Coleman, 1987; White & Reidmann, 1992). Little is known about stepsibling relationships in adulthood. Both substantial contact in adulthood (White & Reidmann, 1992), and more distant relations in adolescence and adulthood have been reported for stepsiblings than for full siblings in nondivorced families (Hetherington, 1999; Hetherington & Jodl, 1994).

There is some evidence that sibling relationships in stepfamilies may be more troubled and less warm than those in nondivorced nuclear families. Little is known, however, about different kinds of sibling relationships in stepfamilies or of their influences on child adjustment. In this *Monograph* we will examine the relationships of full siblings in stepfamilies and nonstepfamilies, and of half siblings and nonrelated stepsiblings in stepfamilies and their association with adolescent adjustment. In addition, gender differences and changes over time in sibling relationships will be explored.

CHILD ADJUSTMENT IN STEPFAMILIES

On average, children in divorced families and stepfamilies, in comparison to those in nondivorced, nuclear families, are more likely to exhibit behavioral and emotional problems, lower social competence, lower self-esteem, less socially responsible behavior and poorer academic achievement (Allison & Furstenberg, 1989; Amato & Keith, 1991a; Anderson et al., 1999; Bray, 1988, 1999; Bray & Berger, 1993; Dornbusch et al., 1985; Fine, Kurdek, & Hennigen, 1992; Fine, Voydanoff, & Donnelly, 1993). The largest and most consistently obtained differences are in externalizing disorders and lack of social responsibility, and to a lesser extent in achievement (Amato & Keith, 1991a; Hetherington & Jodl, 1994). Offspring of divorced and remarried parents also have problems in relationships with parents and peers, and in relationships with romantic partners and spouses in adulthood (Amato, 1999; Amato & Keith, 1991b; Hetherington, 1999). In spite of increased economic resources following a remarriage and the presence of an additional parent figure, the adjustment of children in remarried families differs little from those in divorced families. This leads some investigators to conclude that problems in the adjustment of stepchildren may be attributable to divorce and life in a single-parent family or that the stresses in a stepfamily are sufficient to counter the economic, social, and emotional support a stepparent may bring to the family (see Amato & Keith 1991a for a meta-analysis; see Cherlin & Furstenberg, 1994; Hetherington et al., 1998; Hetherington & Henderson, 1997; Hetherington & Stanley-Hagan, 1995, for recent reviews). In addition, the adjustment of children in stepmother and stepfather families is similar (Brand, Clingempeel, & Bowen-Woodward, 1988; Fine & Kurdek, 1992). Children whose parents have gone through multiple marital transitions show the most severe problems in conduct disorders and achievement (Capaldi & Patterson, 1991; Kurdek, Fine, & Sinclair, 1994, 1995).

Sex differences are not consistently obtained in these studies. When they are found, however, they are more likely to occur with preadolescents than adolescents, and girls are reported to be more adversely affected by being in a stepfamily and are less able to benefit from the presence of a stepfather than are boys (Amato & Keith, 1991a; Clingempeel, Brand, & Ievoli, 1984; Hetherington, 1993; Hetherington & Jodl, 1994; Lee, Burnham, Zimiles, & Ladewski, 1994; Lindner-Gunnoe, 1993; Zill et al., 1993; Zimiles & Lee, 1991).

Problems in offspring adjustment continue long after their parents' marital transitions have occurred (Amato & Keith, 1991b). Adolescents from divorced and remarried families exhibit some of the same externalizing and internalizing problems found in childhood. In addition, in comparison to adolescents in two-parent nondivorced families they initiate sexual activities earlier and are more likely to be teen parents, drop out of school, associate with antisocial peers, and to be involved in substance abuse and delinquent activities (Amato & Keith, 1991a; Conger & Chao, 1996; Demo & Acock, 1996; Elder & Russell, 1996; Hetherington, 1993; Hetherington & Clingempeel, 1992; Hetherington & Jodl, 1994; Kurdek, Fine, & Sinclair, 1994; McLanahan, 1999; McLanahan & Sandefur, 1994; Simons & Chao, 1996; Whitbeck, Simons, & Goldberg, 1996). Even in adulthood, offspring from divorced and remarried families have greater marital instability (Amato, 1999; Amato & Keith, 1991b; Glenn & Kramer, 1985; Hetherington, 1999; McLanahan & Bumpass, 1988; Tzeng & Mare, 1995), lower socioeconomic attainment, less life satisfaction, and more adjustment problems (Amato & Keith, 1991b; Chase-Lansdale, Cherlin, & Kiernan, 1995; Hetherington, 1999).

Children usually report their parents' marital transitions to be traumatic experiences, and most researchers agree that children in divorced and remarried families are at risk for the development of academic, social, emotional, and behavioral problems. There is less consensus, however, on the size of the difference in adjustment between children in divorced and remarried families and those in nondivorced nuclear families. In a 1991 meta-analysis, Amato and Keith (1991a) report relatively modest effect sizes, which were greatly reduced when the adjustment of the child preceding the marital transition was controlled. There is considerable overlap in the adjustment of children from nondivorced, divorced and remarried families. Some more recent studies, however, have reported about a two-fold increase in such things as total behavior problems, externalizing behavior, school dropout, teenage pregnancy, and delinquency (Hetherington & Jodl, 1994; McLanahan, 1999; McLanahan & Sandefur, 1994; Simons & Associates, 1996; Zill et al., 1993). About 10% of offspring from nuclear families experience these problems, compared to 20 to 25% in divorced and remarried families. These problems tend to cluster into a single behavior problem cluster (Jessor & Jessor, 1977; Mekos, Hetherington, & Reiss, 1996). Thus, most children in divorced families and stepfamilies do not develop these problems. They are resilient in the face of their parents' marital transitions, and become reasonably competent individuals functioning within the normal range of adjustment (Emery & Forehand, 1994). In spite of this resiliency, a two-fold increase is not negligible, and although the size of the effects of parental marital transitions on offspring adjustment are modest, they affect large numbers of individuals in many domains of functioning and are long-lasting (Amato, 1999; McLanahan, 1999; Sandefur & McLanahan, 1994). They therefore remain of concern.

There is great variation in children's responses to their parents' marital transitions. On average, children in divorced and remarried families are found to exhibit more problems, fewer competencies, and less well-being than children in nondivorced nuclear families. Problems in adjustment often occur in the immediate aftermath of a marital transition, but also may be triggered by developmental changes and challenges in adolescence. We will study the adjustment of adolescents in stabilized long remarried simple and complex stepfamilies and in nonstepfamilies as they move through adolescence. Gender differences in adjustment also will be examined.

FAMILY PROCESS AND CHILD ADJUSTMENT

In this section we will focus on the potential links between adolescent adjustment and family relationships in stepfamilies and nondivorced families. Researchers have begun to focus on the diversity of children's responses to the challenges and changes accompanying their parents' marital transitions and on factors that undermine or promote their adjustment to their new life situation. In general, family process variables appear to be more powerful predictors of child outcome than are family structure or family type (Avenevoli, Sessa, & Steinberg, 1999). Children, whether living in nondivorced nuclear families, single-parent families, or stepfamilies, exhibit greater well-being, achievement, socially responsible behavior and social competence and fewer behavior problems and psychological disorders when they are raised in a harmonious, supportive family environment (Anderson et al., 1999; Deater-Deckard & Dunn, 1999; Hetherington, 1993, 1999; Hetherington & Clingempeel, 1992; Hetherington & Jodl, 1994). Authoritative parenting characterized by responsive, warm, firm, and consistent discipline benefits children in nondivorced, divorced, and remarried families (Hetherington, 1993; Hetherington & Clingempeel, 1992; Hetherington & Jodl, 1994), although there may be some variations in these effects in different ethnic groups (Avenevoli et al., 1999). The quality of parenting and sibling relationships often is found to moderate or mediate the effects on child adjustment of other stressors such as poverty (McLloyd, 1998), marital conflict (Cowan, Cowan, & Schulz, 1996; Hetherington, 1999), parental depression (Cicchetti & Toth, 1998), or antisocial behavior (Forgatch et al., 1995), and parental marital transitions (Bray, 1999; Bray & Berger, 1993; Hetherington, 1993, 1999; Hetherington & Clingempeel, 1992; Hetherington & Jodl, 1994; Forgatch et al., 1995; Simmons & Associates, 1996). Although there is some evidence that family relationships and process variables may operate differently in different types of families (Avenevoli et al., 1999; Bray & Berger, 1993; Forgatch et al., 1995), the literature is meager. Little is known about how the operation of family risk and protective factors on children's adjustment may vary across nonstepfamilies and different kinds of stepfamilies. This will be a central focus of this *Monograph*.

There is great diversity in the response of children to remarriage. Although most children are resilient in the face of the challenges of remarriage, they also are at greater risk than those in first married families for social, emotional, and academic problems in adjustment. Some of these differences in adjustment between children in first married families and stepfamilies have been attributed to differences in family functioning to problems in the marital relationship exacerbated by the presence of stepchildren, to difficulties in parent-child and stepparent-stepchild relations, and to rivalry and conflict in sibling relations. Less attention has been paid to the role positive marital, parent/stepparent-child, and sibling relationships can play in protecting children and adolescents from adverse consequences of parental marital transitions and in enhancing their well-being. Furthermore, few studies have examined how risk and protective factors in family subsystems and the relationships among subsystems interact over time to produce diverse outcomes in offspring in different kinds of remarried families. Stepfamilies usually have been treated as a homogenous group. The examination of risk and protective relationships and processes in different kinds of stepfamilies and in nonstepfamilies and their contribution to the adjustment of adolescent siblings will be the focus of this study.

In our literature review, we have focused on the functioning and relationships among family subsystems and their association with child adjustment in different types of families. It must be remembered, however, that genetic factors may underlie some of these associations. The partially genetically determined characteristics that make an individual divorce prone and likely to go through multiple marital relationships also may be associated with marital conflict, incompetent coercive parenting, conflictual parent-child relationships, and antisocial or deviant behavior in children. There is a genetic substrate underlying some of the associations among parental characteristics, family relationships, and adolescent adjustment. This shared genetic substrate should be greater for biologically related family members than in nonbiological step relationships. A genetic analysis, however, will not be the focus of this *Monograph*. A behavior genetic analysis of the larger Nonshared Environment in Adolescent Development Study (NEAD) from which the subset of nonstepfamilies and stepfamilies was drawn is presented in Reiss, Neiderheiser, Hetherington, and Plomin (in press).

OVERVIEW OF THE STUDY

The present longitudinal study examines marital, parent-adolescent, and sibling relationships in nonstepfamilies and in simple and complex stepfamily households. The association of these relationships with the adjustment of two adolescent siblings in each household also were studied.

Siblings in this study varied in biological relatedness, with some siblings in stepfamilies being full siblings from the mother's previous marriage, some half siblings, and some stepsiblings. All stepfamilies were in stabilized stepfamilies in which the remarriage had occurred an average of 9 years before and a minimum of at least 5 years prior to the study. Since we were targeting adolescent offspring, it was impossible to match the nonstepfamilies to stepfamilies on length of marriage. Because both types of families were well past the early stages of marriage and family formation and the greatest risk for divorce, however, they were thought to be reasonable comparison groups.

Information on family functioning and children's adjustment was collected twice, 3 years apart, using multiple informants and multiple methods. These included interviews, questionnaires, checklists of behavior symptoms, and observational assessments. Because differences in perspectives were expected, information was sought from parents and target siblings as well as from the children's teachers, in order to obtain a broad view of family and individual functioning. Data available from teachers were incomplete, and were not included in this study.

Data also were collected on many factors outside of the home, such as relationships with nonresidential biological parents, support systems, peers, and life stressors. Since this report is limited to within-household contributions, we did not include these factors in our analyses. We are aware, however, of their importance and they will be discussed in other publications. The sample, although large, is not representative of the population as a whole and has an underrepresentation of ethnic minorities and families living in extreme poverty.

The goals of this study were to examine the following issues: (a) differences in family relationships as well as in the adjustment of family members in nonstepfamilies and simple and complex stepfamily households; (b) changes and stability in family functioning and the adjustment of family members in different family types as children move through adolescence; (c) gender differences in patterns of family functioning and in the adjustment of adolescent siblings in different family types; and (d) family functioning variables associated with the adjustment of adolescent siblings in the different family types.

This *Monograph* continues with an overview of the methods, followed by chapters discussing the marital, parent-child, and sibling family subsystems, the adjustment of the adolescent siblings, the associations among family relationships and their relationship to adolescent adjustment, and a final integrative summary.

II. METHOD

Sandra H. Henderson

Parents and adolescent siblings were assessed using multiple methods and measures in two assessment waves to measure quality of individual adjustment as well as quality of relationships within and across family sub-systems. There were 3 years between Wave 1 and Wave 2 assessments. The data used in this project are part of a national study on the role of differential experiences in adolescent development (Nonshared Environment in Adolescent Development (NEAD); Reiss, Plomin, Hetherington, Howe, Rovine, Tryon, & Hagan, 1994), whose research design and hypotheses have been described elsewhere (Reiss et al., 1994). For the purposes of this study, the data include the largest sample of intensively studied stabilized step-families with adolescent children.

PARTICIPANTS

The subsample from the NEAD study included in this study omitted the families of twins in the original study. The groups of identical and fraternal twins were omitted since there is evidence that family relations and the development of twins may differ from that of singletons and they were not viewed as appropriate comparison groups for the questions addressed in this *Monograph* (Lytton, Singh, & Gallagher; 1995; Mitchell, 1998; Powell, 1993; Rutter & Redshaw, 1991). All other families from NEAD were included in the sample and were comprised of a group of nonstepfamilies and two different types of stepfamilies with at least two same-sex adolescent siblings who were the target adolescents in the study. Siblings were distinguished by age as older adolescent and younger adolescent. In Wave 1 there were 93 nonstepfamilies; 83 simple stepfamilies in which all siblings in the household were the custodial mother's biological children and the custodial father's stepchildren; and 342 complex stepfamilies, in which siblings in the household varied in biological relatedness to custodial mothers and fathers.

The term *nonstepfamilies*, rather than *nondivorced*, is used because a small subset of 26 respondents, both women and men, had previously been involved in marriages with no children. The only children in these households, however, are the biological children of both parents. The two types of siblings pairs in the complex stepfamilies include half siblings, who have the same mother but different fathers, that is, one being the offspring of the mothers' previous marriage and one born to the current union, and unrelated siblings in blended families, one being the child of the mother and one of the father from a previous relationship. It should be noted that this way of defining simple and complex stepfamilies differs from that of some other investigators who would include consideration of the noncustodial parent's remarriage in defining complexity (Bray, 1990). In this study, our operational definition of complexity involves only complexity of sibling relationships within the household.

In order to be considered for the study families were required to meet the following criteria. Spouses had to be legally married; there were no cohabiting families included in the sample. The target adolescent sibling pairs were the same gender, were between 10 and 18 years of age and no more than 4 years apart in age and resided in the household half or more of each week. Older siblings at Wave 1 had a mean of 14.5 years of age, $SD = 2.2$ years, while younger siblings at Wave 1 had a mean age of 12.4 years, $SD = 2.2$ years. Stepfamilies were required to be remarried for at least 5 years and had been married for an average of almost 9 years, and thus were considered restabilized families since all had made it through the early transitional crisis period of remarriage when divorce rates are high (Cherlin & Furstenberg, 1994; Hetherington & Clingempeel, 1992). It was assumed that when stepfamilies have lived together for this duration, family homeostatis and the opportunity for mutual influences of family members and family subsystems would have occurred.

Families were initially recruited for the study through random digit dialing in order to get a nationally representative sample. After screening over 10,000 households, however, only 210 families were eligible and cost became prohibitive. The remainder of families ($N = 510$) were recruited using two national market surveys that contained information on the marital status of parent and age and gender of children. Thus, families were selected from a wide range of geographic regions from the 48 contiguous states, except South Dakota. The extraordinarily large selection pool was necessitated because of the rarity of obtaining siblings who met the above criteria and were in blended families, since only about 13% of fathers have physical custody of their children. The number of male and female children in each family group participating in each assessment wave is given in Table 1.

Sixteen percent of the sample lived in urban areas, 26% in suburban areas, 29% in small towns, and 29% in rural areas. Ethnic composition of the families were 95% European American, 4% African American, and 1% Hispanic American. The Hollingshead Four Factor Indicator of socioeconomic status showed families ranged from lower working-class to upper middle-class, with the mean family income in the $25,000–$35,000 range.

A variety of demographic variables were analyzed to see if families differed by family type (nonstep, simple step, and complex stepfamily). Mothers and fathers did not differ in education level or employment status. Mothers in complex stepfamilies were somewhat younger in age, 36.6 years, as compared to mothers in nonstep and simple stepfamilies who were 38.1 and 39.2 years, respectively, $F(2, 514) = 12.75$, $p < .001$. Similarly, fathers were slightly younger in complex stepfamilies, $M = 39.6$ years, as compared to fathers in simple stepfamiles, $M = 42.7$, $F(2, 512) = 7.79$, $p < .001$, and nonsignificantly younger than father in nonstep families, $M = 40.3$ years. Families differed moderately in total number of children in the family, with 3.2 in nonstepfamilies, 2.4 in simple stepfamilies and 3.6 in complex stepfamilies, $F(2, 515) = 33.63$, $p < .001$. Also, there were differences in marital duration with a mean of 17 years for nonstepfamilies, 7 years for simple stepfamilies, and 9 years for complex stepfamilies, $F(2, 484) = 177.74$, $p < .001$. Correlational analyses were run between marital duration and family process variables, including mothers' and fathers' Positivity/warmth, Negativity/conflict, and Monitoring/control, controlling for age of adolescent. The results revealed no significant findings. This is likely because all families had been married at least 5 years, and many for much longer, even in stepfamilies.

TABLE 1

NUMBER OF FAMILIES AND ADOLESCENTS PARTICIPATING IN EACH WAVE

	Nonstep		Simple		Complex		Total	
	Boys	Girls	Boys	Girls	Boys	Girls	Boys	Girls
Older adolescent:								
Wave 1	47	46	35	48	184	153	266	247
($n = 516$)								
Wave 2	30	27	19	24	87	72	136	123
($n = 259$)								

NOTE. Ns are the same for the younger sibling.

Three years later the sample was reassessed. Actual attrition was very low with only 9%, or 46 of the 518 original families who were eligible to participate at Wave 2 declining to do so. Other families were not included, however, because they no longer met eligibility requirements. First, families had to be nondivorced at Wave 2. Also, since we were interested in the adjustment and family relations of both target siblings, the two siblings had to be residing in the home with their parents at least half of the time in order to be included in the second wave of data collection. Many families did not meet this criterion, because older adolescents from Wave 1 had made a normative transition to college or work by data collection at Wave 2 and resided outside of their family homes. Fifteen of the ineligible families experienced a divorce, 79% of the adolescents had moved out of the home, and the remaining 6% were unable to be classified. This resulted in a reduced sample of 259 nontwin families.

Concern that the two criteria set for collecting data at Wave 2 would result in a biased sample prompted collection of basic data from those families who did not participate in Wave 2. Subsequent attrition analyses were run on demographic variables, as well as parenting composites without observations included (Postivity/warmth, Negativity/conflict, and Monitoring/control) and children's negative adjustment composites (Externalizing and Depressive Symptoms). T-tests revealed there were no mean differences in the demographic characteristics (parents' education, family income, gender of the siblings, and age difference between siblings) for families who participated only at Wave 1 versus families who participated at both Waves 1 and 2. In addition, there were no significant differences in either children's Externalizing or Depressive Symptoms between participants and nonparticipants. There were significant differences in mother's and father's Monitoring/control and Positivity/warmth between the two samples with nonparticipants showing somewhat lower Monitoring/contol and Positivity/warmth than participants. This is not surprising, however, given that adolescents in the nonparticipant group were on average 2 years older than those still in the study at Wave 2, and these two parenting dimensions decrease in intensity with age of child (see Chapter IV). The final sample for this report at Wave 2 consisted of 57 nonstep families, 43 simple stepfamilies and 159 complex stepfamilies.

PROCEDURE

The first wave of data was collected over a period of 15 months by 37 teams of interviewers from the National Opinion Research Center (NORC) who received extensive training on administering measures and conducting videotape sessions. Two interviewers collected the data in two 3-hour sessions in the family's home, with a 1-week interim between the two sessions. Mothers, fathers, and the two siblings each independently completed a battery of questionnaires dealing with family relations, family stressors, and parent and adolescent characteristics and behavior. Family members were given a take-home booklet containing additional measures, which they completed independently between sessions 1 and 2. Parents and adolescents also were videotaped in their homes in a structured problem-solving situation in dyadic, triadic, and tetradic combinations with other family members. All six family dyads—mother/older adolescent, mother/younger adolescent, father/older adolescent, father/younger adolescent, older adolescent/younger adolescent, and mother/father—were videotaped during the first home visit. Only triads and tetrads were conducted during the second visit. For the present study, only observations from the six dyadic interactions were used because (a) preliminary analyses revealed that dyads were more informative than triads or tetrads and (b) triads and tetrads were not videotaped for the second wave of data collection.

The data for Wave 2 were collected in a similar fashion except interviewers visited homes in only one 3-hour session, since there were fewer measures in the Wave 2 battery, and they videotaped only dyadic interactions. In addition, families were mailed one questionnaire booklet prior to the interviewer's visit to be completed before the visit, and also were given another booklet to complete after the home visit and mail in to NORC offices. Fortunately, most of the interviewers who had collected data on Wave 1 families also participated in Wave 2 data collection, thus providing a sense of continuity for families.

Family Type and Ownness

The NEAD project was originally designed to assess the effects of environment and genetics on adolescents' development of depression, conduct disorders, social and academic competence, and self-worth. In order to capture genetic effects, adolescents with varying degrees of genetic relatedness were included. In nonstepfamilies, identical and fraternal twins and nontwin sibling pairs were included. In stepfamilies, genetic variation ranged from unrelated siblings (blended stepfamilies) to half siblings to full siblings.

The focus of this *Monograph* differs from that of the original NEAD study. In the nonstepfamilies, twins were excluded, and in the majority of our stepfamily analyses, we have analyzed the data according to family type rather than sibling genetic relationship, as has been done in previous NEAD studies (e.g., Reiss et al., 1997). In the analyses of sibling relationships, the biological relatedness of siblings to each other is considered. The majority of analyses, however, take into account the parent-adolescent biological relationship ("ownness"), which may differ from sibling genetic relationship. For example, a mother can be the biological mother to both the older adolescent and the younger adolescent in the study, while the father is the biological father to the younger adolescent only. Thus, the siblings are stepsiblings, in this case half siblings, yet the mother's biological relationship to each adolescent is the same.

When looking at stepfamilies, the organization of biological family relationships becomes complex quite rapidly. Initially, when grouping families by family type, not only biological relationships of the targeted sibling but also the biological relationships of other siblings were considered. Based on the complexity of the relationships among family members within stepfamilies, however, too many family groupings emerged (eight in all, see Table 2), and sample sizes within family types became too small to work with.

Therefore, we simplified our categorization into four groups, described below, which account for family type and biological relatedness:

1. *nonstepfamilies*, in which all siblings in the family are biologically related to the mother and father. Almost all of these families involved first marriages, however, 26 respondents had previously been married, but had no children from that relationship;

2. *simple stepfamilies*, in which a remarriage has occurred and all siblings in the family are the custodial mother's biological children and the custodial father's stepchildren;

3. *complex stepfamilies, own*, in which a remarriage has occurred and siblings in the family vary in biological relatedness to custodial mothers and fathers, *and* the parent and adolescent being analyzed are biologically related;

4. *complex stepfamilies, step*, in which a remarriage has occurred and siblings in the family vary in biological relatedness to custodial mothers and fathers,

TABLE 2

SIBLINGS' GENETIC RELATIONSHIP BY FAMILY TYPE

Sibling Genetic Relationship	Family Type							
	Nonstep	Full step	Half step	Blended	Full step/ half step	Full step blended	Full step/ half step/ blended	Half step/ blended
Nonstep (n = 93)	93	—	—	—	—	—	—	—
Full step (n = 182)	—	83	4	—	86	6	—	3
Half step (n = 111)	—	—	37	—	71	—	—	3
Blended (n = 130)	—	—	—	28	—	58	10	34

NOTE. $N = 516$.

and the parent and adolescent being analyzed are not biologically related, that is, are stepkin.

For stepfamily analyses on adolescent adjustment and marital relations, the majority of analyses collapsed groups 3 and 4, creating a three group family type: nonstepfamilies, simple step, complex step, as ownness is not relevant for these analyses. Finally, for stepfamily analyses on siblings, we analyzed by the older adolescent–younger adolescent genetic relationship, rather than family type.

MEASURES

Measures were selected and constructed to collect similar information from different sources and through different methods. Parents completed questionnaire booklets and were offered assistance by the interviewers with some of the more difficult questionnaires when needed. Adolescents were interviewed and completed questionnaires separately in a room out of the hearing of other family members. Assistance was provided for adolescents who had difficulty reading or understanding the questionnaires.

Most measures are well validated and had been used in previous research; however, some measures were modified for our adolescent sample, and others were created specifically for the present study. Data were collected on parent-adolescent, sibling, and marital relationships, positive and negative adolescent adjustment, adult adjustment, and a variety of extrafamilial factors, such as peer relations, social support, and stressful life events. Below are brief descriptions of all measures included in this study. Some measures in the NEAD study are not included in this study. Following the review of measures, within each subcategory a description of the constructs and the measures comprising them will be given. Composites were created through exploratory and confirmatory factor analyses. More details on compositing will be given following the discussion of measures. Table 3 presents a summary of the constructs, including persons reporting, and composites, with Cronbach's alpha coefficients for composites and for the central dimensions of marital, parent-adolescent, and sibling relations, and adolescent adjustment.

Measures of the Marital Relationship

Household Management (HOM; Hetherington & Clingempeel, 1992). The NEAD HOM measure is comprised of two parts and was administered at Wave 1 only. As a result, only cross-sectional analyses using this measure are presented in the marital chapter. In Part 1, parents and adolescents were asked to indicate who in the family helps them perform certain tasks for the adolescent, such as doing the adolescent's laundry, preparing meals and helping with homework, as well as who makes most of the decisions for the adolescent's daily life, such as setting curfew, buying clothes, and religious training. Standardized item alphas for the subscales created for mothers' and fathers' rating of their work for older and younger adolescents ranged from .76 to .88. The second part of the HOM measure was administered only to parents and consisted of two items that assessed how satisfied each partner was with his/her perceived influence in decision making and with the overall division of family jobs.

Locke-Wallace Marital Adjustment Test (Locke & Wallace, 1987). This measure contains one global adjustment question, eight questions measuring areas of possible disagreement, and six items measuring conflict resolution, cohesion, and communication. In addition, for the NEAD battery, 12 items were added concerning disagreement over parenting issues, such as adolescent's allowances, personal appearance, grades, friends, and religious training.

Marital Instability Scale (MIS; Booth, Johnson & Edwards, 1983). The respondent is required to rate on a 4-point Likert scale five situations related to marital instability. These situations range from thinking about separation to having consulted a lawyer about divorce.

Network of Relationships Inventory (NRI; Buhrmester, 1992). This 13-item round-robin scale was designed to assess the subjects' perception of their relations with other family members, including parent, siblings and for the adults, spouses. A Likert-style format is used on items that measure degree of rapport and conflict in the couple relationship.

Child-Rearing Issues: Self and Spouse (CRI; Hetherington & Clingempeel, 1992). This scale consisted of 39 items that assessed how frequently spouses argued or disagreed in the past month over issues of childrearing. Items include spousal conflict over daily routines such as compliance with homework, bedtime, chores, manners, and responses to parental authority and conflict over adolescent issues such as curfews, dating, activities away from home, and use of alcohol, cigarettes, and drugs. On average, Cronbach's alpha coefficients for different family members have been found to be .87 for daily routines, and .75 for adolescent issues (see Hetherington & Clingempeel, 1992).

TABLE 3

Composition of Within- and Across-Wave Composite Variables

| Dimensions | Alphas for Composites | | Assessment Instrument | Scales | Informants |
	Wave 1	Wave 2			
MARITAL RELATIONSHIP COMPOSITES					
Positivity:					
Wife → Husband	.72	.68	Locke-Wallace Marital Adjustmt.	global adjustment	Wife, Husband
Husband → Wife	.67	.77	Network of Relationships Inv.	rapport	Wife, Husband
			Observational coding	positivity:	Observer
				wife to husband	
				husband to wife	
Negativity:					
Wife → Husband	.70	.69	Locke-Wallace Marital Adjustmt.	total disagreement	Wife, Husband
Husband → Wife	.69	.68	Network of Relationships Inv.	conflict	Wife, Husband
			Conflict Tactics Scale	symbolic aggression	Wife, Husband
			Observational coding	negativity:	Observer
				wife to husband	
				husband to wife	
PARENT-CHILD RELATIONSHIP COMPOSITES					
I. Parent behavior toward child					
Positivity:					
Mother → Older child	.66	.73	Expression of Affection	expressive affection,	Mother, Father,
				instrumental affection	Child
Mother → Younger child	.70	.71			
Father → Older child	.74	.73	Parent-Child Relationship	rapport/closeness	Mother, Father, Child
Father → Younger child	.74	.72	Observational coding	positivity:	Observer
				parent to target child	

			Measure	Construct	Reporter
Negativity/Conflict:					
Mother → Older child	.81	.86	Childrearing Issues–I	total conflict	Mother, Father, Child
Mother → Younger child	.70	.71	Childrearing Issues–II	punitive discipline	Mother, Father, Child
Father → Older child	.74	.73	Parent-Child Relationship	conflict	Mother, Father, Child
Father → Younger child	.74	.73	Conflict Tactics Scale	symbolic aggression	Mother, Father, Child
			Observational coding	negativity: parent to target child	Observer
Monitoring/Control:					
Mother → Older child	.75	.76	Child monitoring	knowledge, attempted control, actual control	Mother, Father, Child
Mother → Younger child	.69	.69			
Father → Older child	.76	.78	Observational coding	monitoring & control: parent to target child	Observer
Father → Younger child	.73	.76			
II. Child behavior toward parent					
Positivity:					
Older child → Mother	.79	.74	Parent-Child Relationship	rapport/closeness	Mother, Father, Child
Older child → Father	.73	.71	Network of Relationships	closeness	Child
Younger child → Mother	.75	.74	Observational coding	warmth/support: target child to parent	Observer
Younger child → Father	.70	.69			
Negativity:					
Older child → Mother	.78	.77	Parent-Child Relationship	conflict	Mother, Father, Child
Older child → Father	.75	.74	Network of Relationships	conflict	Child
Younger child → Mother	.72	.71	Observational coding	negativity: target child to parent	Observer
Younger child → Father	.71	.73			

TABLE 3-*continued*

| Dimensions | Alphas for Composites | | Assessment Instrument | Scales | Informants |
	Wave 1	Wave 2			
			SIBLING RELATIONSHIP COMPOSITES		
Positivity:					
Older adolescent	.85	.85	Sib Inventory of Behavior	companionship, empathy,	Mother, Father, Child
Younger adolescent	.84	.87	Conflict Tactics Scale	reasoning	Mother, Father, Child
			Observational coding	positivity: target child to sib	Observer
Negativity:					
Older adolescent	.88	.90	Sib Inventory of Behavior	aggression, rivalry,	Mother, Father, Child
Younger adolescent	.87	.89	Conflict Tactics Scale	avoidance symbolic aggression, aggression	Child
			Observational coding	negativity: target child to sib	Observer
			CHILD ADJUSTMENT COMPOSITES		
I. Negative adjustment					
Depression:					
Older adolescent	.67	.68	Zill Behavior Problems Index	anxious\depressed	Mother, Father, Child
Younger adolescent	.62	.63	Child Depression Inventory	depression	Mother, Father, Child

	Reliability		Instrument	Construct	Observer
Depression			Observational coding	depressed mood: target child to mother / target child to father / target child to sibling	Observer
Antisocial:					
Older adolescent	.68	.69	Zill Behavior Problems Index	antisocial	Mother, Father, Child
Younger adolescent	.62	.63	Observational coding	antisocial behavior: target child to mother / target child to father / target child to sibling	Observer
II. Positive adjustment					
Social Responsibility:					
Older adolescent	.74	.79	Child Competence Inventory	social responsibility	Mother, Father
Younger adolescent	.71	.75	Harter Perceived Competence	prosocial behavior	Mother, Father
Cognitive Agency:					
Older adolescent	.71	.72	Child Behavior Checklist	cognitive	Mother, Father
	.70	.70	Child Competence Inventory	cognitive agency	Mother, Father
Younger adolescent			Harter Perceived Competence	cognitive competence	Child
Sociability:					
Older adolescent	.75	.75	Child Behavior Checklist	social behavior	Mother, Father, Child
Younger adolescent	.72	.78	Autonomous Functioning Checklist	social behavior	Mother, Father, Child
Autonomy:					
Older adolescent	.82	.81	Autonomous Functioning Checklist	maintenance,	Mother, Father, Child
Younger adolescent	.83	.83		self-care, recreation	
Self-Worth:					
Older adolescent	.81	.72	Harter Perceived Competence	global self-worth	Child
Younger adolescent	.78	.68			

Conflict Tactics Scale (CTS; Straus, *1979).* This is a widely used round-robin scale that asks all respondents to rate their conflict resolution tactics with all other respondents; thus the measure assesses parent-adolescent, marital, and sibling dyads in both directions. The measure includes statements that indicate different ways people may act during a disagreement such as crying, hitting, and discussing. Items are summed to create three subscales: reasoning, symbolic aggression, and violence. For the marital chapter, only interspousal symbolic aggression was used. The measure was completed by each husband/wife on their own behavior toward their spouse, as well as their perception of their spouse's behavior toward him/her.

Measures of the Parent-Adolescent Relationship

Childrearing Issues — Part I. This 42-item measure, given to both adolescents and parents, contains statements of areas of potential disagreement between parents and children. Items include the adolescent's behavior, such as behavior at school, lying, etc., as well as rules the adolescent must follow, such as curfew and chores. The measure includes four subscales reflecting conflict around daily routines, adolescent issues, other conflict, and adolescent deviance. Subscales were combined to create a total conflict score. Cronbach's alpha coefficients are reported in Table 3.

Childrearing Issues — Part II. This 43-item measure given to both adolescents and parents assesses different elements of parenting including discipline, control, and communication. Factor analyses revealed three subscales: parent communication, parent punitiveness, and parent yielding to coercion. Discriminant validity checks revealed that parent communication correlated with both parental postivity and negativity, thus it was dropped from future analyses. Punitiveness and yielding to coercion were combined to create a total punitive discipline score.

Conflict Tactics Scale (CTS; Straus, 1979). (See description above under *Measures of the Marital Relationship.*) For the parent-adolescent chapter (Chapter IV), only parent → adolescent and adolescent → parent reasoning and symbolic aggression were used.

Child Monitoring/Control (CM; Hetherington & Clingempeel, 1992). This questionnaire consists of three sections. Each section contains the same 13 items pertaining to different areas of an adolescent's life that a parent may influence or monitor, for example, use of drugs, choice of friends, and health habits. In the first section, how much both the residential mother and father know about their adolescent's life is assessed, which comprises the knowledge subscale. In the second section, residential parents' attempted influence over their adolescent's life is measured, which comprises the attempted control subscale, and in the final section, parents' successful control over their adolescent's life is assessed, which comprises the actual control subscale. Both parents and adolescents complete the scale.

Expression of Affection (EAF; Hetherington & Clingempeel, 1992). This 22-item scale was adapted from one used by Patterson (1982) and requires respondents to indicate if they behaved in the way stated in the past month. Items are grouped into two subscales: expressive affection and instrumental affection. Expressive affection measures items such as spending time alone together, laughing, talking, praising, or giving a hug, while instrumental affection measures joint activities with the adolescent such as shared recreational activities, homework, going for walks, watching television, eating, or going shopping.

Parent-Child Relationship (PCR; Hetherington & Clingempeel, 1992). This 46-item questionnaire consists of items that describe both positive and negative aspects of parent-child relations. Areas of content deal with the way the adolescent and parent relate, for example, how close they are, how well they get along, and how often they disagree. The subscales derived from this measure include: parent → adolescent (*a*) rapport/closeness and (*b*) conflict, as well as adolescent → parent (*c*) rapport/closeness and (*d*) conflict.

Measures of the Sibling Relationship

Sibling Inventory of Behavior (SIB, Schaefer & Edgerton, 1981). This 64-item questionnaire contains items that describe how brothers and sisters behave toward one another. In particular, the frequency of the stated behavior is indicated. On the first 32 items, the adolescents rate their sibling's behavior toward them, using a 5-point Likert scale ranging from 1 = *never* to 5 = *always*. On the second 32 items, the adolescents then rate their own behavior toward their sibling in the manner described above. Items were taken from a measure developed by Schaefer and Edgerton (1981) and modified for use in a prior study of stepfamilies (Hetherington & Clingempeel, 1992). Six subscales are scored in this version: rivalry, aggression, avoidance, companionship, empathy, and teaching.

Sibling Areas of Disagreement (SAD; Hetherington & Clingempeel, 1992). This 16-item scale was constructed by the University of Virginia for the Remarriage Project (Hetherington & Clingempeel, 1992). The first 13 items ask about disagreements with (step)sisters/(step)brothers concerning

39

a variety of topics from activities with friends to choosing a television show, and are added to create a total score.

Conflict Tactics Scale—Sibling Forms (CTS; Straus, 1979). The symbolic aggression subscale of the CTS was completed by mothers, fathers, and adolescents on each target adolescent's behavior toward his/her sibling, as well as his/her perception of the sibling's behavior toward him/her. The physical aggression subscale was not used because of poor distribution on items.

Measures of Adolescent Adjustment and Development

Standardized measures of positive and negative adolescent adjustment were obtained from adolescents, parents, teachers, and observers.

Negative Adolescent Adjustment

Child Depression Inventory (CDI; Kovacs, 1985). This measure consists of 27 items assessing child's self-report of symptoms of depression including feelings of loneliness, sadness, tiredness, and thoughts about suicide during the past 2 weeks. A parallel measure also was given to mothers and fathers. Over the past years, many studies have used the CDI on nonclinical populations (Fauber, Forehand, Long, Burke, & Faust, 1987; Helsel & Matson, 1984; Smucker et al., 1986; Wierzbicki & McCabe, 1988).

Zill Behavior Problems Index (BPI; Zill, 1985). This inventory, derived from items on the Child Behavior Checklist (Achenbach & Edelbrock, 1983), is comprised of five specific subscales describing different aspects of children's behavior including antisocial behavior, anxious/depressed behavior, hyperactive behavior, peer conflict/social withdrawal, and headstrong behavior. In addition, the measure yields two broadband subscales assessing internalizing and externalizing behavior. For the present study, only the general subscales of internalizing and externalizing were used. Mothers, fathers, and adolescents completed the scale.

Positive Adolescent Adjustment

Achenbach Social Competence Scale (CBCL; Achenbach & Edelbrock, 1983). This scale is one portion of the Achenbach Child Behavior Checklist (CBCL), a measure widely used in the study of child and adolescent disorders. The parent version of the competence scale measures child's school performance, activities, friendships and relationships with brothers and sisters. The child version is an 8-item scale in which adolescents list and rate their own activities and school achievements. Two subscales from this measure include the Cognitive Competence subscale, which is an estimate of school grades in several areas, and the Social subscale, which assesses the extent of the adolescent's activity in social organizations, the number of friends, and how well the adolescent gets along with others.

Child Competence Inventory (Hetherington & Clingempeel, 1992). Two subscales from the Child Competence Inventory measuring social responsibility and cognitive agency were used. This measure was developed by Hetherington and Clingempeel (1992) and demonstrated satisfactory validity and reliability. Chronbach's alpha coefficients for different family members reports range from .59 to .72, $M = .66$, for social responsibility and .75 to .84, $M = .79$, for cognitive agency. The subscale of social responsibility asks about the adolescent's adherence to adult norms and values, how well they get along with others and how dependable, honest, understanding, obedient and modest they are. The subscale of cognitive agency assesses the extent to which the adolescent is industrious and oriented to schoolwork, and includes items assessing goal orientation, persistence, self-control, hard work, organization, and enjoyment of intellectual challenge.

Harter Perceived Competence Scale for Children (HPC; Harter, 1982). This scale assesses adolescent's degree of positive self-concept in the areas of cognitive competence, physical appearance, conduct/morality, athletic competence, social acceptance, close friendships, and also includes an overall measure of general self-worth. Children aged 13 and over completed the adolescent version, which contains two additional subscales, romantic appeal and job competence.

Autonomous Functioning Checklist (AFC; Sigafoos, Feinstein, Damond, & Reiss, 1988). This measure was completed by adolescents and both parents and consists of four subscales. The self-care subscale assesses the extent to which the adolescent provides routine care for self or other family members. The maintenance subscale assesses the adolescent's ability to plan and initiate activities on his or her own and to use services such as banks, post offices, or libraries independently. The recreation subscale assesses the extent to which the adolescent pursues leisure and work activities independently, and the social subscale measures activity in social organizations and the social network.

Observational Assessments

Interviewers videotaped 10-minute problem solving interactions of six dyads in the home, including mother-father, mother-older adolescent, mother-younger adolescent, father-older adolescent father-younger adolescent, and older adolescent-younger adolescent, as well as triadic and tetradic interactions. In this study, only dyadic interactions were analyzed.

Family members were asked to check issues that were sources of moderate to intense disagreement between them in their questionnaire booklets. Using these designated areas of conflict, interviewers then asked family members to discuss how arguments about these issues might begin and end and how they might resolve future arguments. Although real problems that family members had identified as topics for their discussion were used, they were kept blind to the origin of the discussion topics. Thus, in the standardized protocol instructions, interviewers introduced the videotape discussion with the following statements: e.g., "All parent and children have occasional disagreements. Two things they *may* disagree about are ___ and ___." It was thought that the use of topics that are real problems, rather than hypothetical problems, for family members would encourage discussion typical of family members' interaction style with each other. By using the families' own problems and videotaping the families in their own homes with the interviewers absent from the discussion, it was hoped this would simulate a disagreement as it would naturally unfold in the home when observers were not present.

Coders were assigned to dyads so that they would not view any family member more than once. For example, a coder might be assigned to code the mother-older adolescent dyad and the father-younger adolescent dyad while another coder would be assigned the mother-younger adolescent dyad and the father-older adolescent dyad, and still another coder would be assigned the sibling dyad and the mother-father dyad. Furthermore, dyads in the same family were assigned at different times so that coders were unlikely to remember the family from previous coding. During the interaction, raters coded each family member's behavior separately, so that in the mother-older adolescent dyad for example, mother → older adolescent behavior was coded separately from older adolescent → mother behavior. Ratings were global assessments based on both the intensity and frequency of behaviors. Over 25% of the data was coded by two coders for reliability purposes.

The Family Interaction Coding System, which was developed for a previous study (Hetherington & Clingempeel, 1992), contains 5-point rating scales developed to assess various aspects of family interactions. Scales included warmth/support, anger/rejection, coercion, involvement, communication, authority/control, assertiveness, self-disclosure, transactional conflict, positive mood, and depressed mood. In addition, several scales were coded only for parents, including child monitoring, parental influence, and parenting styles—authoritative, permissive, authoritarian, and disengaged. Adolescents also were coded on prosocial and antisocial behavior.

Intercoder reliabilities were calculated for each score given to each family member. Reliabilities were assessed in three ways: percentage exact agreement, interclass correlations, and weighted kappas. Weighted kappas were used as they are viewed as more appropriate for rating scales than unweighted kappas (Cohen, 1968). The mean percentage agreement for the factors derived through data reduction and based on the overall ratings used in analyses was 79 (range = 69–91). The mean intraclass correlations was 70 (range = 51–90), and the mean kappa was 61 (range = 50–86).[1]

Data reduction of the observational measures was conducted on the scores of each family member. Confirmatory modeling procedures were employed, based on findings from previous research that has used this coding procedure (Hetherington & Clingempeel, 1992), to create observational composite scores. Composite scores were created for each dyad including: (a) parent-adolescent relationship: mother-older adolescent; mother-younger adolescent; father-older adolescent; father-younger adolescent; (b) marital relationship: mother-father; and (c) sibling relationship: older adolescent-younger adolescent. Two factors, Positivity and Negativity, were identified for all dyads. For all dyads, the composite of negativity included the ratings of anger/rejection, coercion and transactional conflict. The individual ratings that comprised the positivity composite differed somewhat, however, according to dyad.

Positivity in the marital dyad consisted of warmth/support, involvement, communication and self-disclosure. For the parent-adolescent and sibling dyads, positivity of parent to adolescent and adolescent to parent, and of each sibling to the other included ratings of warmth/support, assertiveness, involvement, and communication. In addition, a third factor, monitoring/control, emerged for parent → adolescent dyads, which included authority/control, child monitoring, and parental influence.

Lastly, adolescents' observed ratings of prosocial and antisocial behavior were used as assessments of adolescents' social adjustment and were later combined with paper-and-pencil measures of the same dimensions.

Measures of Adult Adjustment

Center for Epidemiological Studies Depression Scale (CES-D; Radloff, 1977). This 20-item scale assesses respondents' feelings pertaining to depression such as "I felt sad" and reverse-scored "I enjoyed life." The CES-D was

---

[1] Detailed tables of reliabilities are available from the author.

developed to assess depressive symptoms in a large general population study (Radloff, 1977), and is a widely used measure of depressive symptoms in both normal and clinical populations (Orme et al., 1986; Radloff & Terri, 1986). The CES-D has been found to discriminate between clinically depressed and nondepressed individuals (Orme et al., 1986; Radloff & Terri, 1986). The 1-week test-retest correlations in our first wave of data were $r = .68$ for mothers and $r = .65$ for fathers. The internal consistency for the total scores was .69 for mothers and .59 for fathers.

PRELIMINARY ANALYSES AND DATA REDUCTION

Composites were constructed using multiple measures and multiple respondents. To minimize rater bias and increase reliability, composite measures were chosen over individual measures of adolescent adjustment, parenting and sibling and marital relationships. Composite scores have been demonstrated to explain more of the variance in child psychopathology than individual scores (Mathijssen et al., 1998). Data reduction strategies adopted in the Adjustment to Remarriage Project (Hetherington & Clingempeel, 1992) were used to construct the composites for the NEAD project.

Many of the measures collected for this project had been used in the Adjustment to Remarriage Project; thus, we had strong empirical guidelines for grouping certain subscales together. First, exploratory factor analyses were conducted to assess how subscales related to each other as compared to similar analyses run on the same subscales in the Adjustment to Remarriage Project. Analyses were run separately for the marital, sibling, and mother-adolescent and father-adolescent relationship. With few exceptions, similar patterns of factors emerged.

Next, subscale scores were converted into z-scores using the CONDESCRIPTIVE subprogram of SPSS. These z-scores were then summed and divided by the number of scales for that composite. All composite scores of family relationships were standardized across the NEAD sample (without the twins in the original sample) and across both Waves 1 and 2. For Wave 1 analyses, composites were standardized within wave to capitalize on the larger sample size. For the Wave 1–Wave 2 repeated-measures analyses, composites were standardized across waves and included only scales that were collected at both Waves 1 and 2. For all standardizing, each composite has a mean of 0 and a standard deviation of 1.0. Cronbach's alpha coefficients for composite scores of family relationships and adolescent adjustment are reported in Table 3. The following section describes how our different composites were created including marital, parent-adolescent, sibling, and adolescent adjustment composites.

Marital Composites

Marital positivity. Positivity in the marital relationship was measured with (*a*) the Locke-Wallace Quality scale, (*b*) the Locke-Wallace Global scale, and (*c*) the Network of Relationships Inventory. Also, observer ratings of marital positivity, including warmth/support, involvement, communication, and self-disclosure were included.

Marital negativity. The degree of conflict and negativity expressed in the marital relationship was assessed using spouses' reports on (*a*) the Locke-Wallace disagreement subscale, (*b*) the Conflict Tactics symbolic aggression subscales (including both respondent's report of spouse's behavior to respondent and respondent's report of his/her behavior to spouse), and (*c*) the Network of Relationships Inventory conflict subscale. In addition, observer ratings of marital negativity, which included individual reports of anger/rejection, coercion and transactional conflict, were included. Cronbach's alpha coefficients are in Table 3.

Parenting Composites

Parent-adolescent positivity/warmth. The degree of warmth and support in mother-adolescent and father-adolescent relationships was measured using parents' and adolescents' reports on (*a*) the rapport/closeness subscale of the Parent-Child Relationship Scale (Hetherington & Clingempeel, 1992), (*b*) the expressive affection, and (*c*) instrumental affection subscales of the Expression of Affection Scale (Hetherington & Clingempeel, 1992), and (*d*) an observational measure of parents' warmth/support to each sibling, which included individual measures of warmth, communication, assertiveness, and involvement. Cronbach's alpha coefficients are presented in Table 3.

Parent-child negativity/conflict. Parent's negativity and coerciveness toward adolescents was assessed using parents' and adolescents' reports on the (*a*) conflict subscale of the Parent-Child Relationship Scale (Hetherington & Clingempeel, 1992), (*b*) the symbolic aggression subscale of the Conflict Tactics Scale (Straus, 1979), (*c*) the total conflict, and (*d*) punitive discipline subscales of the Childrearing Issues Scale (Hetherington & Clingempeel, 1992), and an observational measure of parents' negativity to each sibling, which included individual measures of coerciveness, hostility, and transactional conflict. Table 3 displays the Cronbach's alpha coefficients for this measure.

Parent-child monitoring/control. Parents' monitoring and control of adolescents' behavior was assessed using parents' and adolescents' reports on the (*a*) knowledge, (*b*) attempted control, and (*c*) actual control subscales of the Child Monitoring and Control Scale (Hetherington & Clingempeel, 1992), and (*d*) an observational measure of parents' monitoring/control, which included individual measures of monitoring, parental influence, and successful control. Cronbach's alpha coefficients are presented in Table 3.

Sibling Composites

Sibling positivity. Siblings' positivity toward each other was measured using parents' and adolescents' reports on the (*a*) companionship, (*b*) empathy, and (*c*) teaching/directiveness subscales of the Sibling Inventory of Behavior. Also used were adolescents' reports on the (*d*) reasoning subscale of the Conflict Tactics Scale. In addition, observational measures of siblings' warmth/support to each other, which included individual measures of warmth, communication, assertiveness, and involvement, were included. Alpha coefficients are presented in Table 3.

Sibling negativity. Sibling negativity was assessed using parents' and adolescents' reports on the (*a*) aggression subscale, (*b*) rivalry subscale, and (*c*) avoidance subscale of the Sibling Inventory of Behavior. Also, adolescents' reports on both the (*d*) symbolic aggression and (*e*) violence subscales of the Conflict Tactics Scale were used. In addition, observer ratings of sibling negativity, which included scores on anger/rejection, coercion, and transactional conflict, were included. Cronbach's alpha coefficients are presented in Table 3.

Adolescent Adjustment Composites

Adolescent Adjustment—Negative

Depressive symptoms. A composite of adolescent Depressive Symptoms was created from (*a*) the Children's Depression Inventory (CDI: Kovacs, 1985), (*b*) the anxious-depressed subscale from the Zill Behavior Problems Index (BPI: Zill, 1985), and (*c*) the Depressed Mood scale from the observational data (Hetherington, Hagan, & Eisenberg, 1992).

Externalizing. The externalizing composite was constructed for the NEAD project from mothers', fathers', and adolescents' report on (*a*) the Zill BPI antisocial subscale and (*b*) the antisocial behavior subscale from the observational data.

Adolescent Adjustment—Positive

Social responsibility. Two subscales were used to assess this domain. Parents' reports of social responsibility from the Child Competence Inventory and procosial behavior from the Harter were included. This index represents the extent to which children adhere to generalized adult social norms and engage in prosocial activity. See Cronbach's alphas in Table 3.

Cognitive agency. This composite consisted of two measures from both parents and two measures from adolescents. Parents' and adolescents' reports on the cognitive subscale of the CBCL were included with adolescents' reports on the cognitive competence subscale of the Harter and parents' reports of the cognitive agency subscale from the Child Competence Inventory. This index represents children's persistence, goal-directed behavior, and performance on academic matters.

Sociability. The composite index of sociability included the social subscales from the CBCL and the Autonomous Functioning checklist as rated by adolescent and both parents. This index assesses positive peer activity, involvement in organized prosocial activity, and the quality of the peer network.

Autonomy. Mothers', fathers', and adolescents' reports on the (*a*) maintenance, (*b*) self-care, and (*c*) recreation subscales of the Autonomous Functioning Checklist (Sigafoos et al., 1988) comprised the autonomy composite. This composite represents the adolescent's engagement in independent and self-reliant activity.

Self-worth The index of self-worth consists of adolescents' report on the Harter Percieved Competence. This index represents adolescents' general tendency to view themselves or their lives positively.

OVERVIEW OF ANALYSES

Two main sets of analyses were conducted. First, analyses were performed within Wave 1 on the full data set of 516 families to capitalize on the large sample size in the first wave. Second, across-wave analyses, on the families who were present in both waves, were performed to assess changes in family relationships and adolescent's adjustment over time.

Grand Mean Standardizing

The measures in the parenting, marital, sibling, and adolescent adjustment composites were standardized for this study in order that direct comparisons among family members' individual and composite reports could be made. The standardization process included deriving a grand mean across all reporters who completed parallel forms on a measure, and then creating a z-score for each measure. First, Wave 1 scores were standardized within-wave to capitalize on the larger sample size and included scores for older adolescent, younger adolescent, mother, father, and observer ratings. The resulting z-scores were used for creating composites for Wave 1 data and were included in all Wave 1 analyses.

Second, in anticipation of running repeated-measures multivariate analyses of variance (MANOVAs) across time periods, scores were standardized across both Waves 1 and 2 and also included scores for older adolescent, younger adolescent, mother, father, and observer ratings. For example, if older adolescents, younger adolescents, mothers, and fathers responded to parallel measures of older → younger sibling negativity, eight scores were standardized together; in this case, older adolescent's report, younger adolescent's report, mother's report and father's report for Wave 1 and Wave 2. Similarly, if older adolescents and mothers responded to the same measures of adolescent → mother negativity, then 4 scores were standardized together including older adolescent's report and mother's report for Wave 1 and Wave 2. Standardizing separately within each wave would have erased possible differences across time, however, by standardizing across waves of data, as well as across reporters, all reporters can be fairly compared to each other and across time periods.

Analytic Plan

Within-wave analyses. MANOVAs were conducted for (a) multireporter, multimeasure composites of family relationships and adolescent adjustment and (b) single reporter, multimeasure composites. Single reporter, multimeasure composites consisted of a single reporter's scores on several subscales, for example, adolescent's report of adolescent-mother instrumental affection, expressive affection, and rapport/closeness, which were combined to create adolescent's report of warmth/positivity. Single reporter composites were included to capture individual reporters' differences in perceptions.

All MANOVAs were calculated with adolescent gender and family type as between-participants factors. Unique sums of squares were used in all analyses because of unequal sample sizes. Significant main effects and interactions of the MANOVAs are presented. In addition, significant univariate results and planned comparisons based on previous research are sometimes discussed in the absence of multivariate effects. The hypotheses that led to such univariate tests of planned comparisons are presented at the beginning of each chapter. In the absence of multivariate effects, however, significant univariate tests should be viewed with caution.

Across-wave analyses. Repeated-measures analyses that parallel the within Wave 1 analyses were conducted at the individual reporter and composite level. Repeated-measures MANOVAs were conducted to assess changes in family relationships and adolescent adjustment from Wave 1 to Wave 2. As in the within-wave analyses, adolescent gender and family type were the between-participants factors. Assessment at Wave 1 and Wave 2, or time, was the within-subject factor. Since within-wave analyses on Wave 1 were conducted using the full sample of 516 participants and since the repeated-measures analyses involved only participants who participated in both waves ($N = 259$), within-wave and across-wave means and standard deviations may differ slightly.

Review of Parallel and Unique Analyses Within Chapters

All chapters included the following analyses. First, within-wave assessments were conducted using MANOVA procedures from the SPSS statistical package, including differences in gender and family type/ownness. Second, stabilities and changes over time (longitudinal findings) are presented, which again may include correlations, repeated-measures MANOVAs (i.e., differences in gender, family type/ownness), and regression or crosslag analyses. Subsequent to descriptive analyses of family subsystems, additional analyses were performed within each chapter exploring questions of particular interest. Specific measures used and analyses performed that differ across chapters are described fully within each chapter. In addition, from a family systems perspective, Chapter VII links all subsystems—marital, parent-adolescent, and sibling—and explores their relation to adolescent adjustment through structural model equation techniques. Similar to MANOVA analyses, both adolescent gender and family type were examined throughout analyses using structural models.

III. MARITAL SATISFACTION, RELATIONSHIPS, AND ROLES

Thomas G. O'Connor and Glendessa M. Insabella

This chapter will focus on the changes, stresses, and adaptation in the marital relationship in stepfamilies and in first marriages. Mean differences and changes over time in marital quality, coparenting relationship, performance of and satisfaction with household work and childrearing tasks, and several indices of individual adaptation are examined. In addition, the relations among these dimensions are explored in first marriages and in couples in diverse types of stepfamilies. A more comprehensive model examining the association of the marital relationship with other family subsystems and with adolescent adjustment is presented in Chapter VII.

As noted in the earlier literature review, spouses in stepfamilies are faced with multiple challenges while trying to build a satisfying marital relationship. They must cope with alterations in residential arrangements and household membership, economic circumstances, and family roles and relationships. Difficulties in building a harmonious, gratifying conjugal relationship may be exacerbated by the presence of children, especially if the children are difficult, resistant, and confrontational, or if they have problems in adjustment (Hetherington & Clingempeel, 1992; White & Booth, 1985). The development of constructive, involved, cooperative coparenting roles may be more difficult in complex stepfamily households where variations in biological relatedness to parents may be associated with differential treatment of children and conflict over childrearing. That is, the cause of differences in relationship quality between nondivorced and remarried couples, if found, are likely the result of problems stemming from parenting roles and family management rather than from the marital relationship as such.

Against the profile of risks, however, it must be remembered that the remarried families in this study are stabilized, that is, they are past the especially stressful years immediately following the remarriage. Many couples with dysfunctional or unhappy marriages would have divorced previously and would not have been eligible for this study. Couples in the current sample of stepfamilies have had on the average almost 9 years to work out their problems and establish a constructive marital relationship. Thus, both the couples in first marriages and stepfamilies have survived the challenges found in the early years of a relationship when declines in marital satisfaction and rates of marital dissolution are greatest (Bumpass, Martin, & Sweet, 1991; Clarke & Wilson, 1994). Nonetheless, couples in first and remarriages have at least two children moving through adolescence, a period when notable realignments in family relations and declines in marital satisfaction may occur (Hetherington, 1993).

This chapter examines whether nondivorced couples and couples in stabilized stepfamilies differ in terms of (a) marital quality as defined by self-reports of conflict and satisfaction as well as observed interactions; (b) negotiation and conflict regarding coparenting roles; (c) absolute levels of, and satisfaction with, division of childrearing responsibilities and household decision making; (d) self-reported levels of depression, alcohol, and marijuana use; (e) correlates of marital quality concurrently and/or longitudinally; and (f) the influence of adolescents' adjustment on marital satisfaction and conflict. Based on previous research reviewed in Chapter I, several hypotheses were proposed. First, it was hypothesized that quality of marital relations as reported by the couple would be similar across family types, but that more negative and less positive interactions in stepfamilies would emerge in observations. Second, it was proposed that couples in simple and complex stepfamilies would report significantly more disagreements regarding childrearing than couples in never-divorced families. Third, it was expected that wives would engage in more household labor and parenting responsibilities than husbands across all family types, but both wives and husbands in stepfamilies would engage in more parenting with their biological child than with their stepchild. Fourth, it was hypothesized that conflict regarding childrearing and satisfaction with household labor would be more strongly associated with marital satisfaction among remarried partners than among partners in first marriages. Fifth, it was predicted that across all family types marital satisfaction and conflict would be significantly associated with satisfaction with division of household responsibilities and household labor, rather than with absolute levels of childrearing tasks. Sixth, it was expected that changes in marital satisfaction would be predicted from depressive symptoms, conflict regarding childrearing, and satisfaction with division of household labor; reciprocally, changes in depressive symptoms would be predicted from the quality of the marital relationship. Finally, it

51

was hypothesized that parents would be more negative and less positive in their marital relations in the presence of an externalizing adolescent, especially in stepfamilies.

METHOD

Sample

The sample included in the analyses in this chapter varies slightly that in from other chapters. Couples were classified as in their first marriage (i.e., never divorced) only if the marriage was the first marriage for both spouses, all adolescents in the household were biologically related to both parents, and if a complete marital history was available. In the classification of nonstepfamilies used in the rest of the *Monograph* some of the spouses had been previously married. All mothers in simple and complex stepfamilies had been married at least once previously and had brought children from their previous relationship(s) into the current remarriage. The majority of fathers in simple and complex stepfamilies had been previously married.

The final sample for this chapter consisted of 80 couples in first marriages, 82 remarried couples in simple stepfamilies, and 287 remarried couples in complex stepfamilies at Wave 1. The corresponding figures for Wave 2 were 51, 43, and 134, respectively (see Chapter II for information on attrition). Simple stepfamilies are known as "traditional" stepfather families because all children in the household are full siblings and were brought into the current family from the mother's previous relationship. In complex stepfamilies, at least one pair of siblings did not share the same degree of biological relatedness to both the mother and the father in the household.

As described above, "ownness" is defined as biological relatedness to the parent. Because this chapter focuses on the marital relationship, a separate ownness variable was computed for each adolescent, describing his or her relationship to both parents in the household. For the older adolescents in stepfamilies, 167 boys and 145 girls were their mothers' biological children and their fathers' stepchildren, whereas 28 boys and 27 girls were fathers' biological children and mothers' stepchildren. The remainder of the targeted older adolescents were biologically related to both the mother and the father in the household: 42 boys and 39 girls in nondivorced families. For the younger adolescents, 113 boys and 114 girls were the biological children of mothers and the stepchildren of fathers, whereas 40 boys and 25 girls were their fathers' biological children and their stepmothers' stepchildren. Eighty-four boys and 73 girls were the biological children of both the mother and the father in the family; however, 42 of these boys and 38 of these girls were from never-divorced families, and 42 boys and 35 girls were from complex stepfamilies. Thus, for analyses using the biological relatedness of the parent to adolescent, there will be a three-group variable for the older adolescent: (a) biologically related to the mother but not to the father; (b) biologically related to both the mother and the father; and (c) biologically related to the father but not to the mother. Because a larger number of the younger adolescents were born to the couple after their remarriage, analyses involving the younger adolescent can begin to tease apart the effects of ownness and family type. A four-group variable of ownness was used for the younger adolescent: (a) biologically related to mother and father's stepchild; (b) biologically related to both mother and father in a never-divorced family; (c) biologically related to both mother and father in a complex stepfamily; and (d) biologically related to father and mother's stepchild.

Data Analysis

Mean differences in marital relationship and individual adjustment variables were examined with family type as a between-family effect and spouse's gender as a within-family effect. Cross-sectional analyses at Wave 1 included all available families. Given the minimal effects of selective attrition (see Chapter II), we report the cross-sectional analyses of Wave 1 using all available families, and this is followed by the repeated-measures analyses including a reduced sample of families that were seen at both waves. The repeated-measures analyses must be considered in light of the differences in power and sample size from that found in Wave 1. In the repeated measure MANOVAs, wave and spouse are within-family effects and family type is the between-family effect.

Within-wave and repeated measures MANOVAs were first run on the marital relationship composites of positivity and negativity measured directionally, that is, Mother → Father and Father → Mother (see Chapter II for more information on the measures included in the composites). Next, parallel MANOVA analyses of the positivity and negativity in the marital relationship based on the individual observational and self report measures were performed. This latter set of analyses allowed examination of whether family type or gender differences in marital quality are specific to an individual reporter or measure.

Analyses of Variance (ANOVAs) were used to analyze variables for which only one index of the construct was available. Univariate contrasts were examined when multivariate F-values indicated a significant effect or when past research and our hypotheses suggested particular planned comparisons.

Following the analyses of the mean levels of positivity and negativity in the marital relationship, mean differences across family type and spouse in other dimensions of the marital relationship (conflict over childrearing, amount of childcare work, and satisfaction with division of household labor) and individual adjustment (alcohol and marijuana usage and depressive symptoms) were analyzed. In the analyses related to childrearing, ownness was included as a between-subjects factor; adolescent's gender also was used as a between-subjects factor in the analyses of the amount of, and satisfaction with, division of childrearing tasks.

Next, the predictors of change in individual differences in the marital relationship and depressive symptoms were examined using regression analyses. This analytic approach complements the repeated-measures ANOVA approach. Whereas the repeated-measures analyses examined changes in the mean level across the whole sample (or subgroups), the regression analyses examined predictors of individual differences over time.

For this chapter, gender and biological relatedness of the target siblings were not included as factors in the analyses because, on average, families included at least one additional (nontarget) child who may not have been of the same sex as the target siblings and whose degree of biological relatedness to the target siblings varied widely in the complex stepfamilies. In addition, no association was predicted between target adolescents' genetic relatedness and marital quality (independent of stepfamily type).

The final set of analyses explored whether the two target adolescents' externalizing behaviors and depressive symptoms were associated with husbands' and wives' marital positivity and negativity concurrently and longitudinally. Husbands' and wives' positivity and negativity were each predicted separately. Both adolescents' behaviors were added to the same model to evaluate the presence of differential effects of each adolescent's adjustment on the marital relationship. Adolescents' gender and dummy variables taking into account family type and biological relatedness were added to the model as main effects and to evaluate two- and three-way interactions. Because biological relatedness varied within families by parent and child, the family type variable was computed for each adolescent separately for mothers and fathers.

RESULTS

Cross-Sectional Analyses of Marital Positivity and Negativity Measures

Table 4 displays the Wave 1 F-values of the multivariate analysis of variance of the marital Positivity and Negativity measures. Table 5 presents the means (SD) and significant contrasts of the F-values from Table 4. Multivariate analyses of the individual observer, self- and spouse reports of marital Positivity and Negativity at Wave 1 reveal consistent patterns as well as some important differences across source (see Table 4).

TABLE 4

F-Values and Significant Levels for Wave 1 Multivariate Analysis
of the Marital Relationship

	Family	Spouse	Interaction
Positivity			
Multivariate	1.42	9.14***	.78
Multivariate df	(8, 840)	(4, 420)	(8, 840)
Univariate			
Observation	3.25*	25.94***	.70
Network Rel	.46	6.20*	1.59
L-W Qual	.66	2.90	.53
L-W Glb	.39	.02	1.18
Negativity			
Multivariate	2.12*	4.69**	2.28*
Multivariate df	(8, 818)	(4, 409)	(8, 818)
Univariate			
Observation	3.88*	.06	3.32*
L-W Dis	.49	11.29**	5.08**
CTS (on spouse)	2.18	3.80	.45
CTS (on self)	2.33	.14	1.24

NOTE. Network Rel = Network of Relationships Inventory, L-W Qual = Locke-Wallace Quality scale, L-W Glb = Locke-Wallace Global scale, L-W Dis = Locke Wallace Disagreements scale, CTS = Conflict Tactics scale, symbolic aggression.

$*p < .05, **p < .01, ***p < .001.$

There was a significant multivariate effect of Family Type at Wave 1 for Negativity. Follow-up univariate analyses indicated that the effect is specific to observations (see Tables 4 and 5). Observers rated spouses in complex stepfamilies as more negative than spouses in nondivorced families. Interestingly, although the multivariate effect for Positivity at Wave 1 is not significant, the univariate effect of observer reports parallels the results for Negativity in indicating that spouses in nondivorced families are significantly more positive than spouses in complex stepfamilies.

There was a robust Spouse effect for both Positivity and Negativity measures. Although all contrasts indicated that wives were comparatively more positive and husbands were comparatively more negative, there was no robust method effect. Thus, the Spouse multivariate effect for Positivity was attributable to observers' reports and self-reports on the Network of Relationship Inventory. The Spouse effects for Negativity were attributable to the disagreement factor from the Locke-Wallace scale (see Tables 4 and 5).

There was one significant Family Type × Spouse interaction for Negativity at Wave 1. Based on observers' reports, husbands were more negative than wives were in simple stepfamilies only. The follow-up analyses of the Locke-Wallace disagreement factor indicated that husbands engaged in more disagreements than wives in simple stepfamilies and in never-divorced families did. In contrast, husbands and wives in complex stepfamilies were

TABLE 5

Means (Standard Deviations) of Marital Relationship Measures

Measures	Nondivorced Families		Simple Stepfamilies		Complex Stepfamilies		Significant Main Effects and Interactions	Significant Contrasts
	Wives	Husbands	Wives	Husbands	Wives	Husbands		
Measures								
Observed Positivity								
Wave 1	.54 (.72)	.38 (.85)	.42 (.75)	.16 (.69)	.35 (.66)	.16 (.72)	spouse:	wives > husbands
Observed Negativity								
Wave 1	−.36 (.82)	−.39 (.89)	−.18 (.80)	−.07 (.79)	−.05 (.82)	−.09 (.86)	family: family × spouse:	CS > ND SS: husbands > wives
Locke-Wallace (Self-Report)								
Quality								
Wave 1	−.09 (1.0)	.03 (.93)	.10 (.91)	.13 (1.0)	−.05 (.99)	.13 (.95)		
Global								
Wave 1	.09 (.90)	.08 (.95)	.08 (.87)	−.03 (.95)	−.04 (.97)	.05 (.91)		
Disagree								
Wave 1	−.12 (.95)	.21 (1.0)	−.23 (.86)	−.01 (1.1)	−.02 (.99)	−.06 (.96)	spouse: family × spouse:	husbands > wives SS, ND: husbands > wives
Network of Relationships (Self-Report)								
Positivity								
Wave 1	.14 (.97)	.00 (.99)	.21 (.86)	.08 (.82)	.04 (1.1)	.03 (.94)	spouse:	wives > husbands
Conflict Tactics Scale								
Report on Spouse								
Wave 1	−.29 (.55)	−.21 (.73)	−.12 (.73)	−.07 (.81)	−.07 (.69)	−.14 (.75)		
Report on Self								
Wave 1	−.14 (.79)	−.05 (.73)	.02 (.91)	.12 (.93)	−.02 (.77)	.15 (.91)		

NOTE. CS = complex stepfamilies, ND = nondivorced families, SS = simple stepfamilies.

equally likely to disagree with their spouses about issues such as finances, expressions of affection, and choice of friends or recreation (see Tables 4 and 5).

One additional measure on an important aspect of the marital relationships, marital instability, also was assessed only at Wave 1 using the Marital Instability Scale. The measure describes the degree to which spouses have pursued the road to separation or divorce (e.g., contacting a lawyer, thinking about divorce). There were no family type differences, but there was a significant Spouse effect, $F(1, 434) = 5.44, p < .05$, which was qualified by a Spouse × Family Type interaction, $F(2, 434) = 4.59, p < .05$ (not tabled). In complex stepfamilies, wives reported more instability in their marriages than did husbands ($M = 3.4$ and 2.5, respectively, approximately one third of a standard deviation difference). Indeed, whereas the highest scores for husbands were reported in nondivorced families ($M = 3.1$), the highest scores for wives were reported in complex stepfamilies ($M = 3.4$). There was no evidence that differences in marital instability were explained by ownness.

A final set of exploratory analyses examined husbands' and wives' marital Negativity and Positivity according to the biological relatedness of the parent to the index adolescent. That is, we examined if having at least one biological child may be a protective factor for marital quality. ANOVA procedures indicated no association between number of biological children (0, 1, or 2) and marital Negativity or Positivity.

Repeated-Measures Analyses of Composites and Individual Measures

Repeated-measures analyses of the observer, self, and spouse reports of the quality of marital relations using the reduced longitudinal sample were conducted. For these analyses, the main effects of Family Type (between-subjects), Wave (within-subjects), and Spouse (within-subjects), the two-way interactions with Family Type and the three-way interaction were examined. Because Family Type and Spouse effects were reported in previous analyses, only Wave main effects and Wave interactions will be reported here.

A main effect for Wave was obtained for both Positivity and Negativity, $F(4, 203) = 17.37, p < .001$, and $F(4, 177) = 3.20, p < .05$, respectively. Lower levels of positivity at Wave 2 compared with Wave 1 were apparent in observers' ratings and in spouse self-reports on the quality subscale of the Locke-Wallace inventory. The findings for Negativity complemented those found for Positivity with a significant main effect for Wave. An increase in negativity over time was evident in self-reports of conflict on the Locke-Wallace scale. Consistent with the findings for Positivity, there were no two-way or three-way interactions that modified these main effects.

Coparenting In Diverse Family Forms:
Cross-Sectional and Longitudinal Analyses

The previous analyses of Negativity examined conflict in relation to the marital relationship. The next set of analyses examines conflict regarding childrearing. The within Wave 1 analysis found a main effect of Family Type for Disagreement About Childrearing, $F(2, 440) = 3.25$, $p < .05$, which was accounted for by less disagreement in the nondivorced couples than in couples in either simple or complex stepfamilies (not tabled). There was not a main effect of Spouse, nor was there a significant Family Type × Spouse interaction. A Family Type main effect was not obtained in the repeated-measures analyses on the reduced longitudinal sample; however, there was a main effect of Wave, $F(1, 218) = 10.01$, $p < .01$, which indicated increasing conflict about childrearing over time. Neither the Spouse main effect nor the Family Type × Spouse or Family Type × Wave interactions were significant at $p < .05$ in the repeated-measures analyses.

It was not possible to assess conflict as a function of ownness using this measure because parents were asked only about general childrearing conflicts and not disagreements related to specific children in the family. A separate measure of conflict about childrearing, based on the Childrearing Issues Scale (see Chapter II), that did assess conflict specific to each child, did not, however, indicate that spouses reported greater conflict about step-children compared to their biological children (not tabled).

Division of Household and Childrearing Responsibilities

The next set of analyses examines a separate component of the marital relationship, the parents' division of childrearing responsibilities. Husbands and wives reported the number of tasks or decisions (e.g., doing laundry, setting curfew) they performed for the older and younger adolescent separately, as well as their overall satisfaction with the division of household chores and decision making. The means, standard deviations, and significant contrasts for the division of childrearing tasks as a function of family type are presented in Table 6. A main effect of Spouse was obtained for the division of tasks for both the older adolescent, $F(1, 442) = 412.65$, $p < .001$, and the younger adolescent, $F(1, 443) = 529.18$, $p < .001$. In both cases, wives reported that they assumed greater childrearing responsibility than husbands. This main effect with older adolescents was qualified by a Spouse × Family Type interaction, $F(2, 442) = 3.12$, $p < .05$, which indicated that husbands in never-divorced families reported greater responsibility for their older adolescent than did husbands in complex stepfamilies (see Table 6). A main effect of Family Type on division of childrearing responsibility was not found for either the older or younger adolescent.

TABLE 6

MEANS (STANDARD DEVIATIONS) OF DIVISION OF CHILDREARING RESPONSIBILITY IN DIVERSE FAMILY TYPES

	Nondivorced Families		Simple Stepfamilies		Complex Stepfamilies		Significant Main Effects and Interactions	Significant Contrasts
	Boys	Girls	Boys	Girls	Boys	Girls		
	(n = 42)	(n = 33)	(n = 35)	(n = 47)	(n = 160)	(n = 127)		
For Older Adolescent:								
Wives' Childrearing Tasks	10.29 (4.48)	10.08 (5.01)	11.23 (4.44)	11.02 (4.93)	11.12 (5.03)	11.21 (4.96)	spouse:	wives > husbands
Husbands' Childrearing Tasks	4.07 (3.54)	3.95 (3.08)	2.86 (2.83)	2.57 (3.35)	3.52 (3.94)	2.52 (3.48)	family type × spouse:	husbands: ND > CS
For Younger Adolescent:								
Wives' Childrearing Tasks	11.67 (5.16)	11.42 (5.61)	11.89 (4.63)	11.83 (5.22)	11.83 (4.94)	12.22 (5.03)	spouse:	wives > husbands
Husbands' Childrearing Tasks	3.86 (3.57)	3.92 (3.14)	2.80 (3.38)	2.49 (3.45)	3.65 (4.06)	2.21 (2.97)		

NOTE. ND = nondivorced families, CS = complex stepfamilies.

Mean differences in the division of childrearing responsibility also were examined by ownness, that is, whether the parent-adolescent relationship was biological or step. When division of childrearing responsibility was examined based on ownness rather than family type, a clear pattern emerged (see Tables 7 and 8). As expected (from Table 6), there was a significant Spouse effect on division of childrearing tasks for both the older adolescent, $F(1, 442) = 252.70$, $p < .001$, and the younger adolescent, $F(1, 441) = 568.56$, $p < 001$. Mothers consistently perform more tasks and make more decisions for the adolescents in the household than do the fathers. This main effect was qualified, however, by a significant Spouse $\times$ Ownness interaction for both the older adolescent, $F(2, 442) = 23.49$, $p < .001$, and the younger adolescent, $F(3, 441) = 4.60$, $p < .01$. Husbands reported that they assumed significantly more childrearing responsibility for adolescents who were their biological children from a previous marriage and least for adolescents who were their stepchildren, older adolescent: $F(2, 445) = 20.38$, $p < .001$; younger adolescent: $F(3, 445) = 7.18$, $p < .001$. Family type does seem to exert an influence, however, as husbands reported being more involved with their biological children in their first marriage than they did with their biological children in complex stepfamilies (see Tables 7 and 8). For mothers, the univariate effect was significant only for the older adolescent, $F(2, 446) = 9.94$, $p < .001$. Mothers reported that they assumed childrearing responsibility more for their biological children from a previous marriage than for either their biological children with their current partner or their stepchildren. Finally, exploratory analyses indicated that there was a consistent Spouse $\times$ Gender of Child interaction, older adolescent: $F(1, 442) = 3.99$, $p < .05$; younger adolescent: $F(1, 441) = 4.96$, $p < .05$. Although mothers performed an equal number of childrearing tasks for boys and girls, fathers were more involved with boys than with girls, older adolescent: $F(1, 446) = 4.60$, $p < .05$; younger adolescent: $F(1, 447) = 8.50$, $p < .01$ (see Tables 7 and 8).

The final set of analyses of the coparenting roles examined satisfaction with division of decision making and childrearing tasks. That is, whereas the previous set of analyses focused on how many tasks or decisions parents undertake for each adolescent, the current set of means analyses examines how satisfied husbands and wives are with the division of these roles and tasks. A significant Spouse effect was obtained, $F(1, 437) = 19.09$, $p < .001$, which indicated that husbands were more satisfied with the division of household responsibilities than were wives ($M = 3.99$, $SD = .95$, and $M = 3.64$, $SD = 1.2$, respectively). There were no family type differences and no differences in satisfaction by biological relatedness to children.

TABLE 7

Means (Standard Deviations) of Division of Childrearing Responsibility as a Function of Ownness and Gender of Older Adolescent: Wave 1

	Wives' Childrearing	Husbands' Childrearing	Significant Main Effects and Interactions	Significant Contrasts
Biological Mother/Stepfather				
Boys (n = 167)	11.62 (4.76)	2.75 (2.95)	spouse:	wives > husbands
Girls (n = 145)	11.55 (4.79)	2.32 (3.18)	ownness × spouse:	wives: bm/sf > bm/bf, sm/bf
				husbands: sm/bf > bm/bf > bm/sf
Biological Mothers and Fathers				
Boys (n = 42)	10.29 (4.48)	4.07 (3.54)		
Girls (n = 39)	10.10 (4.95)	3.85 (3.11)	gender × spouse:	husbands: boys > girls
Stepmother/Biological Father				
Boys (n = 28)	8.29 (4.99)	7.25 (5.52)		
Girls (n = 27)	9.07 (5.42)	3.82 (4.46)		

NOTE. bm/sf = biological mother & stepfather; bm/bf = biological mother & biological father; sm/bf = stepmother & biological father.

TABLE 8

Means (Standard Deviations) of Division of Childrearing Responsibility as a Function of Ownness and Gender of Younger Adolescent: Wave 1

	Wives' Childrearing	Husbands' Childrearing	Significant Main Effects and Interactions	Significant Contrasts
Biological Mother/Stepfather				
Boys (n = 113)	12.51 (4.90)	2.93 (3.50)	spouse:	wives > husbands
Girls (n = 114)	11.86 (5.08)	2.18 (3.02)	ownness × spouse:	husbands: sm/bf; bm/bf, ND > bm/bf, CS; bm/sf
Biological Mother and Father (Nondivorced Families)				
Boys (n = 42)	11.67 (5.16)	3.86 (3.57)	gender × spouse:	husbands: boys > girls
Girls (n = 38)	11.42 (5.61)	3.92 (3.14)		
Biological Mother and Father (Complex Stepfamilies)				
Boys (n = 42)	11.38 (4.61)	3.24 (3.42)		
Girls (n = 35)	13.34 (5.04)	2.00 (3.09)		
Stepmother/Biological Father				
Boys (n = 40)	10.43 (4.84)	5.38 (5.06)		
Girls (n = 25)	11.56 (4.97)	3.20 (3.44)		

NOTE. bm/sf = biological mother & stepfather; bm/bf = biological mother & biological father; sm/bf = stepmother & biological father; ND = nondivorced families; CS = complex stepfamilies.

Depressive Symptoms Among Husbands and Wives in Diverse Family Types

Contrary to expectation, no significant differences by family type or spouse emerged for depressive symptoms. Although there were no main effects, there was a significant Family Type × Spouse interaction at Wave 1, $F(2, 443) = 6.55$, $p < .01$. Husbands in simple stepfamilies reported more depressive symptoms than husbands in complex stepfamilies; within complex stepfamilies, wives reported more depressive symptoms than did husbands. Follow-up analyses were conducted to determine whether, as the above differences suggest, the presence of a biological child was a protective factor for men, and the presence of a stepchild was associated with elevated levels of depression for women. Further analyses failed to support this proposal. For example, within the complex stepfamilies, there was no evidence that ownness or biological constellation was differentially associated with depressive symptoms in men or women.

Alcohol and Marijuana Usage Among Husbands and Wives in Diverse Family Types

Analyses of the frequency of alcohol and marijuana use indicated that there were no differences across family type. Husbands, however, reported more frequent alcohol and marijuana use than wives at Wave 1, $F(1, 430) = 56.16$, $p < .001$, and Wave 2, $F(1, 201) = 19.71$, $p < .001$. The Spouse × Family Type effect was not significant, nor was there any change in drug use over time.

The Relations Among Depression, Satisfaction With Family Roles, Division of Childrearing, and Marital Quality

As expected (and detailed below), there was significant overlap among measures of marital satisfaction and conflict, coparenting, satisfaction with division of childrearing tasks, and depressive symptoms, both cross-sectionally and longitudinally. The concurrent correlations between marital positivity and negativity and depressive symptoms were moderate for both husbands and wives at both waves, and range in absolute value from $r = .22$ to $r = .35$. Despite the mean differences over time noted above for both Positivity and Negativity, stability of individual differences in these composite measures was substantial ($r = .69$ and $.62$ for Positivity for husbands and wives, respectively, and $r = .78$ and $.70$ for Negativity for husbands and wives, respectively, all ps $< .001$).

The hypothesis that the relations among the marital and individual adjustment variables differed across family type and spouse was examined using the Fisher r to z transformation method of comparing correlations. There was no evidence that the pattern of correlations varied across family type or

63

spouse. That is, associations among the processes in the marital relationship were similar across husbands and wives in first marriage families and remarried families. For example, the correlation between conflict regarding childrearing and marital conflict was $r = .50$, .46, and .57 for mothers in never-divorced families, simple, and complex stepfamilies, respectively, and $r = .40$, .62, and .53 for fathers in never-divorced families, simple, and complex stepfamilies, respectively.

The next set of analyses examined the differential ability of spouses' observed behaviors and reports of satisfaction and negativity, aspects of the coparenting relationship, depressive symptoms, and marital history (number of previous marriages) to predict the composite measures of marital Positivity and Negativity measured directionally. Preliminary analyses were conducted to reduce the number of predictor variables in the regression equation from the list of hypothesized predictors for several reasons, including concerns about power, the need to eliminate redundant variables, and colinearity. For example, the length of (re)marriage was entered into preliminary analyses but did not account for any of the variance in the marital relationship for either husbands or wives. The final set of predictors, listed in Tables 9 to 12, is the same for the cross-sectional analyses at Wave 1 and the analyses of change from Wave 1 to Wave 2. As suggested by the Fisher r to z analyses reported above, there was minimal evidence for interactions by family type in the regression analyses. Accordingly, only main effects are reported in Tables 9 to 12. Two dummy variables comparing family types, and for the analyses of change the stability coefficient, are entered on the first step. The second step of the hierarchical regression analyses includes the hypothesized set of predictor variables: depression, division of household work (the average for both children), conflict regarding childrearing, marital instability, the marital history of both partners, and the spouse's reported marital satisfaction and conflict.

Tables 9 and 10 present the cross-sectional predictions of marital Positivity and Negativity at Wave 1 separately for wives and husbands. As hypothesized, individual differences in the marital composite variables were most closely associated with marital process variables rather than with family type and, moreover, a range of marital processes was implicated. Although there were, of course, differences across spouse and affective dimension, it is nonetheless striking that a robust subset of predictors consistently emerges in predicting marital quality. Spouse Positivity and Negativity were consistent and strong predictors of relationship quality in cross-sectional analyses, that is, Positivity and Negativity in relationship quality were reciprocated by husbands and wives. Beyond the effects of reciprocated positivity or negativity, a number of attitudinal predictors emerged for husbands' and wives' reports. Most notably, self-reports of marital instability, conflict about childrearing,

TABLE 9

Predictors of Husbands' Marital Positivity and Negativity, Wave 1

	Wave 1 Positivity		
Step 1	B	SE B	β
Intact vs. step	.10	.09	.06
Intact/simple vs. complex	.05	.05	.04
R^2 for step 1			.00
Step 2			
Spouse Negativity	−.18	.05	−.16***
Spouse Positivity	.36	.04	.40***
Childrearing Conflict	−.05	.02	−.08*
Marital Instability	−.16	.02	−.26***
Depression	−.01	.002	−.09**
Household Work	.05	.02	.08*
Marital History (Husband)	.04	.03	.05
Marital History (Wife)	−.16	.05	−.15**
R^2 for step 2			.62***
R^2 for Final Model			.62***
	Wave 1 Negativity		
Step 1	B	SE B	β
Intact vs. step	.00	.07	.00
Intact/simple vs. complex	−.07	.04	−.05
R^2 for step 1			.00
Step 2			
Spouse Negativity	.72	.04	.65***
Spouse Positivity	.00	.03	.00
Childrearing Conflict	.12	.02	.19***
Marital Instability	.11	.02	.18***
Depression	.01	.002	.08**
Household Work	.00	.02	−.01
Marital History (Husband)	−.01	.02	−.01
Marital History (Wife)	.02	.04	.01
R^9 for step 2			.75***
R^2 for Final Model			.75***

*$p < .05$, **$p < .01$, ***$p < .001$.

and depression also were moderately associated with both relationship positivity and negativity for husbands and wives.

Predicting Individual Differences in Changes in Marital and Individual Adjustment

This next set of analyses examined the factors associated with changes in marital relationship quality (see Tables 11 and 12). For predicting changes in, for example, husbands' marital Positivity, regression analyses were run in which Wave 2 Positivity was regressed onto Wave 1 Positivity and family type in the first step. The remaining predictor variables from Wave 1 were entered in a second block.

TABLE 10

PREDICTORS OF WIVES' MARITAL POSITIVITY AND NEGATIVITY, WAVE 1

	Wave 1 Positivity		
Step 1	B	SE B	β
Intact vs. step	.03	.10	.01
Intact/simple vs. complex	−.08	.06	−.06
R^2 for step 1			.00
Step 2			
Spouse Negativity	−.10	.05	−.09*
Spouse Positivity	.40	.05	.36***
Childrearing Conflict	−.07	.02	−.10**
Marital Instability	−.19	.03	−27***
Depression	−.01	.002	−.11***
Household Work	.08	.02	.13***
Marital History (Husband)	.02	.03	.03
Marital History (Wife)	.03	.06	.02
R^2 for step 2			.62***
R^2 for Final Model			.62***
	Wave 1 Negativity		
Step 1	B	SE B	β
Intact vs. step	.08	.07	.05
Intact/simple vs. complex	.08	.04	.07*
R^2 for step 1			.01*
Step 2			
Spouse Negativity	.58	.03	.65***
Spouse Positivity	−.01	.03	−.02
Childrearing Conflict	.11	.02	.19***
Marital Instability	.05	.02	.09**
Depression	.00	.00	.05*
Household Work	−.02	.01	−.05
Marital History (Husband)	−.03	.02	−.04
Marital History (Wife)	−.04	.04	−.04
R^2 for step 2			.71***
R^2 for Final Model			.72***

*$p < .05$, **$p < .01$, ***$p < .001$.

Significant Wave 1 predictors of a *decrease* in husbands' Positivity were self-reported marital instability and conflict regarding childrearing. For wives' Positivity, the only significant Wave 1 predictor was husband's Negativity, which was associated with a *decrease* in wives' Positivity. Interestingly, for neither wives nor husbands were predictors of *increases* in relationship warmth and satisfaction detected.

Husbands' reports of marital instability predicted an increase in their negativity toward their wives. For wives' Negativity, the only significant predictor of change was a history of multiple marriages; however, the overall block was not significant once the stability was covaried out (i.e., step 2 was not significant). The predictions of change in marital positivity and negativity should be considered in light of the marked over-time stability in

TABLE 11

PREDICTORS OF CHANGE IN HUSBANDS' MARITAL POSITIVITY AND NEGATIVITY

	Wave 2 Positivity		
Step 1	B	SE B	β
Intact vs. step	.06	.12	.04
Intact/simple vs. complex	−.08	.07	−.07
Wave 1 Positivity	.44	.09	.47***
R^2 for step 1			.63***
Step 2			
Spouse Negativity	−.16	.08	−.13
Spouse Positivity	.03	.08	.03
Childrearing Conflict	−.13	.04	−.20***
Marital Instability	−.03	.01	−.15**
Depression	−.01	.01	−.03
Household Work	.00	.01	.00
Marital History (Husband)	.03	.05	.03
Marital History (Wife)	.04	.09	.03
R^2 for step 2			.08***
R^2 for Final Model			.71***
	Wave 2 Negativity		
Step 1	B	SE B	β
Intact vs. step	.06	.12	.04
Intact/simple vs. complex	−.08	.07	−.07
Wave 1 Negativity	.44	.09	.47***
R^2 for step 1			.60***
Step 2			
Spouse Negativity	.15	.09	.14
Spouse Positivity	−.08	.06	−.08
Childrearing Conflict	.06	.09	.11*
Marital Instability	.07	.03	.11*
Depression	.00	.00	.03
Household Work	.00	.03	.00
Marital History (Husband)	−.03	.04	−.04
Marital History (Wife)	.04	.08	.03
R^2 for step 2			.03*
R^2 for Final Model			.63***

$*p < .05, **p < .01, ***p < .001.$

the marital relationship. Because in each case nearly 50% of the variance at Wave 2 was accounted for by the stability of individual differences, the effects of the predictors of change in the marital relationship were only modest.

The Relations Between Children's Adjustment and the Marital Relationship

The final set of regression equations explored whether adolescents' gender, depressive symptoms, and externalizing behaviors influenced the quality of the marital relationship, and whether these child effects varied by

TABLE 12

Predictors of Change in Wives' Marital Positivity and Negativity

	Wave 2 Positivity		
Step 1	B	SE B	β
Intact vs. step	−.19	.16	−.12
Intact/simple vs. complex	.11	.09	.08
Wave 1 Positivity	.36	.08	.36***
R^2 for step 1			.39***
Step 2			
Spouse Negativity	−.16	.08	−.16*
Spouse Positivity	.03	.09	.03
Childrearing Conflict	−.05	.04	−.08
Marital Instability	−.05	.05	−.08
Depression	−.01	.00	−.08
Household Work	.05	.03	.08
Marital History (Husband)	−.07	.05	−.08
Marital History (Wife)	.09	.11	.09
R^2 for step 2			.06*
R^2 for Final Model			.45***
	Wave 2 Negativity		
Step 1	B	SE B	β
Intact vs. step	−.04	.13	−.03*
Intact/simple vs. complex	−.14	.07	−.12*
Wave 1 Negativity	.56	.09	.55***
R^2 for step 1			.50***
Step 2			
Spouse Negativity	.08	.09	.09
Spouse Positivity	−.04	.06	−.05
Childrearing Conflict	.04	.04	.07
Marital Instability	.01	.01	.04
Depression	.00	.00	.05
Household Work	.04	.03	.07
Marital History (Husband)	−.06	.04	−.08
Marital History (Wife)	.14	.09	.14
R^2 for step 2			.03
R^2 for Final Model			.53***

$*p < .05, **p < .01, ***p < .001.$

family type and ownness. Family type was divided into four categories and entered as a three-level dummy variable—separately for each parent and each adolescent—to examine the effects of the biological relations between parents and adolescents and of family. First, hierarchical regressions were run accounting for the effects of gender and family type. The second regression block included both target adolescents' externalizing behaviors and depressive symptoms. Next, all two-way interactions were entered as a block, followed by all three-way interactions in the final step. For parsimony and clarity of presentation, only significant effects were tabled. Because of the large number of predictors, this discussion is focused on highlighting and describing patterns of findings.

Analyses conducted within Wave 1 indicated that family type and gender of the adolescents accounted for only 2% to 4% of the variance (see Table 13 for the cross-sectional results). The final cross-sectional models accounted for 15% to 24% of the variance for husbands' positivity and husbands' negativity respectively. In general, husbands tended to be more negative and less positive with their spouses in the presence of an externalizing adolescent, particularly when the adolescent was their "own" child rather than a stepchild (see Table 13, interaction: Complex-Biological Relation versus Complex-Step Relation × Gender × Younger Adolescent's Externalizing Behavior). These results suggest that parents' marital relations are modestly more sensitive to the behavior problems of their own children rather than the acting out of their stepchildren. Additionally, husbands were more negative in the presence of girls (e.g., see Table 13, interaction: Gender × Younger Adolescent's Externalizing Behavior), while the presence of boys decreased husbands' marital Negativity in stepfamilies (e.g., see Table 13, interaction: Nondivorced versus Stepfamilies × Gender). Thus, children's gender is associated with the interactional pattern between parents. Parents of girls tend to report and demonstrate more marital Negativity than do parents of boys. These gender effects should be interpreted cautiously, however, because it is not possible to conclude that gender per se is the key variable (e.g., many families had one or more other children who may have been the opposite sex of the target adolescents).

The final models predicting the marital relationship longitudinally from Wave 1 variables yielded explained variance ranging from 52% to 67% (see Table 14). The stability of marital Positivity and Negativity was significant in all cases, accounting for 38% to 60% of the variance for wives' Positivity and husbands' Negativity, respectively. Results from the longitudinal analyses tend to support the cross-sectional findings. The presence of externalizing girls was modestly associated with never-divorced wives' increased Negativity and decreased Positivity towards their spouses three years later (e.g., see Table 14, interaction: Nondivorced versus Stepfamily × Gender × Younger Adolescent's Externalizing Behavior) In simple stepfamilies, previous exposure to an acting-out stepchild was related to the husband's diminished Positivity toward his wife 3 years later (e.g., see Table 14, interaction: Simple × Complex × Younger Adolescent's Externalizing Behavior). Living with an externalizing adolescent is likely to exert a disruptive influence on the household, including the marital relationship. In the longitudinal analyses this association seemed most marked for biological daughters and stepsons. In general, the presence of externalizing girls was associated with more conflicted and less harmonious marital relations (e.g., see Table 14, interaction: Gender × Older Adolescent's Externalizing Behavior). Although there were few consistent family

69

TABLE 13

CROSS-SECTIONAL PREDICTION OF MARITAL POSITIVITY AND NEGATIVITY BY ADOLESCENTS' ADJUSTMENT: WAVE 1

Wives' Positivity

Final Model	B	SE B	β
Simple vs. Complex × Younger Dep.	.89	.27	.71***
Simple vs. Complex × Gender × Younger Dep.	-.47	.17	-.57**

Final Model: $F(41, 407) = 2.03$, $p < .001$, $R^2 = .17$
R^2 Change from First Step = .15

Wives' Negativity

Final Model	B	SE B	β
Nondiv vs. Steps	-.20	.06	-.55***
Nondiv vs. Steps × Gender	.12	.04	.51**

Final Model: $F(41, 407) = 2.80$, $p < .0001$, $R^2 = .22$
R^2 Change from First Step = .18

Husbands' Positivity

Final Model	B	SE B	β
Nondiv vs. Steps	.15	.07	.35*
Nondiv vs. Steps × Gender	-.10	.05	-.38*

Final Model: $F(41, 407) = 1.73$, $p < .01$, $R^2 = .15$
R^2 Change from First Step = .13

Husbands' Negativity

Final Model	B	SE B	β
Nondiv vs. Steps	-.27	.06	-.65****
Simple vs. Complex	.21	.10	.38*
Gender × Younger Ext.	.29	.15	.34*
Nondiv vs. Steps × Gender	.17	.04	.66****
Simple vs. Complex × Gender	-.13	.06	-.38*
C. Bio vs. C. Steps × Gender × Younger Ext.	-.39	.18	-.36*

Final Model: $F(41, 407) = 3.12$, $p < .0001$, $R^2 = .24$
R^2 Change from First Step = .22

NOTE. C. Bio = Complex Stepfamily, Biological Relation; C. Step = Complex Stepfamily, Step Relation; Ext. = Externalizing Behaviors; Dep. = Depressive Symptoms; Younger = Younger Adolescent.
$*p < .05$, $**p < .01$, $***p < .001$, $****p < .0001$. Coefficients reported are based on the final model.

TABLE 14

LONGITUDINAL PREDICTION OF MARITAL POSITIVITY AND NEGATIVITY BY ADOLESCENTS' ADJUSTMENT

Final Model	Wave 2 Wives' Positivity			Final Model	Wave 2 Husbands' Positivity		
	B	$SE\ B$	β		B	$SE\ B$	β
Wives' W1 Positivity	.63	.06	.62****	Husbands' W1 Positivity	.74	.06	.69****
Nondiv vs. Steps	.20	.10	.53*	Older Ext.	1.73	.49	1.33****
Simple vs. Complex	.38	.18	.67**	Older Depr.	−.81	.31	−.65**
Nondiv vs. Steps × Younger Ext.	.54	.20	.65**	Younger Ext.	−.74	.29	−.52*
Simple vs. Complex × Gender	−.23	.11	−.64*	Nondiv vs. Steps × Older Ext.	−.44	.20	−.59*
Nondiv vs. Steps × Gender × Younger Ext.	−.38	.13	−.69**	Gender × Older Ext.	−1.05	.28	−1.18***
				Gender × Older Depr.	.51	.19	.67**
				Simple vs. Complex × Younger Ext.	−.75	.26	−.62**
				C. Bio vs. C. Step × Older Depr.	1.04	.44	.62**
				Simple vs. Complex × Gender × Younger Ext.	.45	.16	.57**
				C. Bio vs. C. Step × Gender × Older Depr.	−.71	.27	−.69*

Final Model: $F(42, 185) = 4.72$, $p<.0001$, $R^2 = .52$
R^2 change from First Step = .14

Final Model: $F(42, 182) = 7.47$, $p<.0001$, $R^2 = .63$
R^2 change from First Step = .15

Final Model	Wave 2 Wives' Negativity			Final Model	Wave 2 Husbands' Negativity		
	B	$SE\ B$	β		B	$SE\ B$	β
Wives' W1 Negativity	.70	.06	69****	Husbands' W1 Negativity	.69	.05	.73****
Nondiv vs. Steps × Gender × Younger Ext.	.24	.11	51*				

Final Model: $F(42, 185) = 6.48$, $p < .0001$, $R^2 = .60$
R^2 Change from First Step = .11

Final Model: $F(42, 184) = 8.71$, $p < .0001$, $R^2 = .67$
R^2 Change from First Step = .07

NOTE. C. Bio = Complex Stepfamily, Biological Relation; C. Step = Complex Stepfamily, Step Relation; Ext. = Externalizing Behavior; Depr. = Depressive Symptoms; Younger = Younger Adolescent; Older = Older Adolescent; W1 = Wave 1. Coefficients reported are based on the final model.

$*p < .05$, $**p < .01$, $***p < .001$, $****p < .0001$.

type differences, these findings suggest that gender and biological related-ness interact with adolescents' behavior problems to exert a modest influ-ence on the marital relationship.

To examine further the influence of child-driven effects on the marital relationship, particularly negativity directed at spouses, several cross-lag mod-els were run to analyze the bidirectional effects of adolescents' externalizing behavior and marital negativity. Separate models were run for mothers and fathers and to account for biological relatedness between parent and each adolescent (biological vs. step relation). The stability coefficients were very high for both adolescent Externalizing behavior (r ranges from .40 to .66, $p < .05$) and marital Negativity (r ranges from .69 to .88, $p < .001$). The cross-lag path predicting marital Negativity at Wave 2 from adolescents' Externalizing behavior at Wave 1 (while controlling for the stability of marital Negativity) was significant at the $p < .05$ level in only one of the eight models; the younger adolescents' Externalizing behavior modestly predicted their biological fathers' marital Negativity 3 years later ($\beta = .12, t = 2.14$).

The reverse pattern was also supported in one of the eight models. Step-mothers' marital Negativity predicted older adolescents' Externalizing 3 years later ($\beta = .36, t = 2.11, p < .05$) even after controlling for the stability of adolescent Externalizing. The sample size for this model, however, was very small at Wave 2 ($n = 17$).

Taken together the regression and cross-lag results provide suggestive evidence for a bidirectional model of adolescent behavior and marital negativity effects, but the magnitude of the effect is modest and not consis-tent across patterns of biological relatedness or spouse. It may be that this effect is moderated by, among other factors, ownness and gender. Alter-natively, the inconsistent pattern may have resulted from a small sample size. Replication of this bidirectional association is therefore needed.

DISCUSSION

The discussion of the findings is defined by six conceptual areas: assess-ments of marital quality, children's effects on the marriage, household work and its association with ownness, the connections between relationship and individual adjustment, gender differences in the marriage, and longitudinal assessment of change in marital quality.

Marital Quality of Never-Divorced Couples and Remarried Couples

Consistent with previous research on marital relations in newly remar-ried couples (Hetherington & Clingempeel, 1992) and couples in stabilized remarriages (Bray & Berger, 1993), the quality of marital relations in nondivorced families and stepfamilies was found to be far more similar than different in this sample of nondivorced and long-established stepfamilies. The few differences in the marital relationship across family type were detected in coparenting aspects of the relationship and in the associations between adolescent's adjustment and the marital relationship. Although family type differences in marital quality based on observer reports were found, the effect was apparent only in Wave 1 (see Bray & Berger, 1993; Hetherington & Clingempeel, 1992).

The similarity in marital satisfaction (positivity) and conflict (negativity) in first marriages and remarriages, despite marked differences in marital histories, tasks of the relationship, and quality of other relationships within the family (e.g., see Chapter IV), is illustrated in three ways. First, the overall quality of the marital relationship or marital satisfaction was similar in both groups. Differences in relationship quality were not apparent in individual measures or in self- and partner reports. Nonetheless, it is striking that these findings replicate, in a very specific way, those of Bray and Berger (1993) and Hetherington and Clingempeel (1992) regarding observers' impressions of marital interaction quality. It is not clear whether these findings suggest that remarried partners may be biased in their reports (for instance, spouses may report high satisfaction because they compare their current relationship to a previously broken marriage) or whether marital relations in stepfamilies are more negative and less positive in observed interactions because they may be more likely to discuss conflicts about childrearing, an area that is very clearly more difficult for spouses in remarried families to resolve —perhaps especially in time-limited observational sessions. Whatever the source of this difference, it is clear that a comprehensive assessment of marital quality requires multimethod and multireport design (see Matthews, Wickrama, & Conger, 1996).

A second finding that underscores the similarity in first marriages and remarriages is that marital relationship quality was equally stable across family and marital type. Furthermore, the cross-sectional and longitudinal relations among marital quality, coparenting roles, and individual adjustment were similar, suggesting that marital processes were similar across family type. In general, marital quality was better predicted from factors reflecting the nature of the marital relationship, such as spouses' behaviors and reported satisfaction and disagreements, especially disagreements regarding childrearing. Third, although family type differences were observed in terms of spouses' satisfaction with coparenting roles and division of responsibility for childrearing, the differences appeared to be a function of the biological relationship of the parent and child rather than family (or marital) type per se. For example, both mothers and fathers displayed a tendency to be more engaged with the parenting tasks involving their biological child, particularly if the child was not a biological child of the spouse. This is a novel finding, and suggests that further attention be given to the moderating influence of parental "ownness."

It is important to consider the absence of differences in marital quality in light of the fact that marriages and remarriages were long established. There is now evidence that the early years of a first marriage or a remarriage are a high-risk period for separation (e.g., Clarke & Wilson, 1994), although divorces tend to occur more rapidly in remarriages, especially those with children (Cherlin & Furstenberg, 1994; Tzeng & Mare, 1995). The current findings extend the findings reported by Clarke and Wilson (1994) in suggesting that there may be a convergence of first marriagess and remarriages over time.

Although the major finding in this chapter is the relative *absence* of family type effects, the few differences and interactions that were detected suggest that husbands and wives in different family constellations do experience the coparenting relationship differently. Consistent with previous reports (Schultz, Schultz, & Olson, 1991), conflict regarding childrearing was more commonly reported by spouses in simple and complex remarried families than in nondivorced families. Feelings of depression also were more common in husbands in simple stepfamilies and wives in complex stepfamilies. Thus, there are stresses associated with being a stepparent or adjusting to parent-child relations in complex stepfamilies. Kurdek (1996) reported that there is a "spillover" effect in stepfamilies in which the quality of the marital relationship suffered as a result of conflict regarding childrearing. The absence of differences in marital satisfaction, however, indicates that this effect was not found in the current study. Nonetheless, it is noteworthy that for all marriages individual differences in conflict about childrearing were concurrently associated with both affective dimensions of marital quality, and they were one of the few predictors of a decrease in marital satisfaction and increase in conflict across the 3-year period.

A "Child Effects" and Family Effects Model of Marital Quality

There was some evidence that adolescents' externalizing behavior was associated with marital quality, as numerous investigations have shown. The novel question addressed in this chapter was whether children's behavior was associated with a change in marital quality. Although the findings are complex, they do provide some evidence that children's behavior does influence marital quality and vice versa, and that these patterns of influence may vary by biological relatedness between parent and adolescent and adolescent gender. The central implication of these results is that further research on the association between marital quality and children's adjustment should examine a bidirectional model, a proposal consistent with a systems model of family development.

Ownness and Division of Household Work

There was considerable evidence that ownness, or whether the parent-child relationship was biological or step, was associated with men's and women's household work and adoption of responsibility for the child's development (e.g., setting curfew). Both husbands and wives accepted more responsibility if they brought the child into the marriage from a previous relationship. This contrast was minor, however, compared to the overwhelming difference in participation of household chores and childcare between husbands and wives. Regardless of family type or ownness, women adopted greater responsibility for childrearing. Nonetheless, these data suggest that biological (versus step) relatedness should be included in the list of factors that modify, however slightly, the marked differences between spouses in the amount of household work and childrearing responsibility they perform (Thompson, 1991). Thus, all of the above differences are consistent with the hypothesis that differences between first and remarried partners have more to do with coparenting tasks and household management than with the marital relationship as such.

Marital Relationship, Relationship History, and Individual Adjustment

There was little evidence that spouses in remarriages may have divorce-prone personalities (Capaldi & Patterson, 1991), nor was there evidence that additional stresses and conflict that remarried spouses face adversely affect individual adjustment. Indeed, the only finding regarding individual adjustment that replicated at both waves was that wives reported more depression than their husbands in complex stepfamilies did. The reasons for this are not clear, but it is possible to rule out some explanations. For example, it was not the case that husbands' or wives' experience of depressive symptoms was associated with presence of a stepchild or, conversely, that the presence of a biological child buffered against depression in stepfamilies. It is important to note that although family type differences in depressive symptoms had been reported (Hetherington & Clingempeel, 1992, reported elevated levels of depression in newly remarried families), much of the previous research has focused on the transition years, during which maladjustment may be particularly likely. Family type may not be associated with depressive symptoms in long-established marriages.

Despite the absence of group differences, individual differences in depressive symptoms were, as expected, correlated with marital relationship quality and coparenting concurrently for both men and women in never-divorced families and remarried families. Finally, it is important to recall that the levels of depressive symptoms were well below clinical level for all but a small number of spouses. Accordingly, variation in depressive symptoms and changes over time should not be connected with severe mal-adjustment, but with variation in mild depressive experiences.

Marital history, or the number of previous relationships, has been found to correlate both with individual adjustment and with relationship quality, including likelihood of further divorce (Amato, 1996; Capaldi & Patterson, 1991; O'Connor, Hawkins, Dunn, Thorpe, & Golding, 1998). Although the number of previous marriages was not associated with depressive symptoms, there was some evidence that wives' marital history was associated with lower levels of husbands' positivity and an increase in wives' negativity over time. The findings that wives' but not husbands' marital history was related to relationship quality and change may reflect the slightly wider distribution of the number of previous relationships for women.

Differences Between Husbands and Wives

There were marked and consistent differences between husbands and wives in marital relationship quality and coparenting roles. Wives in never-divorced families engaged in and reported less negativity and more positivity than their husbands. These differences, which were not limited to observations or self- or partner reports, are consistent with what other authors suggest are more global differences in the extent to which men and women are expressive and affectionate in marriage (Gottman, 1993).

Spouse differences in marital quality were frequently modified by a Spouse × Family type interaction, suggesting that a model based only on gender is too simplistic to explain these findings. Similarly, it is striking that there were more spouse by family type interactions than there were main effects of family type. Four findings are especially interesting in this regard. First, wives in complex stepfamilies reported that they had thought about marital dissolution and had pursued getting a divorce more than did their husbands, or husbands and wives in other family types. Second, it was only in complex stepfamilies that the frequently reported sex difference in depressive symptoms were found. Third, unlike their peers in nondivorced families and simple stepfamilies, women in complex stepfamilies were more similar to their husbands in terms of the level of conflict and closeness they reported. Finally, in contrast to other studies, there was minimal evidence that the quality of marital relations, coparenting, or satisfaction with household management was significantly less salient for husbands than it was for wives. The above pattern of findings suggests that, on the one hand, main effects models of gender require considerable revision and, on the other, that family type is a strong modifier of gender effects.

Longitudinal Change

One clear and significant finding that applied equally to all marriages was the marked drop in quality over time. A decrease in marital quality was observed across measures and reporters, including observations of marital interactions, self- and spouse reports on questionnaires, and a measure of conflict regarding childrearing. This mean change in the affective quality of long-established marriages complements the well-known drop in quality in the initial years of marriage (Kurdek, 1998). Other research has linked changes in marital quality and family stress to transition in the family life cycle; adolescence is reported to be a particularly stressful period. It is not obvious, however, what life cycle changes these marriages were experiencing. Most families included at least one additional child, thus precluding simple relations with the transition through adolescence and toward leaving home. All families, however, had at least two adolescents present, which may incur stressors, conflicts, and realignments in family relations that undermine the marital relationship. Furthermore, these parents are in early midlife, a time when reevaluations of life situations, including intimate relations, work, and attainment often occur. It may be, for example, that the declines in marital satisfaction are only partly associated with stresses and strains and lack of support within the family. A mean decrease in marital quality also was reported in a large sample of couples at various life stages and, as in the current study, a mean decrease was found despite very stable individual differences (Johnson, Amoloza, & Booth, 1992). Johnson et al. (1992) suggested that the mean decrease may reflect a developmental change, although it is equally unclear in that study what the mechanism is for a developmental change. Available reviews of marital relationship change (e.g., Karney & Bradbury, 1995) document a number of plausible processes, but more research on the mechanisms of change is needed. Finally, it is noteworthy that although several predictors of increases in negativity and decreases in positivity in the marital relationship were identified in the regression analyses, there were no factors associated with a positive change in the marital relationship. Thus, both group and individual difference analyses highlight a decline in the quality of the marital relationship. A drop in marital satisfaction may have implications for individuals' well-being, but it does not necessarily lead to separation (e.g., Heaton & Albrecht, 1991).

For both husbands and wives in all family types, conflict regarding childrearing was a relatively robust predictor of a decrease in marital satisfaction. Thus, conflict in coparenting roles may show "spillover" effects on the marital relationship quality over time. Whether this process in turn leads to marital dissolution, as suggested by the report of Block, Block, and Morrison (1981), must await further follow-up study. The short time period between waves in this study and the limited number of reported separations do not permit conclusions to be drawn.

A final note regarding the longitudinal analyses is that there was no evidence of differential drop in marital satisfaction, conflict over child-rearing, or other aspects of the marital relationship as a function of family type.

Summary

The current study is one of the few attempts to examine the quality of marital relations in long-remarried families in diverse types of stepfamilies and compare them to long-established marriages in never-divorced families using a multimeasure, multirespondent design, which included observations. Early in a remarriage the new stepparent is often in a position of greater marginality than the biological parent is, and the marital relationship may be less central than in nonstepfamilies. Thus, the important differences between first marriages and remarriages may be in the salience rather than in the quality of the marital relationship. This will be explored as relations among family subsystems and child adjustment are examined in subsequent chapters.

IV. PARENT-ADOLESCENT RELATIONSHIPS IN NONSTEP-, SIMPLE STEP-, AND COMPLEX STEPFAMILIES

Sandra H. Henderson and Lorraine C. Taylor

A substantial body of research has documented the difficulties that families encounter when they go through a marital transition (Bray, 1990; Furstenberg & Cherlin, 1991; Hetherington, 1993; Hetherington & Clingempeel, 1992). Findings indicate that, during the initial years following remarriage, family members have difficulty negotiating new family roles and relationships and that some of the most problematic relations occur between parents and adolescents (see Hetherington & Stanley-Hagen, 1996, for a review). As noted in the introductory chapter of this *Monograph* (Chapter I), there may be temporary perturbations in relations between the bio logical parent and child and more long-lasting ones in relations between stepchildren and stepparents and in sibling relations (Bray, 1991; Hetherington, 1989, 1991, 1993; Hetherington & Clingempeel, 1992.)

In this chapter, characteristics and differences in the parent-adolescent relationship in nonstep-, simple step-, and complex stepfamilies of relatively long duration will be described. In addition, gender differences and the role of biological relatedness, which we refer to as "ownness," in relationships will be examined. Changes in the parent-adolescent relationship and the frequently described realignments in family relationships as children move through adolescence (Baumrind, 1991) also will be explored. The following hypotheses were based on the theoretical conceptualizations and empirical findings reviewed in Chapter I of this *Monograph*.

First, because divorce occurs earlier in remarriages than in first marriages, it was assumed that many dysfunctional families would have dropped out of the sample of stabilized stepfamilies. It was hypothesized that, in general, long-term, restabilized simple stepfamilies would show evidence of primarily positive family relationships and would show few differences from nonstepfamilies. This is in contrast to studies that have found significant differences between nondivorced families and stepfamilies early in a remarriage (e.g., Hetherington & Clingempeel, 1992).

Second, it was predicted that most differences found in parent-adolescent relationships in stepfamilies would be due to the complexity of family composition in the household. It was expected that more complicated family configurations would lead to greater challenges, lack of cohesion and difficulties in negotiating roles and relationships in stepfamilies, and hence to more conflict and less supportive, warm engagement among parents and adolescents in complex stepfamilies than in simple step- or nonstepfamilies.

Third, it was hypothesized that differences in the biological relatedness between parent and adolescent would contribute to differences in levels of positivity and negativity in their relationship. It was predicted that parents of adolescents who were biologically related would be more involved, and thus show higher levels of warmth and monitoring than parents of adolescents who were not biologically related. Predictions about "ownness" and negativity were similar, with stepparents expected to show higher levels of negativity than biological parents.

Fourth, it was hypothesized that children's move from early to late adolescence would be accompanied by parental distancing. Distancing would be reflected in decreased levels of conflict, as well as decreased levels of warmth, monitoring, and control by mothers and fathers over time. In addition, it was predicted that adolescents' distancing behavior would be shown in decreased Positivity/warmth and increased Negativity/conflict toward parents as adolescents were striving to become more autonomous and were more resistant to parental controls.

Fifth, as others have demonstrated (Forehand & Nousiainen, 1993), it was expected that mothers would be more involved in childrearing than fathers. Mothers were predicted to show greater Postivity/warmth and Monitoring/control than fathers to both girls and boys.

Sixth, parent's differential childrearing was examined. It was hypothesized that there would be greater differential parenting, or nonshared parenting as it is often referred to, where mothers and fathers treat siblings differently, in families who had adolescents of varying biological relatedness to parents. Specifically, within families, it was expected that the biological child would receive higher levels of Positivity/warmth, characterized by affection, support and involvement, from a biological parent, while a stepchild in the same family would receive less Positivity/warmth. In addition, mothers and fathers were expected to show greater Negativity/conflict with their stepchildren than with their own adolescents. In families where adolescents shared the same biological relatedness to parents, no significant differences in parenting were predicted.

METHOD

Two phases of analyses were conducted. The first included cross-sectional MANOVAs for Wave 1 to capitalize on the larger sample of families, followed by repeated-measures MANOVAs which utilized "time" or "wave" as the repeated measure and involved only the families present in both waves (see Table 1, Chapter II). Adolescent gender and family type (nonstep, simple step, complex step/own, complex step/step) were between-subjects factors in MANOVAs. Univariate tests were run following significant multivariate effects and for planned comparisons. Separate analyses for older and younger siblings were performed.

It is important to note that all MANOVAs were also calculated on individual reporters' composite scores (e.g., child's reports on several subscales of mother-adolescent negativity), as well as at the subscale level by reporter. Results of the individual reporter composite MANOVAs revealed the same pattern of results as the multireporter, multimeasure composites, and thus are not presented.

For analyses of reporter at the subscale level, we used raw scores rather than standardized scores. Analyses at the subscale level, however, also were largely similar to those run at the composite level, with only a couple of subscales yielding no results rather than different results. Again, because these analyses did not provide any additional information regarding source of report, they were not presented. Information on individual reporter-level composite and subscale MANOVAs are available from the first author.[2]

In addition, cluster analyses were performed on parenting dimensions to reveal different styles of parenting (e.g., authoritative, permissive, etc.). MANOVAs were run on the resultant parenting styles by child sex and family type/ownness. We found many interesting results, but for the sake of parsimony, did not include tables in this chapter; however, all results are available from the authors.[3]

The next set of analyses included an exploration of differential parenting within families and examined whether nonshared parenting is greater in families with adolescents of varying biological relatedness to parents.

---

[2] Cross-sectional and repeated-measures MANOVA results for individual reporters are available from the first author.

[3] Results from cluster analyses are available from the authors.

As discussed in Chapter II (Method), three primary indices of parenting were assessed, including Positivity/warmth, Negativity/conflict and Monitoring/control. These parenting dimensions have been identified both theoretically and through past research as important in understanding the dynamics of the parent-adolescent relationship (Baumrind, 1972; Hetherington & Clingempeel, 1992; Avenevoli, Sessa, & Steinberg, 1999). Parenting dimensions were assessed through questionnaire data and through observational ratings that were combined to yield multimethod/multirespondent composite measures. Similar MANOVAs also were performed on adolescents' behavior to parent using parent, adolescents', and observers' reports.

Also as noted in Chapter II, we constructed different categories of family type and biological relatedness, depending on the research question and the dyad being analyzed. For parent-adolescent relations, we constructed family type/ownness as follows:

1. *nonstepfamilies*, in which all siblings in the family are biologically related to the mother and father

2. *simple stepfamilies*, in which a remarriage has occurred and all siblings in the family are the custodial mother's biological children and the custodial father's stepchildren;

3. *complex stepfamilies, own*, in which a remarriage has occurred and siblings in the family vary in biological relatedness to custodial mothers and fathers, *and* the parent and adolescent being analyzed are biologically related;

4. *complex stepfamilies, step*, in which a remarriage has occurred and siblings in the family vary in biological relatedness to custodial mothers and fathers, *and* the parent and adolescent being analyzed are not biologically related, that is, are stepkin.

A discussion of adolescent gender, family type, parent-adolescent biological relatedness, and differences in parent-adolescent relationships within waves is presented below followed by an examination of the stability and change in parent-adolescent relationships across time. Finally, analyses of nonshared parenting are described and examined.

RESULTS

Before examining the effects of family type, ownness, and child gender on parenting, we looked at the relationship between our main dimensions of parenting and the length of marriage, given the possibility that differences in quality of parent-child relationship may be due to the amount of time parents, children, and stepchildren have been together. As noted in Chapter

II, there were differences in marital duration, with a mean of 17 years for nonstepfamilies, 7 years for simple stepfamilies and 9 years for complex stepfamilies. Thus, we calculated correlation coefficients between parenting dimensions (Positivity/warmth, Negativity/conflict, and Monitoring/control) and marital duration, controlling for age of adolescent. The analyses revealed that there were no differences in quality of parenting related to the length of the parent's marriage despite the differences in marital duration in each family type. This is likely because families had been married at least 5 years, and many, including stepfamilies, had been married for much longer, with nonstepfamily marriages ranging up to 37 years, simple stepfamily marriages to 15 years and complex stepfamily marriages to 17 years.

In addition, we also looked at the importance of including age of adolescent in our MANOVAs. Again, we calculated correlation coefficients between parenting (Positivity/warmth, Negativity/conflict, and Monitoring/control) and age of adolescent. The results revealed very modest correlations ranging from .09 to .20, but with most falling around .12. We decided to exclude age as a variable in the MANOVAs because (a) the correlations with parenting were low to moderate, and (b) after including age groups, cell sizes in repeated-measures analyses would have been too small to interpret.

Within-Wave Analyses

The multivariate analyses of multimethod/multirespondent composites of mother's and father's parenting with older and younger siblings are presented in Table 15. This is followed by Tables 16 and 17, which present means, standard deviations, and significant contrasts for these analyses for older and younger adolescents, respectively.

Gender differences. Differences in parents' relations with sons and daughters are frequently reported with infants and young children; however, gender differences in the parents' treatment of children once they have reached adolescence are obtained less often and consistently. In this study of parent-adolescent relationships, it was found that girls received more warmth and support and greater monitoring from mothers than did boys (see Tables 16 and 17).

Family differences in parent-adolescent relationships. A notable finding relating to parent-adolescent relationships in this study was the relative lack of differences in parenting related to being in a stepfamily or a nonstepfamily. Instead, the biological relationship between parent and adolescent was stronger in determining differences in parenting than family type. There were no systematic differences in mother's treatment of her biological adolescents in nonstep-, simple step-, and complex stepfamilies,

TABLE 15

F-Values and Significance Levels for Multivariate Analyses of Multimethod/Multirespondent Composites of Parenting of Older and Younger Adolescents in Wave 1

| | Family Type | | | | Gender | | | |
| | Older | | Younger | | Older | | Younger | |
	Mother	Father	Mother	Father	Mother	Father	Mother	Father
Multivariate	7.74**	5.61***	6.06***	5.37***	3.06*	.22	1.98	.15
Multivariate df	(9,1512)	(9,1512)	(9,1512)	(9,1512)	(3,503)	(3,503)	(3,503)	(3,503)
Univariate								
Positivity/warmth	18.73***	14.59***	12.95***	16.07***	7.51***	.30	2.02	.21
Negativity/conflict	2.56*	3.17*	3.86**	.17	.18	.02	.72	.17
Monitoring/control	2.82*	3.81**	2.36	4.08**	4.32*	.03	4.30*	.11

*$p < .05$, **$p < .01$, ***$p < .001$; all gender × family type interactions were nonsignificant.

TABLE 16

MEANS (STANDARD DEVIATIONS) OF THE MULTIMETHOD/MULTIRESPONDENT COMPOSITES OF PARENTING TO OLDER ADOLESCENTS IN WAVE 1

Composite Report:
Mothers → Older adolescent

	Nonstep (NS) (n = 93) cl-own		Simple Step (SS) (n = 83) cl-own		Complex Step (CO) (n = 272) cl-own		Complex Step (CS) (n = 65) cl-step		Significant Main Effects and Interactions	Significant Contrasts and Planned Comparisons
	Boys	Girls	Boys	Girls	Boys	Girls	Boys	Girls		
Positivity/warmth	.35 (.48)	.54 (.49)	.35 (.43)	.55 (.47)	.27 (.57)	.36 (.50)	-.19 (.52)	-.07 (.72)	family:	NS, SS, CO > CS
									sex:	girls > boys
Negativity/conflict	.08 (.62)	.14 (.49)	.11 (.54)	.17 (.64)	.25 (.63)	.18 (.56)	-.02 (.59)	.03 (.54)	family:	CO > CS
Monitoring/control	.05 (.55)	.18 (.68)	.05 (.60)	.14 (.48)	.00 (.55)	.19 (.49)	-.16 (.78)	-.08 (.68)	sex:	girls > boys
									family:	NS, SS, CO > CS

Composite Report:
Fathers → Older adolescent

	Nonstep (NS) (n = 93) cl-own		Simple Step (SS) (n = 83) cl-step		Complex Step (CO) (n = 67) cl-own		Complex Step (CS) (n = 270) cl-step		Significant Main Effects and Interactions	Significant Contrasts and Planned Comparisons
	Boys	Girls	Boys	Girls	Boys	Girls	Boys	Girls		
Positivity/warmth	.05 (.55)	.24 (.50)	-.20 (.65)	-.26 (.60)	.01 (.55)	.05 (.52)	-.26 (.65)	-.30 (.56)	family:	NS, CO > SS, CS
Negativity/conflict	-.15 (.54)	-.14 (.54)	-.17 (.54)	-.10 (.58)	-.31 (.51)	-.36 (.55)	-.07 (.58)	-.12 (.53)	family:	CS > CO
Monitoring/control	-.04 (.49)	.06 (.69)	-.20 (.64)	-.29 (.65)	-.09 (.64)	-.21 (.66)	-.26 (.66)	-.21 (.63)	family:	NS > SS, CS

*p < .05, **p < .01, ***p < .001; numbers in parentheses are standard deviations.

TABLE 17

Means (Standard Deviations) of the Multimethod/Multirespondent Composites of Parenting to Younger Adolescents in Wave 1

Composite Report: Mothers → Younger adolescent

	Nonstep (NS) (n = 93) c2-own		Simple Step (SS) (n = 83) c2-own		Complex Step (CO) (n = 269) c2-own		Complex Step (CS) (n = 68) c2-step		Significant Main Effects and Interactions	Significant Contrasts and Planned Comparisons
	Boys	Girls	Boys	Girls	Boys	Girls	Boys	Girls		
Positivity/warmth	.28	.35	.36	.46	.19	.26	-.12	-.07	family:	NS, SS, CO > CS; SS > CO
	(.30)	(.52)	(.49)	(.39)	(.48)	(.52)	(.69)	(.70)		
Negativity/conflict	-.02	.15	.03	.11	.24	.18	-.04	-.01	family:	CO > CS
	(.45)	(.52)	(.52)	(.67)	(.64)	(.53)	(.44)	(.74)		
Monitoring/control	.26	.23	.25	.42	.15	.33	.04	.16	sex:	girls > boys
	(.56)	(.66)	(.61)	(.43)	(.52)	(.50)	(.53)	(.45)		

Composite Report: Fathers → Younger adolescent

	Nonstep (NS) (n = 93) c2-own		Simple Step (SS) (n = 83) c2-own		Complex Step (CO) (n = 178) c2-own		Complex Step (CS) (n = 159) c2-step		Significant Main Effects and Interactions	Significant Contrasts and Planned Comparisons
	Boys	Girls	Boys	Girls	Boys	Girls	Boys	Girls		
Positivity/warmth	.02	.05	-.34	-.20	-.04	-.04	-.34	-.41	family:	NS, CO > SS, CS
	(.46)	(.53)	(.63)	(.54)	(.58)	(.58)	(.53)	(.51)		
Negativity/conflict	-.28	-.20	-.28	-.15	-.17	-.28	-.19	-.26		
	(.37)	(.49)	(.40)	(.61)	(.53)	(.45)	(.47)	(.46)		
Monitoring/control	.17	.10	.01	.01	.01	.11	-.14	-.09	family:	NS > CS
	(.51)	(.59)	(.64)	(.51)	(.65)	(.56)	(.61)	(.59)		

$*p < .05$, $**p < .01$, $***p < .001$; numbers in parentheses are standard deviations.

rather, differences occurred between mother's parenting toward biological versus stepchildren. Similarly, there were few differences in father's behavior toward his biological children in nonstep- and stepfamilies, but differences emerged in his treatment of stepchildren. Some family type differences did emerge, however, in adolescents' behavior toward fathers. In the discussion to follow, it should be remembered that adolescents in simple stepfamilies are always the mother's but not the father's biological children, whereas adolescents in complex stepfamilies can belong to either one or both parents.

Family differences in mother-adolescent relationships. The strength of biological ownness as a predictor of relationship quality can be seen in analyses of the mother-adolescent relationship. At the multimethod/multireporter composite level, in relations with both older and younger siblings, mothers and their own adolescents in nonstep, simple step and complex step/own family types were significantly higher in positivity than mothers and stepchildren in complex stepfamilies (see Tables 16 and 17). The former three family types consist of biological mother-adolescent relationships in both nonstep- and stepfamilies, while the latter consists of a nonbiological relationship in a stepfamily. Thus, the effect is one of biological relatedness rather than family type, with mothers being more warm and supportive of their biological offspring than their stepchildren. In addition, mothers also monitored their older biological adolescents significantly more than their stepchildren. Moreover, in complex stepfamilies, mothers had more conflictual relationships with their own children than with their stepchildren. This finding is consistent with past studies that report both greater negative and positive affective engagement of biological parents with their own adolescents than of stepparents with stepchildren (e.g., Hetherington & Clingempeel, 1992).

Family differences in father-adolescent relationships. In examining the tables for fathers, as with mothers and adolescents, there were few family type differences in father-adolescent relationships. The data indicate that differences in parenting are associated with differences in the biological relationship between father and adolescent.

Composite analyses revealed that fathers displayed more warmth and support to their biological offspring than to their stepchildren. Similarly, fathers monitored their stepchildren less than their biological children in nonstepfamilies. Interestingly, fathers in complex stepfamilies were more negative toward their older stepchildren than toward their older biological children, which was opposite to the pattern found for mothers and adolescents. Also, biological fathers in nonstepfamilies showed higher levels of

87

monitoring than did biological fathers or stepfathers in stepfamilies, a rare family type difference (see Tables 16 and 17).

An interesting finding is the absence of gender by family type inter-actions for mothers' and fathers' with sons and daughters. Other studies have found that stepdaughters have more problems in interactions with stepparents and in accepting stepparents (Brand et al., 1988; Hetherington, 1993; Hetherington & Clingempeel, 1992; Vuchinich et al., 1991), but in long-established stepfamilies with adolescent offspring this does not seem to be the case.

Mothers' and Fathers' Parenting

We did not include mothers' and fathers' parenting together in our analyses of family type and biological ownness because of the complexities involved in creating meaningful categories that made sense for older and younger adolescents, as well as across time from Wave 1 to Wave 2. We were interested, however, in any differences between mothers' and fathers' childrearing, so we ran a set of analyses using a different breakdown of ownness and family type. The breakdowns are slightly different for older versus younger adolescents because of our sample, and we were not able to conduct analyses across time because of small cell sizes. The breakdown for older adolescents is as follows: (a) nonstepfamily, biologically related to both mother and father; (b) simple stepfamily, biologically related to mother, step to father; (c) complex stepfamily, biologically related to mother, step to father; and (d) complex stepfamily, step to mother, biologically related to father. For younger adolescents: (a) nonstepfamily, biologically related to both mother and father; (b) simple stepfamily, biologically related to mother, step to father; (c) complex stepfamily, biologically related to mother and father; (d) complex stepfamily, biologically related to mother, step to father; and (e) complex stepfamily, step to mother, biologically related to father.

MANOVAs were calculated with parent sex as a within-subjects factor and child sex and family type/ownness as between-subjects factors on all of the parenting dimensions. Tables for these analyses, which are largely repetitive with those previously discussed, are not presented for the sake of parsimony; however, results indicated large main effects of parent sex. Mothers showed higher levels of Positivity/warmth [older, $F(1, 503) = 166.46$, $p < .001$; younger, $F(1, 503) = 219.52$, $p < .001$], Negativity/conflict [older, $F(1, 503) = 132.43$, $p < .001$ younger, $F(1, 503) = 187.48$, $p < .001$], and Moni-toring/control [older, $F(1, 503) = 54.67$, $p < .001$; younger $F(1, 503) = 100.19$, $p < .001$] in all family types and to both girls and boys than did fathers. This strong main effect is particularly interesting because it holds across biologi-cal relationship; thus, stepmothers also are higher on the three parenting dimensions than are biological fathers. For older adolescents, there was an interaction of Parent Sex × Child Sex for Positivity/warmth, $F(1, 503) = 4.16$, $p < .05$, and Monitoring/control, $F(1, 503) = 6.97$, $p < .01$, with mothers showing greater positivity and monitoring/control to girls than to boys. There were no differences for younger adolescents or with fathers. Also, there were no interactions with family type/ownness.

A set of MANOVAs also was calculated for child to parent behavior, with both mothers and fathers in the same analyses. Again, the within-subjects factor was Parent Sex, while Child Sex and family type/ownness were between-subjects factors. Analyses were run on adolescent → parent positivity and negativity, and results were similar to the parent → adolescent results reviewed above; specifically, children were more positive [older, $F(1, 503) = 140.78, p < .001$; younger $F(1, 503) = 140.46, p < .001$] as well as more negative [older, $F(1, 503) = 111.63$, $p < .001$; younger, $F(1, 503) = 154.99$, $p < .001$] to their mothers than to their fathers. There were no interactions with child sex or family type/ownness.

Across-Wave Analyses

Repeated-measures MANOVAs of multimethod/multirespondent composites of mother's and father's parenting with older and younger siblings were conducted and are summarized below. Results revealed parallel main effects of family type/owness to those found in Wave 1 analyses. In addition, there were no Wave × Family Type or Gender interactions, so multivariate and means tables are not presented. Wave effects found are discussed below.

Stability and change over time in parent-adolescent relationship. Significant wave effects were found across all composite dimensions of mothers' parenting toward older adolescents with decreases in mothers' Positivity/warmth, $F(1, 248) = 134.48$, $p < .001$, Negativity/conflict, $F(1, 248) = 7.68$, $p < .01$, and Monitoring/control, $F(1, 248) = 80.54, p < .001$, from Wave 1 to Wave 2. Effects also were found for younger adolescents across maternal parenting dimensions, indicating an overall Wave 1 to Wave 2 decrease in mother's Positivity/warmth, $F(1, 248) = 77.73$, $p < .001$, and Monitoring/control, $F(1, 248) = 33.60$, $p < .001$. Mothers' decreased levels of parenting toward adolescents were not differentiated by adolescents' gender, family type, or biological relatedness.

Fathers, too, showed a trend toward increasing disengagement from their adolescents across time. From Wave 1 to Wave 2 with both younger and older adolescents, fathers declined in Positivity/warmth, older, $F(1, 247) = 125.91, p < .001$; younger, $F(1, 247) = 47.99$, $p < .001$, and Monitoring/control, older, $F(1, 247) = 89.39$, $p < .001$; younger, $F(1, 247) = 68.83, p < .001$. Like mothers, fathers' distancing from their adolescents was not differentiated by adolescents' gender, family type, or biological relatedness.

Adolescent behavior toward mothers and fathers. Analyses of adolescents' behavior toward mothers revealed both older and younger adolescents display less positivity and affection with stepmothers in comparison to children with biologically related mothers (see Tables 18 to 20). In addition, older and younger adolescent girls were more positive and warm to their mothers than were boys. Younger adolescent girls also were somewhat more negative with mothers than were boys. Analyses of the adolescents' behavior toward fathers find that younger and older adolescents were more positive and warm to biological fathers than to stepfathers. Adolescents living in nonstepfamilies were significantly more warm toward their fathers than were stepchildren with stepfathers in complex stepfamilies.

Repeated-measures analyses revealed a similar pattern of results so are not presented in tables. There were no significant interactions of wave with child gender or family type; however, there were significant main effects for wave, with adolescents' warmth to parents declining over time.

Nonshared Parenting

After demonstrating differences in the quality of parent-adolescent relationships between families, we wanted to explore how differently parents treat children within the same family and whether any differences can be explained by variation in family type. First, we looked at the means, standard deviations, and range of relative differences in parenting within families based on difference scores of our main parenting indices of Positivity/warmth, Negativity/conflict, and Monitoring/control. The relative difference score was computed by subtracting the younger sibling's score from the older sibling's score.

Means of the relative difference scores revealed that all of the parenting dimensions tended to be distributed around zero and had an adequate range of differences from −2.42 to 1.94. Recall that with relative difference scores, a positive number means that the older sibling is receiving more of a particular parenting dimension, while a negative difference score indicates that the younger sibling is receiving more. In summary, the means from these analyses reveal that within families, some parents favor the older child and some the younger, but there is no systematic significant older/younger birth order effect.

The next question we wanted to address was whether differences in ownness within families were related to differences in parenting. A set of correlation coefficients was calculated between ownness and differential parenting with mothers' and fathers' data examined separately. Differences in ownness were scored as follows: a 0 represented no differences in ownness between siblings; a 1 indicated that the younger sibling is a biological child and the older sibling is a stepchild; and a −1 indicated that the older sibling

TABLE 18

F-Values and Significance Levels for Multivariate Analyses of Multimethod/Multirespondent Composites of Adolescent's Behavior to Parents in Wave 1

| | Family Type | | | | Gender | | | |
| | Older | | Younger | | Older | | Younger | |
	Mother	Father	Mother	Father	Mother	Father	Mother	Father
Multivariate	4.61**	4.10***	3.14**	4.27***	4.82***	.62	3.70**	1.54
Multivariate df	(6,1008)	(6,1008)	(6,1008)	(6,1008)	(2,504)	(2,504)	(2,504)	(2,504)
Univariate								
Positivity/warmth	10.53***	10.81***	6.77***	11.56***	10.45***	.00	5.77*	.03
Negativity/conflict	2.09	2.00	1.83	.25	2.12	1.32	3.31+	2.40

*$p < .05$, **$p < .01$, ***$p < .001$, +$p < .07$; all gender × family type interactions were nonsignificant.

TABLE 19

MEANS (STANDARD DEVIATIONS) FOR THE MULTIMETHOD/MULTIRESPONDENT COMPOSITES OF OLDER ADOLESCENT'S BEHAVIOR TO PARENTS IN WAVE 1

	Nonstep (NS) (n = 88) cl-own		Simple Step (SS) (n = 80) cl-own		Complex Step (CO) (n = 269) cl-own		Complex Step (CS) (n = 64) cl-step		Significant Main Effects and Interactions	Significant Contrasts & Planned Comparisons
	Boys	Girls	Boys	Girls	Boys	Girls	Boys	Girls		
Composite Report: *Older adolescent → Mothers*										
Positivity/warmth	.28	.69	.30	.53	.25	.41	−.39	−.06	family:	NS, SS, CO > CS
	(.83)	(.72)	(.68)	(.72)	(.86)	(.87)	(.75)	(1.07)	sex:	girls > boys
Negativity/conflict	−.01	.12	.03	.30	.18	.18	−.09	−.07		
	(.74)	(.67)	(.68)	(.87)	(.85)	(.77)	(.79)	(.67)		

	Nonstep (NS) (n = 87) cl-own		Simple Step (SS) (n = 79) cl-step		Complex Step (CO) (n = 67) cl-own		Complex Step (CS) (n = 266) cl-step		Significant Main Effects and Interactions	Significant Contrasts and Planned Comparisons
	Boys	Girls	Boys	Girls	Boys	Girls	Boys	Girls		
Composite Report: *Older adolescent → Fathers*										
Positivity/warmth	.05	.28	−.13	−.40	−.05	.10	−.32	−.43	family:	NS, CO > SS, CS
	(.79)	(.73)	(.96)	(.72)	(.79)	(.72)	(.93)	(.89)		
Negativity/conflict	−.29	−.15	−.30	−.11	−.38	−.39	−.15	−.11		
	(.72)	(.75)	(.80)	(.86)	(.66)	(.80)	(.81)	(.78)		

*$p < .05$, **$p < .01$, ***$p < .001$; numbers in parentheses are standard deviations.

TABLE 20

Means (Standard Deviations) for the Multimethod/Multirespondent Composites of Younger Adolescents' Behavior to Parents in Wave 1

	Nonstep (NS) (n = 88) cl-own		Simple Step (SS) (n = 79) cl-own		Complex Step (CO) (n = 261) cl-own		Complex Step (CS) (n = 66) cl-step		Significant Main Effects and Interactions	Significant Contrasts and Planned Comparisons
	Boys	Girls	Boys	Girls	Boys	Girls	Boys	Girls		
Composite Report: Younger adolescent → Mothers										
Positivity/warmth	.14	.25	.13	.38	.07	.18	−.42	−.13	family:	NS, SS, CO > CS
	(.51)	(.67)	(.63)	(.71)	(.77)	(.77)	(.80)	(1.06)	sex:	girls > boys
Negativity/conflict	−.08	.18	−.15	.07	.16	.11	−.15	.02	sex:	girls > boys
	(.58)	(.83)	(.66)	(.83)	(.89)	(.74)	(.54)	(.81)		

	Nonstep (NS) (n = 93) cl-own		Simple Step (SS) (n = 83) cl-step		Complex Step (CO) (n = 67) cl-own		Complex Step (CS) (n = 270) cl-step		Significant Main Effects and Interactions	Significant Contrasts and Planned Comparisons
	Boys	Girls	Boys	Girls	Boys	Girls	Boys	Girls		
Composite Report: Younger adolescent → Fathers										
Positivity/warmth	−.05	−.02	−.52	−.39	−.15	−.12	−.47	−.59	family:	NS, SS, CO > CS
	(.63)	(.80)	(.74)	(.82)	(.79)	(.85)	(.78)	(.75)		
Negativity/conflict	−.41	−.19	−.43	−.16	−.25	−.25	−.19	−.28		
	(.50)	(.71)	(.61)	(.84)	(.72)	(.69)	(.73)	(.66)		

*$p < .05$, **$p < .01$, ***$p < .001$; numbers in parentheses are standard deviations.

is a biological child and the younger sibling is a stepchild: this coding system has been used in previous research (Henderson, Hetherington, Mekos, & Reiss, 1996). Again, differential parenting was represented by relative difference scores, which were computed by subtracting the younger sibling's score from the older sibling's score (e.g., mother → older child Positivity/warmth — mother → younger child Positivity/warmth), thus a positive or high number means that the older sibling is receiving more of the parenting dimension and the younger sibling is receiving less, while a negative or low number means that the younger sibling is receiving more and the older sibling is receiving less.

Correlational results presented in Table 21 reveal that mothers were more supportive and affectionate and also more negative and coercive with their own child than with their stepchild, reflecting the pattern of findings from between-family MANOVA analyses. For example, in Table 21, the correlation coefficient of −.40, $p < .01$, between differences in owness and mother's differential positivity means the following: a positive value on parenting indicates that the older sibling is receiving more Positivity/warmth and the younger sibling is receiving less, thus a negative correlation with owness indicates that as warmth to the older sibling goes up, it is more likely to be related to the older child being the biological child. The inverse is also true: as mother's Positivity/warmth goes down, it is more likely that the older child is the stepchild given that a −1 on owness means the older child is biological and the younger child is a stepchild. Similarly, the correlations for fathers indicated that fathers were more warm and more controlling with their biological children; these findings corroborate with previous findings from between-family analyses.

Parent-adolescent absolute differences by gender and family type. Having demonstrated that parents do treat biological children differently than their stepchildren *within the same family*, we turned to our last question: Are there smaller or larger differences in parenting as a result of family type? To this end, we ran two sets of repeated-measures MANOVAs, this time using *absolute difference* scores computed from composite parenting scores to determine size of differences, as opposed to relative difference scores used above. It was necessary to use absolute differences rather than relative differences because with regard to the mother-adolescent relationship there was only one group in which the older adolescent was a stepchild. Thus, when using a relative difference score of older adolescent minus younger adolescent, there would have been a confounding factor of owness for that group of older stepsiblings and younger biological siblings. With absolute difference scores, we preserve the magnitude of differential treatment between older and younger siblings without building in a bias based on owness. For example, if the older child had a score of 20 and the younger

TABLE 21

CORRELATIONS OF DIFFERENCES IN OWNNESS AND RELATIVE DIFFERENCES
IN PARENTING TO OLDER ADOLESCENTS/YOUNGER ADOLESCENTS

	Wave 1 Differences in Ownness	Wave 2 Differences in Ownness
Mother's differential parenting: (Older adolescent/Younger adolescent)		
Positivity/warmth	−.40**	−.49**
Negativity/conflict	−.17**	−.07
Monitoring/control	−.05	−.05
Father's differential parenting: (Older adolescent/Younger adolescent)		
Positivity/warmth	−.35**	−.33**
Negativity/conflict	−.09	.06
Monitoring/control	−.20**	−.21**

$*p < .05, **p < .01, ***p < .001.$

child one of 10, the score would be 10. Similarly, if the older child had a score of 10 and the younger child had one of 20, the score is still 10. In each case, the score of 10 represents the magnitude of difference between treatment of the older child versus the younger child. These scores are subsequently related to family type and ownness as described below.

For mothers, family type was coded 0 when both siblings were biological offspring of the mother and lived in a nonstepfamily, 1 when both siblings were biological offspring of the mother but lived in a stepfamily, and 2 when one sibling was a biological offspring and one was a stepchild. For fathers, family type was coded 0 when both siblings were biological offspring of the father and living in a nonstepfamily, 1 when both siblings were stepchildren and lived in a stepfamily, and 2 when one sibling was a biological offspring and one was a stepchild.

F-values and means for cross-sectional MANOVAs calculated on parent's absolute differential treatment by adolescent gender and family type are reported in Tables 22 and 23. Results reveal that the largest discrepancy in parental treatment for both mothers and fathers occurred in families in which there was one biological child and one stepchild. These results reveal that biological offspring in nonstep- and stepfamilies are treated with more similar amounts of Positivity/warmth, Negativity/conflict and Monitoring/control by mothers and similar degrees of Positivity/warmth and Monitoring/control by fathers as compared to families where there is one biological child and one stepchild. For example, in Table 23, mothers' absolute difference scores for Positivity/warmth range from .39 to .46 in nonstep- and simple stepfamilies—both family types in which both siblings are biologically related to the mother. This is a significantly smaller difference (absolute difference: |older sibling − younger sibling|) than the means of .61 and .66 in complex

TABLE 22

F-Values and Significance Levels for Absolute Differences in Parenting of Older-Younger Adolescents in Wave 1

	Gender	Family Type	Family × Gender
Mother-adolescent:			
Multivariate	1.28	6.21***	.62
Multivariate *df*	(3,505)	(6,1010)	(2,505)
Differences in Positivity/warmth	.36	7.85***	.06
Differences in Negativity/conflict	.64	7.98***	.89
Differences in Monitoring/control	2.75*	5.35	.85
Father-adolescent:			
Multivariate	.90	2.63*	1.26
Multivariate *df*	(3,505)	(6,1010)	(2,505)
Differences in Positivity/warmth	.06	5.70**	.13
Differences in Negativity/conflict	2.54	1.43	3.26*
Differences in Monitoring/control	.47	3.11*	.95

$*p < .05, **p < .01, ***p < .001.$

TABLE 23

Means for the Multimethod/Multirespondent Composites of Parent-Adolescent Absolute Differences Scores—Wave 1

	Nonstep (NS) Both sibs bio		Simple Step (SS) Both sibs bio		Complex Step (CS) One sib bio, one sib step		Significant Main Effects and Interactions	Significant Contrasts and Planned Comparisons
	Boys	Girls	Boys	Girls	Boys	Girls		
Mother's Absolute Difference Scores								
Positivity/warmth	.39	.40	.44	.46	.60	.66	family:	CS > NS, SS
	(.23)	(.30)	(.36)	(.41)	(.42)	(.66)		
Negativity/conflict	.35	.41	.50	.46	.61	.70	family:	CS > NS, SS
	(.28)	(.35)	(.40)	(.44)	(.59)	(.58)		
Monitoring/control	.44	.39	.45	.43	.66	.52	sex:	boys > girls
	(.34)	(.30)	(.36)	(.35)	(.50)	(.45)	family:	CS > NS, SS
Father's Absolute Difference Scores								
Positivity/warmth	.33	.37	.44	.44	.51	.51	family:	CS > NS, SS
	(.26)	(.30)	(.33)	(.33)	(.42)	(.47)		
Negativity/conflict	.36	.46	.33	.48	.50	.44	family ×	NS, SS:
	(.27)	(.44)	(.33)	(.47)	(.39)	(.39)	sex:	girls > boys
Monitoring/control	.37	.42	.44	.51	.52	.48		CS: boys > girls
	(.34)	(.30)	(.36)	(.35)	(.50)	(.45)	family:	CS > NS, SS

$*p < .05, **p < .01, ***p < .001$; numbers in parentheses are standard deviations.

stepfamilies wherein one sibling is biological and one is a stepchild. In addition, in Wave 1, there is a greater discrepancy with male sibling pairs than with female sibling pairs in mother's monitoring and control. Wave 1 analyses also reveal that in families with one biological child and one stepchild, fathers treat boys with greater differential negativity than girls.

Repeated-measures analyses reveal a similar pattern of main effects for mothers and adolescents and thus are not presented in tables. Repeated-measures results indicate main effects of ownness at both waves with mothers using significantly less *differential* Positivity/warmth, $F(3, 248) = 18.25$, $p < .001$, and Monitoring/control, $F(3, 248) = 3.26$, $p < .02$, with their two biological siblings in nonstep- or simple stepfamilies than they do in complex stepfamilies with one biological child and one stepchild. Similarly, fathers use less differential Positivity/warmth, $F(3, 247) = 8.10$, $p < .001$, with siblings when there is not a discrepancy in biological ownness. There were no wave effects or interactions.

In sum, these analyses on nonshared parenting reveal that (*a*) parents treat siblings differently, (*b*) parents are significantly more likely to treat siblings differently when siblings differ in their biological relationship to the parent, and (*c*) parent's differential treatment of siblings is not due to family type.

DISCUSSION

Past research has clearly delineated the differences in family functioning between newly remarried families and nondivorced families (Bray & Berger, 1993; Hetherington, 1995; Hetherington & Clingempeel, 1992; Hetherington & Jodl, 1994). In general, this research has demonstrated that parent-adolescent relationships in recently remarried families face many stresses and are often characterized by less parental control, monitoring, and warmth and more negative behavior in parent-adolescent interactions than those found in nondivorced families. Although relationships between biological parents and adolescents in stepfamilies improve over time as has been demonstrated previously (Hetherington & Clingempeel, 1992), those between stepparents and stepchildren tend to remain more problematic and disengaged.

The analyses in this study present a descriptive picture of parent-adolescent relationships in reestablished, long-term stepfamilies, which appear to be somewhat different than those found in recently formed stepfamilies. In fact, our data show that relationships between biologically related parents and adolescents in long-established stepfamilies are similar to those in nonstepfamilies, whereas relationships between stepparents and stepchildren remain more troubled. Biological relatedness, rather than family type, seems to be associated with different patterns of parent-adolescent relationships, although there is some indication that being in a complex stepfamily may exacerbate problems in parent-adolescent relations to some extent.

Mothers and fathers are significantly more warm and supportive with their biological children regardless of family status. They feel closer to their

97

adolescents, have more rapport with their adolescents and enjoy spending time together. They also are more likely to control and monitor their biological adolescents' activities, behaviors and associations. They are emotionally and behaviorally involved in their adolescents' lives. It may be that parents who have had a much longer time getting to know their biological child also have had greater opportunity to develop shared activities and interests, and have a stronger sense of attachment, involvement and shared family history—all of which may lead to deeper feelings of closeness and warmth than in the relationships parents share with stepchildren. It should be remembered, however, that these stepfamilies have been together for an average of 9 years, a sufficient time for establishing a bond if it is ever to occur.

It may not just be the shared history of biologically related parents and children that draws them closer together. Biologically related parents and children are genetically more similar than stepparents and stepchildren and genetically based similarities in characteristics and interests may promote more engagement and positive ties. Evolutionary psychologists also would argue that this greater involvement and commitment of biological parents with their children is based on the need to facilitate intergenerational transmission of their genes.

Interactions between stepparents and children have also, although less consistently, been found to be characterized by higher levels of conflict and negativity than parents and adolescents in nonstepfamilies (Hetherington & Clingempeel, 1992; Hetherington & Jodl, 1994). While some studies show that stepfathers are less concerned, involved, and critical of their adolescents than are nondivorced fathers, we found fathers in stepfamilies not only were less affectionate but also were much harsher with nonbiological children— they were more coercive, angry, and negative with their nonbiological children than with their biological children. Stepchildren reciprocated with less warmth toward stepfathers. The father-stepdaughter relationship, in particular, has previously been identified as problematic in newly constituted stepfamilies (Brand et al., 1988; Bray & Berger, 1993; Hetherington & Clingempeel, 1992; Hetherington & Jodl, 1994); however, in the present study, fathers were equally negative with both stepdaughters and stepsons.

Interestingly, mothers were less negative with their stepchildren than with their biological children. In our sample, the only stepmothers were those in blended families where mothers were dealing not only with their own adolescents, but with their husband's children from a previous relationship. This may be an especially difficult situation for mothers. As others have noted, stepmothers seem to encounter more challenges in stepfamilies than do stepfathers (Furstenberg, 1987; Furstenberg & Nord, 1987; Santrock et al., 1988; Visher & Visher, 1978). Remarried fathers initially may expect mothers to take on the traditional role of primary caretaker (Fine et al.,

1993; Thomson, McLanahan, & Curtin, 1992; Waldren, 1986; Whitsett & Land, 1992), which is thought to create more tension and negativity between stepmothers and stepchildren who dislike having a mother replacement. In these long-term remarried families, however, this is not the case. In addition, more affectionate relationships also were found with greater warmth by the adolescent toward the mother in biologically related dyads in stepfamilies than with stepchildren and stepmothers. Both stepchildren and stepmothers may be coping by distancing in these long-established stepfamilies.

Although girls were more likely than boys to receive greater warmth, support, monitoring, and control from mothers, this seemed to run across families, and gender by family type interactions were rarely found. This corroborates the finding that differences in the parenting of boys and girls in response to remarriage are unlikely to be found in adolescence, although they sometimes have been found with preadolescents and younger children (Bray & Berger, 1993; Hetherington & Clingempccl, 1992).

Our findings also concur with previous work that has demonstrated differences in mother-child versus father-child relationships (Almeida & Galambos, 1991; Forehand & Nousiainen, 1993; Wierson, Armistead, Forehand, Thomas, & Fauber, 1990). As compared to fathers, mothers were both more positive and negative with their children. Mothers also were more positive with girls than with boys. In addition, mothers took a larger role in monitoring and controlling their adolescent's life than did fathers, especially for older girls. This main effect finding is particularly interesting because it holds for stepmothers, as well; thus, although stepmothers and adolescents are less positive and negative with each other than biologically related mothers and adolescents, our findings suggest they still build more affectively intense relationships, both positive and negative, than do fathers and children. Stepmothers also assume a greater role in monitoring and control than biological fathers do. A similar result was seen in Chapter III, in which wives take on a greater share of childrearing and household responsibilities than husbands, regardless of family type or ownness.

Past studies have indicated that it is not just the absolute level of warmth, negativity, control, and monitoring that affects adolescent adjustment, but also that differential treatment of siblings by parents is important (Henderson et al., 1996; Mekos, Hetherington, & Reiss, 1997; Tejerina-Allen, Wagner, & Cohen, 1994). In this study the greatest differential treatment was found in stepfamilies where one adolescent was biologically related to a parent but the other sibling was not.

Overall, these analyses give a picture of reestablished stepfamilies functioning fairly well, although somewhat differently than nonstepfamilies. Furthermore, it appears that with long-term stepfamilies, acceptable roles, relationships, and responsibilities among family members have been satisfactorily established, resulting in fewer family type differences than can be found among more recently reconstituted families. In newly remarried families, differences are found between mothers and their biological children in simple stepfamilies and in nondivorced families (Bray & Berger, 1993; Hetherington & Clingempeel, 1992) that were not obtained in these longer married stepfamilies. The stepfamilies most likely to show perturbations in family functioning were those that were most complex. The biological relationship of the parent and adolescent emerged, however, as having importance for the affective quality of parenting as demonstrated through both between- and within-family analyses. Despite past difficulties, parents and biological adolescents in stabilized stepfamilies exhibit a caring, involved, supportive relationship that is less likely to be found for stepparents and stepchildren, who remain less engaged and emotionally involved with each other even after a long period of time together.

V. SIBLING, HALF SIBLING, AND STEPSIBLING RELATIONSHIPS IN REMARRIED FAMILIES

Edward R. Anderson

In this chapter, differences in the quality of sibling relationships among full biological siblings, half siblings, and unrelated stepsiblings living in remarried households are examined. These relationships are further contrasted with those of full biological siblings living in nonstepfamily households.

There is a wide array of sibling relationships that can appear in remarried families, and the nature of these relationships is often ambiguous. This ambiguity is illustrated by children's responses to a seemingly simple question: Who is in your immediate family? Furstenberg (1988) found that 41% of children excluded their stepsiblings from their lists of immediate family members. Interestingly, Furstenberg finds that these exclusions were unrelated to the length of time spent living in a stepfamily.

Few children in the population have the entire array of sibling relationships. Cherlin and McCarthy (1985) report that only 6% of remarried couples under age 40 in 1980 had three sets of children; that is, the custodial parent's children from a previous marriage, mutual children from the current remarriage, and the stepparent's children from a previous marriage. Nevertheless, it seems likely that most stepfamilies will *eventually* contain more members than the most common pattern of stepfather, custodial mother, and one or more full siblings. Bumpass (1984b) found that the acquisition of a half sibling occurred for one third of those children entering a stepfamily within 4 years; two thirds of children in stepfamilies eventually have either a half sibling or a step sibling. Although in this study only three types of sibling relationships in stepfamilies are involved in the targeted sibling pairs, as will be recalled from the methods chapter in this volume (Chapter II, Table 2), almost two thirds of the targeted siblings are embedded in stepfamilies with a more complex array of sibling relationships.

In contrast to data on parent-child relationships, few studies of stepfamilies have included assessments of sibling relationships. Differences among full siblings, half siblings, and stepsiblings, and the associations between sibling relationships and adolescent adjustment rarely have been explored. Clinical reports and what little research is available suggest that such sibling relationships may play an important role as risk and protective factors in the adjustment of children confronting the challenges in remarried families. Based on previous literature as reviewed in the introduction to this *Monograph*, the following hypotheses were investigated.

First, relative to nonstepfamilies, relationships between full biological siblings in stepfamilies will be marked by more hostility, coercion, and rivalry, and by less support and involvement.

Second, in stepfamilies, relative to full biological siblings, stepsibling relationships will evidence less negative behavior but also more distance and less positive behavior. In stepfamilies, relative to half siblings, stepsibling relationships should be less negative but also less positive. Relationships between half siblings should be more like those of full biological siblings than relationships between stepsiblings.

Third, across all sibling configurations, girl pairs should evidence greater empathy, support, and involvement than boy pairs.

Fourth, across time, sibling relationships should become more disengaged, with declining levels of both positivity and negativity. Levels of both positivity and negativity should be greater in sibling pairs closer in age than pairs further apart.

Fifth, the quality of the sibling relationship should be a significant predictor of adolescent adjustment over time.

Sixth, the extent to which adolescents are similar in adjustment to their sibling should depend on the quality of the sibling relationship.

METHOD

As noted previously, all of the sibling dyads involved same-sex siblings, with an age difference of no more than 5 years. Furthermore, the birth order of the adolescent varied. We use the terms "older" and "younger" to indicate the relative birth status of the adolescent, but this does not imply that the older adolescent is the eldest sibling in the family. Three levels of biological relatedness were examined. *Full siblings* are adolescents who share the same biological mother and father (i.e., are full biological relatives). *Half siblings* are adolescents who share one biological parent. *Stepsiblings* are adolescents who are biologically unrelated. In addition, full siblings reside in either stepfamily or nonstepfamily households. In stepfamilies, the full sibling pair have a residential stepparent. Table 24 provides the mean ages and mean age differences of the siblings for the analyses presented here. Significant main effects of family type were found for the age of the younger sibling, $F(3, 508) = 9.4$, $p < .001$, and the age difference between siblings, $F(3, 508) = 15.8$, $p < .001$. Follow-up tests revealed that younger half-siblings tended to be younger ($M = 12.0$ years, $SD = 1.8$) compared to stepsiblings ($M = 13.3$ years, $SD = 2.1$) or full siblings in remarried families ($M = 12.7$ years, $SD = 2.0$). Furthermore, stepsiblings were older than full siblings in intact families ($M = 12.3$ years, $SD = 1.8$). In addition, the age difference between stepsiblings ($M = 1.8$ years, $SD = 1.1$) was smaller than the age difference in any other group. The age difference between half siblings ($M = 2.6$, $SD = .84$) also was greater than that between full siblings in remarried families ($M = 2.2$, $SD = .82$). As a consequence, the age of the younger sibling and the age difference between siblings were used as covariates when examining mean differences between family types. Analyses with and without covariates are both presented.

The sibling relationship was assessed by children's, siblings', and parents' reports on a revised version of the Sibling Inventory of Behavior (Schaefer & Edgerton, 1981) used by Anderson and Rice (1992). Because of the extensive battery of instruments in the NEAD study, the inventory was reduced somewhat from the version used previously by Anderson and Rice (1992), but the six factors identified in the previous version were replicated in the current study. These factors were: Rivalry (e.g., "is jealous of sibling," "tattles on sibling," median $\alpha = .77$), Aggression (e.g., "gets angry with sibling," "fusses and argues with sibling," median $\alpha = .80$), Embarrassment/Avoidance (e.g., "is embarrassed to be with sibling in public," "acts ashamed of sibling," median $\alpha = .85$), Teaching/Directiveness (e.g., "teaches sibling new skills," "tries to teach sibling how to behave," median $\alpha = .67$), Empathy (e.g., "is pleased by progress sibling makes," "shows sympathy when things are hard for sibling," median $\alpha = .88$), and Companionship (e.g., "has fun with sibling," "treats sibling as a good friend," median $\alpha = .88$). Factor analysis indicated the existence of two broad dimensions underlying these scales: Positivity (Directiveness, Empathy, and Companionship), and Negativity (Rivalry, Aggression, and Avoidance). Composite measures of Positivity and Negativity were thus computed for each rater by taking the mean of the standardized measures comprising the factors. In addition, observational measures of Positivity and Negativity also were used. These composite observational measures parallel those described for parent-adolescent relationships.

Correlations among raters on these composites of Positivity and Negativity ranged from .18 to .61 (median $r = .40$), with the strongest correlations not surprisingly found between mother's and father's reports.

TABLE 24

MEANS (STANDARD DEVIATIONS) FOR ADOLESCENTS' AGES ACROSS SIBLING GROUPS

	Full: Nonstep		Full: Remarried		Half siblings		Stepsiblings	
	Boys	Girls	Boys	Girls	Boys	Girls	Boys	Girls
Older Adolescent	14.7	14.6	14.8	15.1	14.6	14.6	15.1	15.0
Age	(1.8)	(1.9)	(2.0)	(2.0)	(1.8)	(2.0)	(2.0)	(2.0)
Younger Adolescent	12.3	12.2	12.6	12.9	12.0	12.1	13.4	13.2
Age	(1.6)	(1.9)	(2.0)	(2.1)	(1.6)	(2.0)	(1.9)	(2.0)
Age difference	2.4	2.4	2.2	2.2	2.6	2.5	1.8	1.7
	(0.9)	(1.0)	(0.8)	(0.8)	(0.9)	(0.8)	(1.1)	(1.2)
N	46	49	87	95	60	49	74	56

Multimethod/multirespondent composite measures of Positivity and Negativity based on all raters were computed taking the mean of the standardized composite for each respondent (including observers). The correlations among the resulting composite variables for the older and younger adolescent were very high, with a correlation of .88 on the Positivity composite and .93 on the Negativity composite. Thus, these composite variables appear to represent relationship indices rather than unique measures of individual behavior. Consequently, for analyses involving the Positivity and Negativity composites, the scores for the older and younger adolescent were combined into a relationship index. Correlations between the older and younger adolescent on the individual dimensions also were high, with correlations of .81 for Rivalry, .89 for Aggression, .90 for Companionship, .79 for Empathy, and .54 for Avoidance. Correlations between siblings on observed Positivity ($r = .56$) and Negativity ($r = .91$) were also high. Directiveness, however, was only modestly correlated between siblings ($r = .34$). In light of these findings, for analyses involving individual dimensions, variables were combined to form a relationship index with the exception of Directiveness.

RESULTS

Results will be presented first for within-wave differences in sibling relationships across family type/relatedness. Analyses will include both composite variables and individual dimensions. Differences across source of report also will be examined. Second, developmental changes in sibling relationships will be investigated. Third, using both cross-sectional and longitudinal models, the relations between individual child adjustment and sibling relationship quality will be examined. Finally, analyses will be presented which focus on the similarity between siblings on adjustment variables.

Within-Wave Differences in Sibling Relationships

Composite variables. Differences in the positivity and negativity composite variables were examined using a 2 (gender) × 4 (sibling relatedness/family type) multivariate analysis of variance. Means and standard deviations are given in Table 25.

Multivariate tests revealed a main effect of gender, $F(2, 507) = 13.8$, $p < .001$. This multivariate effect was due primarily to gender differences in overall Positivity, $F(1, 508) = 23.55$, $p < .001$, with more positive behaviors between girls ($M = .05$, $SD = .56$) than between boys ($M = -.20$, $SD = .59$).

In addition, multivariate tests revealed a main effect of sibling relatedness, $F(6, 1014) = 13.26$, $p < .001$. Only the univariate test for Negativity was significant, $F(3, 508) = 21.57$, $p < .001$. Follow-up tests using Tukey's honestly significant difference test indicated that less negative behavior occurred in stepsibling relationships ($M = -.08$, $SD = .55$) than in any of the other three groups ($M = .38$, $SD = .57$). There was no significant interaction of relatedness and gender on the composite variables. The effects of gender on Positivity and of relatedness on Negativity remained significant after controlling for age and age difference.

Individual dimensions. To analyze scores on the individual dimensions, four separate multivariate analyses were conducted. First, the three dimensions of relationship Negativity (Rivalry, Aggression, Avoidance) were analyzed. Next, the two dimensions of relationship Positivity (Empathy, Companionship) were analyzed. Third, the observational composite indices of relationship Positivity and Negativity were analyzed. Finally, the individual scores for older and younger adolescent Directiveness were analyzed in a repeated-measures analysis.

Table 26 shows the means, standard deviations, and significant effects for these four analyses. A multivariate effect of family type was found for the Negativity dimensions, $F(9, 1524) = 14.7$, $p < .001$, and all three follow-up univariate tests also were significant, Rivalry: $F(3, 508) = 12.3$, $p < .001$; Aggression: $F(3, 508) = 36.9$, $p < .001$; Avoidance: $F(3, 508) = 1.8$, $p < .01$. In all three cases, stepsiblings evidenced the least Negativity. For Rivalry and Aggression, stepsiblings were significantly different from all other groups; for Avoidance, stepsiblings scored lower compared to full siblings in stepfamilies. Only one other pairwise comparison was significant: Rivalry was lower among half siblings compared to full siblings in stepfamilies.

Among the variables measuring relationship Positivity, there was a significant multivariate effect of gender, $F(2, 507) = 35.9$, $p < .001$. Only the univariate test for Empathy, however, was significant, $F(1, 508) = 19.6$, $p < .001$. Empathy was higher in relationships between girls ($M = .12$, $SD = .66$) than in relationships between boys ($M = -.29$, $SD = .66$).

105

TABLE 25

MEANS (STANDARD DEVIATIONS) FOR COMPOSITE MEASURES OF SIBLING RELATIONSHIP QUALITY, UNADJUSTED FOR COVARIATES

	Full: Nonstep		Full: Remarried		Half siblings		Stepsiblings		Significant Main Effects and Interactions	Significant Contrasts
	Boys	Girls	Boys	Girls	Boys	Girls	Boys	Girls		
Positivity	-.10	.06	-.17	.02	-.34	.08	-.16	.07	gender	girls > boys
	(.51)	(.54)	(.54)	(.49)	(.62)	(.55)	(.64)	(.67)		
Negativity	.25	.34	.52	.33	.42	.31	-.09	-.07	family type/ relatedness	full: nonstep; full: remarried; half-siblings > stepsiblings
	(.64)	(.56)	(.59)	(.51)	(.56)	(.56)	(.58)	(.51)		

TABLE 26

Means (Standard Deviations) for Composite Measures of Sibling Relationship Quality, Unadjusted for Covariates

	Full: Nonstep		Full: Remarried		Half siblings		Stepsiblings		Significant Main Effects and Interactions	Significant Contrasts
	Boys	Girls	Boys	Girls	Boys	Girls	Boys	Girls		
Rivalry	.00 (.73)	.06 (.72)	.24 (.67)	.16 (.63)	-.03 (.57)	-.01 (.59)	-.33 (.68)	-.18 (.57)	family type/relatedness	full: nonstep; full: remarried; half siblings > stepsiblings; full: remarried > half siblings
Aggression	.15 (.82)	.19 (.64)	.33 (.62)	.20 (.64)	.18 (.61)	.03 (.65)	-.56 (.86)	-.48 (.58)	family type/relatedness	full: nonstep; full: remarried; half siblings > stepsiblings
Avoidance	.09 (.62)	.05 (.69)	.25 (.64)	.18 (.60)	.25 (.64)	.04 (.68)	-.10 (.57)	.02 (.64)	family type/relatedness	full: remarried > stepsiblings
Empathy	-.20 (.57)	.12 (.67)	-.28 (.65)	.15 (.62)	-.36 (.63)	.17 (.63)	-.30 (.73)	.05 (.75)	gender	girls > boys
Companionship	-.15 (.69)	-.06 (.67)	-.18 (.66)	-.20 (.64)	-.39 (.73)	-.07 (.66)	-.16 (.85)	-.10 (.78)		
Observed Positivity	-.35 (.60)	-.29 (.60)	-.45 (.51)	-.32 (.45)	-.67 (.63)	-.31 (.61)	-.45 (.49)	-.12 (.62)	gender; family type/relatedness	girls > boys; stepsiblings > half siblings; full: nonstep; full: remarried > half siblings
Observed Negativity	.39 (1.0)	.87 (.94)	.65 (.89)	.66 (.79)	.79 (.88)	.73 (.89)	.11 (.90)	-.01 (.93)	family type/relatedness	half siblings > stepsiblings
Older Directiveness	.18 (.51)	.21 (.59)	.03 (.69)	.14 (.64)	.07 (.62)	.35 (.68)	-.03 (.78)	-.27 (.77)	gender; family type/relatedness	girls > boys; full: nonstep; full: remarried; half siblings > stepsiblings
Younger Directiveness	-.18 (.54)	-.03 (.59)	-.15 (.62)	-.12 (.53)	-.35 (.62)	.03 (.64)	-.28 (.63)	-.16 (.65)	adolescent status; family type/relatedness × adolescent status	older > younger; full: nonstep; full: remarried; half siblings (older > younger); stepsiblings (older = younger)

NOTE. Older = Older Adolescent; Younger = Younger Adolescent.

Among the observational composites, there were multivariate effects of gender, $F(2, 490) = 15.7$, $p < .001$, and family type/relatedness, $F(6, 980) = 8.8$, $p < .001$. Consistent with the analyses presented so far, the gender difference was significant only for Positivity, $F(1, 491) = 18.7$, $p < .001$, with girl pairs displaying more positive behavior in their interactions ($M = -.27$, $SD = .56$) compared to boy pairs ($M = -.48$, $SD = .56$). Univariate tests of family type/relatedness were significant for both observed Positivity, $F(3, 491) = 3.9$, $p < .05$, and observed Negativity, $F(3, 491) = 16.0$, $p < .001$. Follow-up tests indicated that half sibling relationships were less positive ($M = -.51$, $SD = .65$) compared to stepsiblings ($M = -.31$, $SD = .57$). Moreover, stepsibling relationships were observed to be much less negative ($M = .06$, $SD = .91$) compared to all other groups ($M = .69$, $SD = .89$).

Finally, several significant effects were found in the measures of individual Directiveness. First, a main effect of gender was found, $F(1, 508) = 11.9$, $p < .001$, with more Directiveness found in relationships between girls ($M = .04$, $SD = .54$) than between boys ($M = -.13$, $SD = .54$). A main effect of family type/relatedness also was found, $F(3, 508) = 4.5$, $p < .01$, with Directiveness lower among stepsiblings ($M = -.20$, $SD = .60$) compared to all other groups ($M = .00$, $SD = .52$). Not surprisingly, older adolescents were more directive ($M = .07$, $SD = .69$) than younger adolescents ($M = -.16$, $SD = .61$), in the significant effect of adolescent status, $F(1, 508) = 13.8$, $p < .001$. Finally, a family type/relatedness by adolescent status interaction was found, $F(3, 508) = 4.1$, $p < .01$. The difference in Directiveness between older and younger siblings was smaller among stepsiblings ($M = .06$, $SD = .78$) compared to all other groups ($M = .28$, $SD = .66$). This last difference, however, was no longer significant once age of the younger child and age differences were controlled.

Thus, a consistent picture emerges from these cross-sectional analyses. First, relationships between girls are more positive than relationships between boys, and this difference is found on observational as well as self-report data. It should be noted, however, that this difference arises only on the dimension of empathy, which involves communication, support, and information-sharing, and not on the measure of companionship, which assesses involvement in mutual activities. Girl pairs, did, however, report more directiveness than boy pairs, but there were no gender differences on measures of negativity. Second, across family type/relatedness, stepsibling relationships are reported to be less negative than other relationships, and independent observers confirm this difference. Stepsiblings were less directive than other siblings, but there were no differences across family type/relatedness on positivity.

Differences by source of report. Differences in sibling relationship quality as a function of source of report was explored in repeated-measures analyses using source of report (mother, father, older adolescent, younger adolescent, and observer) and adolescent status (older vs. younger) as repeated-measures factors. Because mean differences in the behavior of older and younger adolescents were of interest, in this analysis the relationship variables were disaggregated into separate scores for the older adolescent and the younger adolescent. Results from these tests are presented in Table 27. The significant main effects for relatedness on Negativity, and for gender on Positivity remained in these analyses. In addition, a main effect of adolescent status was obtained for Negativity, with older adolescents being rated as more negative ($M = .26$) than younger adolescents ($M = .19$).

Significant reporter effects, and significant reporter-by-adolescent status interactions appeared for both Positivity and Negativity. Means for these comparisons are plotted in Figures 1 and 2. As shown, reports from independent observers were more negative and less positive than reports from parents, with reports from adolescents in between. In addition, reports from adolescents about themselves were more positive and less negative than their reports about their siblings. For Negativity, all reporters viewed the older adolescent as more negative than the younger, except for the self-reports of older adolescents. For Positivity, the difference between ratings of the self and ratings of the sibling was more dramatic.

Three other significant effects were obtained, which were quite small relative to the other findings (see Table 27). For negativity, there were significant gender-by-reporter, and relatedness-by-gender-by-reporter interactions.

TABLE 27

F-VALUES AND SIGNIFICANCE LEVELS FOR REPEATED-MEASURES ANALYSES
EXAMINING SOURCE OF REPORT AND ADOLESCENT STATUS EFFECTS

	Negativity	Positivity
Relatedness	22.13***	1.28
Gender	0.33	22.61***
Reporter	36.96***	51.32***
Adolescent status	49.19***	0.28
Relatedness × gender	0.57	0.75
Relatedness × reporter	1.40	1.80*
Relatedness × adolescent status	0.44	0.40
Gender × reporter	2.47*	2.01
Gender × adolescent status	0.80	0.77
Reporter × adolescent status	52.19***	61.55***
Relatedness × gender × reporter	2.19**	0.83
Relatedness × reporter × adolescent status	1.42	1.38
Relatedness × gender × adolescent status	0.95	0.15
Gender × reporter × adolescent status	0.53	0.92
Relatedness × gender × reporter × adolescent status	1.31	1.26

*$p < .05$, **$p < .01$, ***$p < .001$.

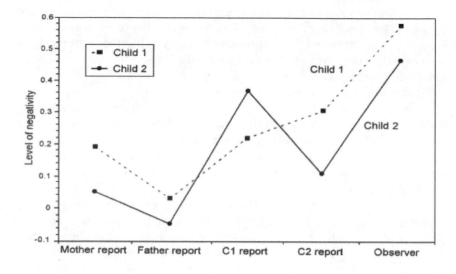

FIGURE 1.—Means for composite measures of sibling Negativity by reporter.

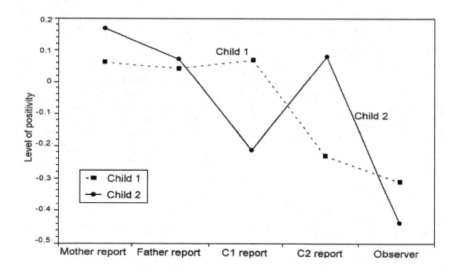

FIGURE 2.—Means for composite measures of sibling Positivity by reporter.

First, gender differences were larger in reports obtained from adolescents, with boys reporting greater Negativity than girls. For younger adolescent reports, these differences were largest for full siblings in stepfamilies. For Positivity, there was a small relatedness-by-reporter interaction. Reports from older adolescents and mothers were more positive about relations in nonstepfamilies; reports from younger adolescents were more positive about stepsiblings.

Thus, there is a consistent trend for adolescents to report more positive and less negative behavior about themselves than their siblings. Parents and observers, however, report that older adolescents are more negative and less positive than their younger siblings. The least favorable scores for both younger and older adolescents appeared in the observational data relative to the self-report data.

Developmental Changes in Sibling Relationships

We examined developmental changes in sibling relationships in three ways. First, the correlations of sibling relationship variables with adolescent's age, and the difference in ages between siblings were examined. Next, the stability of sibling relationship variables was examined. Third, repeated-measures analyses of the sibling relationship variables were conducted.

Correlations with age and age differences. As a first look at changes in sibling relationships over time, correlations between adolescent's age and sibling age differences with the composite variables are given in Table 28. As seen, less negative relationships occurred for older adolescents. Levels of Aggression, Rivalry, and Avoidance all decreased with age. Positivity was

TABLE 28

CORRELATIONS OF AGE AND AGE DIFFERENCE WITH SIBLING COMPOSITE VARIABLES

	Age of Older Adolescent	Age of Younger Adolescent	Older Adolescent's – Younger Adolescent's Age
Positivity	.05	.10*	−.09*
Negativity	−.18***	−.20***	.05
Rivalry	−.36***	−.37***	.02
Aggression	−.27***	−.33***	.15***
Avoidance	−.17***	−.23***	.14***
Companionship	−.09*	.00	−.18***
Empathy	.16***	.16***	−.01
Older Adolescent's Directiveness	−.21***	−.30***	.21***
Younger Adolescent's Directiveness	−.08*	.02	−.19***

*p < .05, **p < .01, ***p < .001.

less consistently related to age. Although Empathy between adolescents increased with age, levels of Companionship were either unrelated or declined with age. Directiveness on the part of the older sibling also declined with age. In general, larger age differences were associated with more Aggression and Avoidance, and less Companionship between siblings. In addition, larger age differences were associated with greater Directiveness from older adolescents, and less Directiveness from younger adolescents. These findings are consistent with the notion that larger age differences between siblings are associated with more hierarchical relationships, including more aggressiveness and less companionship. Neither Rivalry nor Empathy, however, was associated with the age difference between siblings.

Stability of sibling measures. Correlations of the individual dimensions across time ranged from .59 for Companionship to .72 for Rivalry and Empathy. Older adolescent and younger adolescent Directiveness had stability coefficients of .48 and .56, respectively, while the observational measure of Positivity and Negativity had stability coefficients of .40 and .33, respectively. The overall composites had stability coefficients of .66 for Positivity and .63 for Negativity, indicating moderate to high stability for these measures of sibling relationships.

Repeated-measures effects. Repeated-measures analyses of variance of the composite sibling dimensions of Positivity and Negativity and of the six individual dimensions were conducted. The main effects described in the cross-sectional analyses for Wave 1 were replicated in the longitudinal analyses with the smaller sample. In addition, for both composite variables, there was a main effect of wave, $F(1, 249) = 22.7$ and 75.4, $p < .001$, for Positivity and Negativity, respectively. Over time, sibling relationships became less positive (Wave 1 $M = -.07$, $SD = .53$; Wave 2 $M = -.21$, $SD = .64$), but also less negative (Wave 1 $M = .30$, $SD = .57$; Wave 2 $M = .02$, $SD = .60$). This pattern of disengagement did not interact with family type. Finally, for sibling Negativity only, a gender-by-wave interaction was obtained, $F(1, 249) = 6.1$, $p < .05$. The decline in Negativity observed over time was larger for pairs of boys (Wave 1 $M = .37$, $SD = .61$; Wave 2 $M = .00$, $SD = .66$) than pairs of girls (Wave 1 $M = .24$, $SD = .51$; Wave 2 $M = .05$, $SD =. 54$). Among the individual dimensions, the decline over time occurred for all dimensions except Avoidance, Empathy, and the observational measure of Positivity. The gender-by-wave interaction occurred on all Negativity variables except Avoidance.

Thus, the evidence suggests that sibling relationships undergo transformation across this age range. All dimensions of negativity showed decreases over time, as did measures of directiveness and companionship. Empathy between siblings, however, did not show this change, and suggests that siblings over time become engaged in more mutual disclosure relative to involvement in shared activities.

Relation of Sibling Variables to Adolescent Adjustment

In this section, the relation between sibling variables and adolescent adjustment is examined. First, within-wave correlations between composite sibling relationship variables and adolescent adjustment are presented. In addition, we examine whether gender and family type/biological relatedness moderates the relation between sibling relationship quality and adjustment. Second, using the findings from the cross-sectional analyses as a guide, we examine longitudinal relations between sibling relationship quality and adolescent adjustment.

Cross-sectional findings. The within-wave correlations between sibling relationship variables and adolescent's adjustment are presented in Table 29. Not surprisingly, Positivity was associated with lower levels of Externalizing and Depressive Symptoms, and higher levels of Social Responsibility, Cognitive Agency, Sociability, Autonomy, and Self-Worth. Opposite relations were found for Negativity. These relations held for both older and younger adolescents. Directiveness was least likely of the individual dimensions to be associated with adjustment.

We next examined whether gender and family type/biological relatedness moderated the relation between sibling relationship quality and adolescent adjustment. Because of the large number of variables measuring adjustment, these analyses were limited to those variables that showed the strongest correlational results: Externalizing and Social Responsibility.

Following the procedures recommended by Aiken and West (1991), continuous variables were centered to minimize collinearity and maximize interpretability, and categorical variables used unweighted effects coding. Main effects and interactions were entered simultaneously in each regression equation; separate regressions were conducted for Externalizing and Social Responsibility.

Results of the regressions are presented in Table 30. As shown, Negativity and Positivity were significantly related to Externalizing. Only Positivity was significantly associated with Social Responsibility. Gender moderated the association between Positivity and Externalizing for younger children. The association of Positivity with Externalizing was stronger for boys ($\beta = -.35$) than for girls ($\beta = -.18$). This moderating effect was not seen for Social Responsibility.

Family type/relatedness moderated the association between sibling's Negativity and Social Responsibility. Follow-up tests revealed that this association was less strong for both older and younger stepsiblings compared to

TABLE 29

WITHIN-WAVE CORRELATIONS BETWEEN COMPOSITE SIBLING RELATIONSHIP VARIABLES AND ADOLESCENTS' ADJUSTMENT VARIABLES

	Positivity	Negativity	Rivalry	Aggression	Avoid.	Compan.	Empathy	OA Dir.	YA Dir.
Older Adolescents' Adjustment									
Externalizing	-.35***	.41***	.30***	.29***	.33***	-.23***	-.34***	-.19***	-.09*
Depressive Symptoms	-.17***	.23***	.23***	.17***	.25***	-.29***	-.16***	-.16***	-.00
Social Responsibility	.46***	-.24***	-.12**	-.14***	-.29***	.37***	.50***	.39***	-.23***
Cognitive Agency	.22***	-.12**	-.04	-.01	-.13**	.13**	.25***	.21***	-.04
Sociability	.27***	-.14***	-.10*	-.13***	-.15***	.14***	.33***	.22***	.10*
Autonomy	.21***	-.17***	.16***	-.18***	-.14***	.07*	.30***	.15***	.12**
Self-Worth	.13**	-.14***	-.06	-.05	-.12*	.09*	.14***	.07	-.01
Younger Adolescents' Adjustment									
Externalizing	-.30***	.34***	.25***	.25***	.28***	-.21***	-.31***	-.16***	-.16***
Depressive Symptoms	-.19***	.20***	.24***	.18***	.24***	-.21***	-.19***	-.03	-.20***
Social Responsibility	.38***	-.18***	-.09*	-.11**	-.20***	.28***	.42***	.29***	.28***
Cognitive Agency	.21***	-.10**	-.03	-.06	-.11**	.14***	.24***	.03	.17***
Sociability	.24***	-.11**	-.11**	-.18***	-.14***	.17***	.27***	-.01	.26***
Autonomy	.21***	-.15***	-.17***	-.19***	-.14***	.11**	.29***	-.04	.28***
Self-Worth	.16***	-.11**	-.02	-.08*	-.09*	.18***	.13***	.10*	.13***

NOTE. Avoid. = Avoidance/Embarrassment, Compan. = Companionship, OA Dir. = Older Adolescents' Directiveness, YA Dir. = Younger Adolescents' Directiveness.
*p < .05, **p < .01, ***p < .001.

TABLE 30

Regression Results for Main and Moderating Effects of Sibling Relationship Variables on Adolescents' Adjustment

| | Externalizing | | Social Responsibility | |
	Older	Younger	Older	Younger
Main effects				
Sibling's Negativity	.32***	.27***	−.05	−.01
Sibling's Positivity	−.18***	−.15**	.42***	.35***
Moderating effects				
Gender × Negativity	.04	.03	.01	−.09
Gender × Positivity	−.03	−.10*	.05	.02
Family type/relatedness × Negativity	−.03	.06	.09*	.13**
Family type/relatedness × Positivity	−.05	−.07	.06	.08
R^2	.20	.16	.22	.16
$F(6, 509)$	21.60***	16.00***	24.10***	16.70***

*$p < .05$, **$p < .01$, ***$p < .001$.

other groups (older adolescent βs = −.22 vs. −.34 for stepsiblings and other groups, respectively; younger adolescent βs = −.12 and −.18). This moderating effect was not significant for Externalizing.

Longitudinal findings. Anderson et al. (1992) reported significant longitudinal relations between sibling relationship quality and adolescent adjustment for a sample of adolescents in remarried families. In that study, all adolescents in stepfamilies were full biological siblings from the mother's previous remarriage, and were in the early years of a remarriage. Because similar measures were used in this study, we sought to replicate these findings with the current sample, encompassing a broader age range, a longer time span between waves, different sibling types, and more long-term remarriages.

To test for the presence of longitudinal relations, a series of structural equation models were conducted. The null model consisted of only within-variable stability coefficients, as presented in Figure 3. Subsequently, a series of models, nested within the null model, were estimated that tested the presence of cross-lag relations. These models tested for the longitudinal relation between relationship quality and later adjustment, and between adjustment and later relationship quality. Externalizing and Social Responsibility were examined in separate models. Results of these tests are presented in Table 31.

For Externalizing, two models showed significant improvement over the stability model. These two models included prospective relations between relationship quality and later adjustment, first for the older adolescent only, and second for both the older adolescent and the younger adolescent. The model including cross-lag relations between relationship quality and the

115

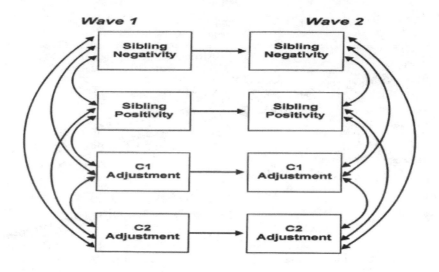

FIGURE 3.—Within-variable stability model for sibling relationship quality and adolescent adjustment.

TABLE 31

CROSS-LAG STRUCTURAL EQUATION MODEL RESULTS FOR SIBLING RELATIONSHIP QUALITY AND ADOLESCENT ADJUSTMENT

	Model results		Difference from Stability model	
	χ^2	df	χ^2	df
Externalizing				
Stability only	23	12		
Relationship quality → Older Adol. adjustment	14	10	9*	2
Relationship quality → Ynger Adol. adjustment	20	10	3	2
Relationship quality → Old & Yng adjustment	10	8	13*	4
Older Adol. adjustment → relationship quality	22	10	1	2
Ynger Adol. adjustment → relationship quality	22	10	1	2
Old & Yng adjustment → relationship quality	22	8	1	4
Reciprocal lagged relations	8	4	15	8
Social Responsibility				
Stability only	49	12		
Relationship quality → Older Adol. adjustment	46	10	3	2
Relationship quality → Ynger Adol. adjustment	48	10	1	2
Relationship quality → Old & Yng adjustment	38	8	11*	4
Older Adol. adjustment → relationship quality	43	10	6*	2
Ynger Adol. adjustment → relationship quality	40	10	9*	2
Old and Yng adjustment → relationship quality	36	8	13*	4
Reciprocal lagged relations	25	4	24*	8

NOTE. Older Adol. or Old = Older Adolescent's; Ynger Adol. or Yng = Younger Adolescent's.
*$p < .05$.

younger adolescent's later adjustment was not a significant improvement. Examination of the cross-lag coefficients in the model including both the older and younger adolescent revealed one significant parameter, the cross-lag path linking sibling Positivity to the older adolescent's later Externalizing. Thus, the improvement in fit for the model including both the older adolescent and the younger adolescent appeared to be primarily the result of including paths for the older adolescent. These tests indicate that sibling relationship quality is associated with later Externalizing only for the older adolescent. Specifically, Positivity in the relationship is associated with lower Externalizing at Wave 2 ($\beta = -.15$). This result may be indicative of the buffering effect of caring for a younger sibling, consistent with the findings of Werner (1993).

In cross-sectional analyses, gender moderated the relation between sibling Positivity and Externalizing. A two-group structural equation model was conducted to determine if this moderating effect was present longitudinally. The model allowing separate estimates by gender ($\chi^2 = 75$, $df = 42$) was not a significant improvement over the model in which path coefficients were constrained to be equal ($\chi^2 = 76$, $df = 44$). Thus, the association between relationship quality and later Externalizing does not appear to differ by gender.

For Social Responsibility, five models yielded a significant improvement over the stability model. All three models involving prospective relations between children's Social Responsibility and later sibling relationship quality were a significant improvement. In addition, the model including prospective relations between relationship quality and later Social Responsibility for both the older and younger adolescent was also a significant improvement. Not surprisingly, then, the model of reciprocal lagged relations also was a significant improvement. Examining this latter model, three cross-lag coefficients were significant: the paths linking sibling Positivity to later Social Responsibility for the older and younger adolescent, and the path linking the younger adolescent's Social Responsibility to later Positivity. No other cross-lag paths were significant.

In cross-sectional analysis, family type/relatedness moderated the relation between sibling Negativity and Externalizing. A four-group structural equation model was conducted to determine if this moderating effect was present longitudinally. Allowing separate path coefficients across groups ($\chi^2 = 123$, $df = 100$) did not yield a significant improvement over the equality model ($\chi^2 = 133$, $df = 112$). Thus, the association of sibling relationship quality with later Social Responsibility does not appear to differ across family type/relatedness.

Thus, there is evidence that sibling relationship quality is related to adolescent adjustment. Longitudinal data demonstrate that relationship quality predicts later adjustment, controlling for earlier levels of adjustment. Both older and younger adolescents showed greater social responsibility when their sibling relationships had been positive, although some of this process is bidirectional, with more positive sibling relationships occurring for children who earlier had shown higher social responsibility. In addition, having a positive sibling relationship was associated with lower externalizing for older adolescents at the later wave. There was inconsistent evidence that these effects were moderated by gender or family type/relatedness, with longitudinal analyses failing to replicate the significant cross-sectional findings.

Similarity Between Siblings

We also investigated whether the similarity between siblings in Externalizing and Social Responsibility was dependent upon sibling relationship quality. Social learning theory would predict that similarity between siblings on adjustment variables would increase to the extent that the relationship between them is positive. To test this idea, we included a term representing the interaction between sibling relationship quality and the older adolescent's behavior following the regression procedures described previously. The regression coefficient associated with the older adolescent's adjustment (i.e., the extent to which the younger adolescent's adjustment can be predicted from the older adolescent's adjustment) indicates the overall similarity between siblings, whereas the interaction term tests whether this similarity is dependent on the level of relationship quality. Because similarity also may depend on gender or family type/relatedness, terms representing these interactions also were included. Results are presented in Table 32.

Not surprisingly, there was a moderately strong association between the behavior of the older and younger adolescent for both variables. In neither case, however, was the similarity dependent on the relationship quality between siblings, as measured by overall Positivity and Negativity. Similarity between siblings was moderated by gender for both Externalizing and Social Responsibility. In both cases, the similarity between siblings was stronger for

TABLE 32

REGRESSION RESULTS FOR MAIN AND MODERATING EFFECTS RELATING OLDER ADOLESCENT'S ADJUSTMENT TO YOUNGER ADOLESCENT'S ADJUSTMENT

	Externalizing	Social Responsibility
Older adolescent's adjustment	.31***	.45***
Gender × older adolescent's adjustment	.09*	.08*
Family type/relatedness × older adolescent's adjustment	−.10*	−.04
Sibling Negativity × older adolescent's adjustment	.04	−.03
Sibling Positivity × older adolescent's adjustment	.04	.06
R^2	.12	.22
$F(5, 510)$	14.50***	29.60***

*$p < .05$, **$p < .01$, ***$p < .001$.

boys (βs = .37 and .50 for Externalizing and Social Responsibility, respectively) than for girls (βs = .19 and .32 for Externalizing and Social Responsibility). In addition, family type/relatedness moderated similarity in Externalizing. Follow-up tests revealed that less similarity occurred between stepsiblings (r = .17) than in other groups (r = .38). This moderating effect of family type/relatedness was not found for Social Responsibility.

To examine the similarity between siblings over time, cross-lag models were conducted for Externalizing and Social Responsibility. As in the previous analyses, the null model consisted of only within-variable stability coefficients. For Externalizing, a model allowing a cross-lag path from older adolescent Externalizing to younger adolescent Externalizing resulted in a significant improvement (χ^2 = 0.3, df = 1) over the null model (χ^2 = 9.3, df = 2). The model allowing a cross-lag path from the younger adolescent to the older adolescent was not a significant improvement (χ^2 = 9.2, df = 1). The results of the saturated model are given in Figure 4. Similar results were identified for Social Responsibility. The model allowing a cross-lag path from the older adolescent to the younger adolescent resulted in a better fit (χ^2 = 3.3, df = 1) compared to the stability model (χ^2 = 29.2, df = 2), but the alternative cross-lag path was not a significant improvement (χ^2 = 29.2, df = 1). Results of the saturated model are presented in Figure 5.

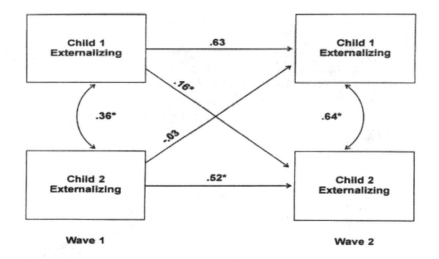

FIGURE 4.—Cross-lag regression results for sibling similarity in Externalizing.

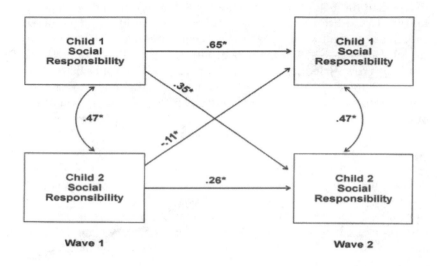

FIGURE 5.—Cross-lag regression results for sibling similarity in Social Responsibility.

Multiple-group structural models were conducted to test whether the moderating effects of gender and family type/relatedness found in the cross-sectional data were present longitudinally. Allowing separate cross-lag relations for gender or family type/relatedness did not improve the fit of the model. Thus, none of the cross-sectional moderating effects were significant in the longitudinal data.

The findings concerning similarity between siblings showed that, over time, the adjustment of older siblings predicted that of younger siblings, but not the reverse. The extent of similarity between siblings did not appear to be associated with the degree of positivity or negativity in the relationship. There was inconsistent evidence that similarity was related to gender or family type/relatedness, with longitudinal data failing to replicate the cross-sectional findings.

DISCUSSION

The hypotheses presented at the outset were largely supported by the analyses, but with some notable exceptions. In this study comparing different sibling relationships in remarried families to biological siblings in nonstepfamilies, unrelated stepsiblings showed little evidence that relationships were anything other than benign. In the analysis of the multimethod/multirespondent composites, the stepsibling group was less negative compared to the other three groups, and there were no differences in overall Positivity or on Companionship and Empathy. On the individual dimensions, stepsibling relationships exhibited less Rivalry and less Aggression than all other groups, and less avoidance and embarrassment of each other than among full siblings in stepfamilies. These differences also were noted by independent observers, with stepsibling relationships showing much less Negativity compared to other groups. Moreover, stepsibling relationships showed less Directiveness compared to other relationships. This does not necessarily imply that stepsibling relationships were less hierarchical; the difference in Directiveness between older and younger siblings was not significant once age differences were controlled. More likely, stepsiblings in these long-term stepfamilies have managed to develop what Ihinger-Tallman (1987) described as successful "satellite" relationships, providing support and companionship, with less negativity. Other studies note that stepsibling relationships are relatively benign or even positive (Ganong & Coleman, 1994; White & Reidman, 1992).

The relationships of half siblings were more like those of full siblings than stepsiblings, a finding in accord with the reports of Ganong and Coleman (1988, 1994). Although half sibling relationships showed somewhat less rivalry than full siblings, and were observed to be less positive than stepsiblings, the composite analyses showed no differences between full and half siblings, and no other differences emerged. Thus, adolescents in these long-term families appear to make few distinctions about whether a sibling is "half" or "full," a result suggested by Ganong and Coleman (1994).

Previous studies of full siblings in newly formed stepfamilies have found such relationships to be more negative than those of full siblings in nonstepfamilies (e.g., Anderson & Rice, 1992). In this study, with longer term stepfamilies, and with a larger age range of siblings, this difference was not as apparent. Results of composite Positivity and Negativity variables showed no differences between full siblings in stepfamilies and nonstepfamilies. Further, no differences between full sibling in stepfamilies and nonstepfamilies emerged in any of the individual dimensions, including observational data. Thus, overall levels of negativity between full siblings appear to have abated in these long-term stepfamilies, a marked contrast to earlier studies. Future longitudinal work on stepfamilies that follows sibling relationships over the long term is needed to determine whether these differences across studies are due to differential selection or adjustment over time.

As was found in other studies, especially the Hetherington and Clingempeel study (Anderson & Rice, 1992), which used similar measures to those in this study, relationships between girls were characterized by more Positivity than those of boys. This difference in Positivity also was found among observational reports. In addition, relationships between girls showed more Directiveness on the part of both older and younger adolescents. Gender differences were not apparent, however, with respect to negative behaviors of Aggression, Rivalry, and Avoidance. Importantly, no interactions between gender and sibling relatedness were found on the composite variables, individual dimensions, or observational reports. Thus, in this study, gender was a main effect, with girl pairs displaying more positive behavior than boy pairs. It should be kept in mind that this study did not examine cross-sex sibling pairs, which may reveal greater gender differences.

As was found in Anderson and Rice (1992), sibling relationships became more disengaged as children moved further into adolescence. Levels of both Positivity and Negativity declined significantly over time, with the decrease in Negativity being more pronounced for boys than for girls. Not all dimensions showed this change, however. Notably, the constructs of Avoidance and Empathy did not show a significant decline over time. Furthermore, although sibling relationships were observed to be less negative over time, there was no significant change in observed Positivity. In part, these changes likely reflect the measurement used. The Sibling Inventory of Behavior was originally developed for a younger sample of children, and may not fully represent the range of behaviors characteristic of adolescent sibling relationships, which may involve more mutual information-sharing, self-disclosure, and verbal support, rather than companionate behavior and shared time. The dimension of Empathy, however, most closely taps this domain (e.g., shows sympathy, helps adjust to new situations, is concerned about sibling's welfare and happiness), and importantly, did not decrease over time. Thus, not all aspects of the sibling relationship are declining in frequency over time, and it may therefore be more accurate to conclude that the relationship is transforming rather than disengaging. Future work which includes measurement of constructs associated with more mature peer relationships would shed light on the specific ways sibling relationships change over adolescence.

That the quality of sibling relationships is important for development is reflected in the findings relating sibling variables to adolescent adjustment. Within-wave analyses showed moderately strong relations between adolescent adjustment and the quality of sibling relationships. Adolescents with a sibling relationship characterized by more Positivity and less Negativity showed lower Externalizing and Depressive Symptoms, and higher Social Responsibility, Cognitive Agency, Sociability, Autonomy, and Self-Worth. Longitudinal analyses for both older and younger adolescents showed a prospective relation between having a positive sibling relationship and later Social Responsibility, controlling for earlier levels of adjustment. This finding replicates that of Anderson et al. (1992) with a younger sample of more recently formed stepfamilies. Given that the current study also has a longer time interval (3 years compared to 2 years), this replication is noteworthy. In addition, having a positive sibling relationship was associated with lower Externalizing for older adolescents, controlling for earlier adjustment. Werner (1993) has reported that enforced caretaking is associated with resilience in the face of stress. Given that older adolescents were more likely to evidence directiveness than younger adolescents, a similar process may be present in these data. Having responsibility for caretaking of a younger sibling may thus have important benefits. Finally, there was evidence that at least some of the association between sibling relationship quality and adolescent adjustment is bidirectional. The younger adolescent's Social Responsibility predicted later sibling Positivity, over and above previous levels of Positivity. The specific processes by which this occurs, however, await future data. It may be, for example, that more socially responsible adolescents are making more positive overtures to their siblings, who in turn respond favorably. Alternatively, having a more social responsible younger sibling may elicit more empathy and support from older siblings. Observational tests of this dynamic might shed light on these alternatives.

There was some evidence that sibling relationship quality had differential implications for adolescent adjustment depending on gender and family type/relatedness. The inverse relation between Positivity and Externalizing was stronger for boys than for girls. In addition, the inverse relation between sibling Negativity and adolescent Social Responsibility was not as strong among stepsiblings. Neither of these findings, however, was replicated in the longitudinal analyses, so they should be considered cautiously. This lack of replication may be the result of lower power in the longitudinal data, the attrition of subjects over the course of the study, or the length of time between assessments.

The prospective relation between sibling relationship quality and later adjustment implies that there are beneficial effects for both older and younger adolescents of having a positive sibling relationship, but the particular mechanism remains unknown. Adolescents may, for example, feel more valued and perceive greater support as a function of having a positive sibling relationship, which may promote more socially responsible behavior. Alternatively, adolescents may directly socialize their siblings by providing guidance or information, setting and enforcing standards for behavior, or serving as role models. There is evidence for this latter process in other research, but the data suggest that older adolescents are more likely than younger adolescents to be acting as socialization agents. For example, older brothers influence their younger brothers' drug behavior and delinquency (Brook, Whiteman, Gordon, & Brook, 1989; Duncan, Duncan, & Hops, 1996; Rowe & Gulley, 1992) and older siblings serve as a reference group for shaping adolescents' attitudes about sexuality (East, 1996; East, Felice, & Morgan, 1993; East & Shi, 1997; Rowe, Rodgers, Meseck-Bushey, & St. John, 1989). In

123

this study, there were prospective longitudinal relations between the earlier adjustment of older adolescents and the later adjustment of younger adolescents, but no prospective relations were found for the alternative path. Such a finding is consistent with the notion that older adolescents provide socialization for their younger siblings, and younger siblings are more likely to model and imitate the behavior of their older siblings. Greater imitation of the older sibling by the younger sibling would be in accord with the experimental findings by other investigators (Lamb, 1977; Samuels, 1977).

The mechanisms linking sibling relationship quality to later adjustment also can involve other relationships in the family. For example, characteristics of the parents and their relationship may influence the relationship between siblings, which in turn influences adaptation. In a sequential analyses of four-person family interactions in the NEAD data, we have found that marital distress was associated with differential involvement of the siblings in family conflict (Greene & Anderson, 1999). Thus, aspects of other family relationships may affect the extent of positivity and negativity in the sibling relationship.

Social learning theory (e.g., Bandura, 1969) suggests that the potency of a model should be greater when relationships are close. In support of this, Rowe and Gulley (1992) found that similarity between siblings on measures of delinquency and substance use is related to high sibling warmth. Similarly, East (1996) found that a warm and close relationship with an older child-bearing sister was associated with early sexual activity in younger sisters. There was no evidence in this study, however, that closeness in the sibling relationship affected the likelihood of adolescents showing behavior similar to their siblings. Moreover, there was no evidence in this study that negative aspects of the relationship—such as aggression and rivalry—promoted similarity in externalizing behavior, something also reported by East (1996). Not all studies find that closeness moderates the extent of similarity. Rowe et al. (1989) found no evidence of greater sibling similarity on sexuality as a function of time together, although this is likely a poor marker for sibling closeness. It may be that more subjective feelings of closeness are important for similarity between siblings.

Similarity between siblings may, of course, arise for reasons other than socialization experiences. For example, both Externalizing and Social Responsibility have been found to have substantial heritability coefficients (Reiss et al., in press). There is reason to believe, however, that the sibling relationship holds a unique place among family relationships. In other analyses of NEAD, it has been found that shared environment effects are prominent in sibling relationships, something not identified in other family relationships. Genetic analyses in the NEAD data show less genetic influence for sibling negativity than for negativity in other family relationships (Plomin, Reiss, Hetherington, & Howe, 1994; Reiss et al., in press), and the relation between sibling negativity and externalizing behavior is explained mostly through shared environmental factors, in contrast to findings with parental negativity (Pike, McGuire, Hetherington, Reiss, & Plomin, 1996; Reiss et al., in press). Moreover, the contribution of shared environment to sibling relationships becomes stronger over time (Reiss et al., in press). Thus, the sibling relationship is unique from parent-child and marital relationships in the importance of shared environment. Reiss et al. (in press) have speculated that sibling relationships are maintained via a tit-for-tat reciprocity, which creates an equal or shared environment for siblings. The very high correlations in the composite measures of Positivity and Negativity in part reflect this reciprocity. Furthermore, this reciprocity in sibling relationships is thought to be based on a fundamental need to keep things equal (Reiss et al., in press). It is this dynamic that is believed to override strong genetic influences in sibling relationships. When asymmetries occur in sibling relationships, however, the relationship may be more sensitive to genetic influence or nonshared environmental influence (Reiss et al., in press).

In this study, in the cross-sectional analyses, similarity between siblings was moderated by gender and family type/relatedness. Although these moderating effects did not hold in the longitudinal analyses (perhaps as much for methodological reasons as substantive), they shed some light on the mechanisms at work in sibling relationships. Among boy pairs, similarity was higher, and the association between sibling relationship quality and adjustment was greater. Based on the conclusions of Reiss et al. (in press), it can be speculated that shared environment factors, in particular, reciprocity in sibling relationships, is more critical for relationships between brothers. This greater reciprocity may be responsible for the higher similarity of brothers. In this study, however, reciprocity was not assessed directly, but rather inferred from the high correlations among scores for the older adolescent and the younger adolescent, and no differences in the pattern of correlations occurred across gender. A more direct assessment might reveal differences in reciprocity between girl and boy pairs. In addition, it must be kept in mind that this study included only same-sex sibling pairs. Opposite-sex sibling pairs may show less reciprocity and more asymmetry, and thus would be more susceptible to nonshared or genetic effects, as suggested by Reiss et al. (in press).

In contrast, stepsiblings were less similar to one another, and the association between sibling relationship quality and adjustment was weaker than in other groups. It may be that genetic or nonshared factors are more critical in the establishment of stepsibling relationships. Studies of stepsiblings in the early stages of remarriage as they become acquainted will be needed to reveal how or whether reciprocity becomes established.

125

In sum, in these long-term stepfamilies, stepsibling relationships stand out as a unique group. They exhibited less Negativity, specifically less Aggression and Rivalry, than other sibling relationships, but appeared equally as positive. In contrast, there were few differences in the relationships among half siblings, and full siblings in stepfamilies and nonstepfamilies. As was found with parent-child relationships, biological ownness thus plays a critical role in the quality of sibling relationships. Girl pairs exhibited more Empathy and Directiveness in their relationships than boy pairs, but other aspects of relationship quality were comparable. Over time, adolescent sibling relationships exhibited less Rivalry, Aggression, and Companionship, but levels of Empathy remained similar to before, and the decline in Negativity was sharper for boys. Finally, the quality of the sibling relationship was related to later adolescent adjustment, controlling for earlier levels of adjustment. Both older and younger adolescents who had a positive relationship with a sibling showed greater Social Responsibility at the second wave. In addition, there was evidence that younger siblings took on characteristics of their older siblings, but the reverse was not found. Future work can elucidate the more specific mechanisms by which positive sibling relationships have their effect on adolescent development.

VI. ADOLESCENT ADJUSTMENT IN NONSTEPFAMILIES AND STEPFAMILIES

Monica J. Skaggs and Kathleen M. Jodl

In this chapter, the adjustment of the two target adolescents in nonstep-families and in simple and complex stepfamilies is examined as a function of family type and adolescent gender. Stability and change in adjustment over the 3-year period between Wave 1 and Wave 2, as children move further into adolescence, also are studied. On the basis of past research findings (see Chapter I), the following hypotheses regarding adolescent adjustment were proposed.

First, we hypothesized that adolescents from nonstepfamilies would be more socially responsible, academically competent, and have fewer emotional and behavior problems than those from simple and complex stepfamilies (Amato, 1991; Brand, Clingempeel, & Bowen-Woodward, 1988; Bray, 1988, 1998; Bray & Berger, 1993; Hetherington, 1993, 1999; Hetherington & Clingempeel, 1992; Hetherington & Jodl, 1994; Lee, Burkham, Zimiles, & Ladewski, 1994; Zill, Morrison, & Coiro, 1993; Zill & Peterson, 1983). Since children who have been in divorced, one-parent households grow up faster and are more independent (Weiss, 1979) and since youths in stepfamilies, especially daughters, leave home earlier (Cherlin & Furstenberg, 1994; Hetherington, 1999), the adolescents in stepfamilies also were expected to be more autonomous. Furthermore, children from complex stepfamilies were expected to be less competent and show more behavior problems than those from simple stepfamilies because of the greater number of adaptive challenges experienced in complex stepfamilies (Hetherington & Jodl, 1994). No family type differences were predicted in sociability and self-worth, since these are rarely and inconsistently reported in the research literature.

Second, we expected that girls would display more cognitive agency, sociability, social responsibility, and depressive symptoms than boys (Cicchetti, Rogosch, & Toth, 1997; Cicchetti & Toth, 1998; Hetherington, 1991a, 1993). We hypothesized, however, that boys would have higher levels of self-worth and externalizing than girls (Kazdin, 1997; Loeber & Stouthamer-Loeber, 1998; Moffitt, 1993). Research has shown that girls place increasingly more emphasis on appearance as they move through adolescence (Eccles, Wigfield, Harold, & Blumenfeld, 1993; Stipek & Daniels, 1990). In addition, girls perceive a greater disparity between their physical attractiveness and the importance they place on appearance, thereby creating lower general self-esteem (Harter, 1990). Therefore, we not only expected that girls would have lower levels of self-worth than boys, but also girls' self-worth would diminish over time. Thus, we predicted that although there would be some main effects for both family type and gender on adolescents' adjustment, there would be no differential effect of living in a stepfamily on the adjustment of boys and girls (no family type by gender interaction). Although there is some evidence that preadolescent girls may be more adversely affected than preadolescent boys by their parents' remarriage (Hetherington, Cox, & Cox, 1985; Hetherington & Jodl, 1994), gender differences in the effects of being in a stepfamily on adjustment are rarely found in adolescence (Bray & Berger, 1993; Hetherington & Clingempeel, 1992; Hetherington & Jodl, 1994).

Finally, we hypothesized that children would become more sociable, socially responsible, and autonomous over time (Morrison & Masten, 1991; Steinberg & Silverberg, 1986). We expected that externalizing behavior, particularly for boys, would increase over adolescence (Loeber & Stouthamer-Loeber, 1998; Moffitt, 1993), and that depressive symptoms, in girls, would increase (Cicchetti, Rogosch, & Toth, 1997). Moreover, since adolescents begin to devalue academic achievement by the junior high school years (Crockett, Losoff, & Petersen, 1984), we predicted that cognitive competence would decline over time.

METHOD

In this chapter, five areas of positive adolescent adjustment and two areas of problematic adjustment are examined. The positive domains included autonomy, cognitive agency, sociability, social responsibility, and self-worth. The problem behaviors included externalizing behavior and depressive symptomatology. The full definitions and the instruments and procedures used to assess these dimensions are described in Chapter II. Multireporter, multimeasure composites of each domain of adolescent adjustment were used in the analyses included in this chapter.

Multivariate and subsequent univariate analyses of variance for gender and family type effects of multimethod, multi-informant composites of the seven areas of adolescent adjustment were used to examine the within-wave differences in adjustment at Wave 1 ($N = 516$). Repeated-measures MANOVAs were performed to examine across-wave differences in adjustment of adolescents present in both waves ($N = 259$). Composites used for Wave 1 and 2 for all analyses only included measures included in both waves of data collection. Analyses were conducted separately for the older and younger adolescent. Similar separate analyses were conducted for mother, father, adolescent, and observer reports. In considering individual reporter analyses, it should be noted that only mother and father reports were available for social responsibility; only adolescent reports were available for self-worth; and observer reports were present only for depressive symptoms and externalizing behavior.

Family type differences were examined using three categories. The ownness breakdown for complex stepfamilies used in the parent-child analyses was not applicable for most analyses in this chapter because of the use of multiple reporter composites. The ownness issue can only be examined when one reporter's view is taken into account. Therefore, in this chapter, analyses using multiple reporter composites included three family types: nonstepfamilies, simple stepfamilies, and complex stepfamilies. In analyses for mothers' and fathers' individual reports, however, family type was further broken down by ownness to indicate whether the parent was reporting on an adolescent to whom he/she was biologically related. We expected that parents would perceive their own child more positively and less negatively than their stepchild.

RESULTS

Cross-Sectional Analyses of Multimethod, Multirespondent Composites

Multivariate analyses of multimethod, multirespondent composite indices of adolescent adjustment for Wave 1 for the older and younger adolescent are presented in Table 33. Means, standard deviations, and significant group differences for these analyses are presented in Tables 34 and 35, for the older and younger adolescent, respectively.

Gender differences. MANOVAs of multirespondent, multimeasure composites of adjustment for the older adolescent indicated that girls were consistently more competent than boys, as shown in Table 34. Analyses for the larger sample in Wave 1 indicated that girls were more socially responsible, sociable, autonomous, and higher in cognitive agency than boys. Despite

129

TABLE 33

<small>F-Values and Significance Levels for Multivariate Analyses of Adolescent Adjustment: Wave 1 Cross-Sectional Analyses for the Older and Younger Adolescents</small>

| | Family Type | | Gender | |
	Older	Younger	Older	Younger
Multivariate	3.19***	2.41**	10.25***	8.20***
Multivariate df	(2,471)	(2,452)	(1,471)	(1,452)
Univariate				
Social Responsibility	10.63***	12.10***	4.90*	6.74*
Cognitive Agency	6.68**	4.05*	9.82**	11.26**
Sociability	ns	ns	5.43*	ns
Autonomy	ns	ns	27.27***	23.05***
Self-Worth	ns	ns	ns	ns
Externalizing	5.71**	3.23*	5.61*	6.84**
Depressive Symptoms	ns	ns	9.60**	ns

<small>*p < .05, **p < .01, ***p < .001; none of the gender by family type interactions were significant.</small>

their higher levels of competence than boys, girls also exhibited more depressive symptoms. As expected, boys demonstrated more externalizing behavior than did girls.

Parallel analyses were conducted for the younger adolescent from each family (see Table 35). The same pattern of results as found for the older adolescent also was found for the younger adolescent. No significant gender differences in sociability and depressive symptoms were noted, however, between younger girls and boys. Despite their age differences, the younger and older adolescents demonstrated very similar patterns of adjustment.

Family type differences. Examination of differences across nonstepfamilies and stepfamilies indicated that adolescents from nonstepfamilies exhibited more competent behaviors and less problem behaviors than adolescents living in complex stepfamilies. In the rare case when adolescents in simple stepfamilies differed from those in nonstepfamilies or complex stepfamilies, simple stepfamilies tended to be intermediate between the other two family types.

Family type effects for the older adolescent revealed that adolescents from nonstepfamilies were reported to be more socially responsible than those from simple and complex stepfamilies (see Table 34). In addition, adolescents from simple stepfamilies were more socially responsible than adolescents from complex stepfamilies. For younger adolescents, those from nonstepfamilies were more socially responsible than adolescents from complex stepfamilies (see Table 35). Both younger and older adolescents from nonstepfamilies were higher in cognitive agency and lower in externalizing than those from complex stepfamilies. These findings suggest that complex relations in stepfamilies present adaptive challenges that put adolescents at

TABLE 34

MEANS (STANDARD DEVIATIONS) FOR ADOLESCENT ADJUSTMENT AT WAVE 1 FOR THE OLDER ADOLESCENT

	Nonstep		Simple		Complex		Significant Main Effects and Interactions	Significant Contrasts
	Boys	Girls	Boys	Girls	Boys	Girls		
Social Responsibility	.37	.53	.13	.19	-.27	.18	family:	NS > SS > CS
	(.88)	(.81)	(.81)	(.94)	(.97)	(.83)	gender:	girls > boys
Cognitive Agency	.20	.40	-.06	.25	-.16	.10	family:	NS > CS
	(.70)	(.72)	(.75)	(.78)	(.81)	(.64)	gender:	girls > boys
Sociability	-.08	-.07	-.01	.29	-.14	.02	gender:	girls > boys
	(.66)	(.76)	(.77)	(.70)	(.62)	(.62)		
Autonomy	-.03	.30	-.01	.31	-.04	.35	gender:	girls > boys
	(.62)	(.55)	(.62)	(.70)	(.61)	(.56)		
Self-Worth	-.16	-.03	.22	-.14	-.01	-.12		
	(.91)	(.77)	(.72)	(.66)	(.77)	(.81)		
Externalizing	-.16	-.23	.07	-.06	.23	-.08	family:	CS > NS
	(.56)	(.47)	(.61)	(.64)	(.73)	(.61)	gender:	boys > girls
Depressive Symptoms	-.02	.06	-.15	.16	-.06	.16	gender:	girls > boys
	(.58)	(.53)	(.44)	(.57)	(.57)	(.67)		

NOTE. NS = nonstepfamily; SS = simple stepfamily; CS = complex stepfamily.

TABLE 35

MEANS (STANDARD DEVIATIONS) FOR ADOLESCENT ADJUSTMENT AT WAVE 1 FOR THE YOUNGER ADOLESCENT

	Nonstep		Simple		Complex		Significant Main Effects and Interactions	Significant Contrasts
	Boys	Girls	Boys	Girls	Boys	Girls		
Social Responsibility	.19	.55	−.13	−.01	−.28	−.01	family:	NS > CS
	(.78)	(.76)	(.83)	(.86)	(.85)	(.84)	gender:	girls > boys
Cognitive Agency	.09	.26	−.24	.13	−.21	.07	family:	NS > CS
	(.66)	(.75)	(.77)	(.56)	(.77)	(.68)	gender:	girls > boys
Sociability	−.03	.04	.13	.15	.01	.03		
	(.68)	(.64)	(.79)	(.56)	(.62)	(.63)		
Autonomy	−.27	.02	−.27	.11	−.32	.04	gender:	girls > boys
	(.66)	(.61)	(.65)	(.61)	(.61)	(.62)		
Self-Worth	.06	.10	.04	−.08	.12	−.03		
	(.74)	(.61)	(.66)	(.64)	(.73)	(.70)		
Externalizing	−.10	−.27	.04	−.04	.17	−.14	family:	CS > NS
	(.57)	(.42)	(.77)	(.68)	(.68)	(.56)	gender:	boys > girls
Depressive Symptoms	−.11	−.09	−.14	.05	.03	.08		
	(.54)	(.58)	(.54)	(.45)	(.62)	(.53)		

NOTE. NS = nonstepfamily; SS = simple stepfamily; CS = complex stepfamily.

risk for problems in adjustment. After a period of disruption and destabilization, family relations in stepfamilies become more harmonious and less conflictual over time (Bray & Berger, 1993; Hetherington & Jodl, 1994). Research has shown, however, that family functioning and relationships in stepfamilies continue to differ from those in nondivorced families. In addition, exploratory analyses revealed that adolescents from both types of stepfamilies report more negative life events than adolescents from non-stepfamilies, however, there was no difference in the number of negative life events experienced by adolescents from simple stepfamilies compared to those from complex stepfamilies. Consistent with past research (e.g., Bray & Berger, 1993), the present study demonstrates that children and adolescents in complex stepfamilies are more likely to have conflictual, distressed family relationships, as well as more problems in adolescent adjustment.

As predicted, no differences were found in sociability or self-worth, and the hypothesized difference in autonomy did not emerge. It is notable that the effects of being in a stepfamily are similar for boys and girls, as evidenced by the absence of significant family type by gender interactions. Studies have shown that girls and boys adjust to remarriage differently, with preadolescent girls having more trouble forming relationships with step-fathers and perceiving a disruption in the mother-daughter bond (Bray & Berger, 1990; Bray & Berger, 1993; Hetherington, Cox, & Cox, 1982). Given the length of the remarriages in this study, these initial differences in adjustment between boys and girls appear to have dissipated.

Cross-Sectional Analyses of Multimethod, Individual Respondent Composites

MANOVAs for individual reports of adolescent adjustment are presented in Table 36 for the older adolescent and Table 37 for the younger adolescent. Since no significant findings for observer reports were obtained for externalizing and depressive symptoms, these results are not tabled. It should be noted that each of the dimensions was rated by observers using a single scale and these behaviors, unless extreme, are difficult to identify in a 10 min observational session.

Gender differences. The most consistent findings for all reporters was that mothers, fathers, and adolescents each reported that for both the older (see Tables 38 and 39) and younger (see Tables 40 and 41) adolescent, girls were more autonomous than were boys. All family members, with the exception of fathers of older adolescents, reported that boys exhibited more externalizing behavior than did girls. Mothers and fathers agreed that younger and older girls were higher in cognitive agency than were boys. Discrepancies occurred in the rating of depressive symptoms, with adolescents and mothers agreeing that, as expected, with the older adolescents,

TABLE 36

F-Values and Significance Levels for Multivariate Analyses of Adolescents', Mothers' and Fathers' Reports of Adjustment at Wave 1 for the Older Adolescent

	Family Type			Gender		
	Adolescent	Mother	Father	Adolescent	Mother	Father
Multivariate	1.79*	4.36***	3.31***	9.04***	9.02***	4.88***
Multivariate df	(2,469)	(2,491)	(2,467)	(1,469)	(1,491)	(1,467)
Univariate						
Social Responsibility	N/A	15.23***	4.23**	N/A	6.18*	5.68*
Cognitive Agency	ns	8.31***	6.26***	ns	6.87**	9.89**
Sociability	ns	8.70***	ns	ns	ns	ns
Autonomy	ns	ns	ns	19.18***	11.09**	8.09**
Self-Worth	ns	N/A	N/A	ns	N/A	N/A
Externalizing	ns	7.59***	7.42***	9.09**	5.56*	8.86**
Depressive Symptoms	ns	2.69*	ns	11.75**	10.30**	ns

*$p < .05$, **$p < .01$, ***$p < .001$; none of the gender-by-family type interactions were significant.

TABLE 37

F-Values and Significance Levels for Multivariate Analyses of Adolescents', Mothers' and Fathers' Reports of Adjustment at Wave 1 for the Younger Adolescent

	Family Type			Gender		
	Adolescent	Mother	Father	Adolescent	Mother	Father
Multivariate	ns	3.10***	2.08**	7.28***	5.62***	6.65***
Multivariate df	(2,454)	(2,492)	(2,473)	(1,454)	(1,492)	(1,473)
Univariate						
Social Responsibility	N/A	9.77***	9.82***	N/A	7.64**	4.50*
Cognitive Agency	ns	ns	ns	ns	8.45**	15.07***
Sociability	ns	5.34***	ns	ns	ns	ns
Autonomy	ns	3.21*	ns	18.45***	11.12**	14.72***
Self-worth	ns	N/A	N/A	ns	N/A	N/A
Externalizing	ns	6.33***	4.87**	8.23**	7.91**	7.60**
Depressive Symptoms	ns	7.75***	2.80*	ns	ns	ns

*$p < .05$, **$p < .01$, ***$p < .001$; none of the gender-by-family type interactions were significant.

girls showed more depressive symptoms than did boys, whereas no reporters found gender differences in depressive symptoms for the younger adolescent. There is a considerable body of research indicating increasing gender differentiation in depressive symptoms over the course of adolescence (Gjerde, 1995; Lewinsohn et al., 1994). Mothers and fathers agreed that both older and younger girls were more socially responsible than boys (see Tables 39 and 41). It should be noted, however, that for the most part, even when family members' perceptions of significant gender differences in adjustment differed, their views were in the same direction.

TABLE 38

MEANS AND STANDARD DEVIATIONS FOR ADOLESCENT ADJUSTMENT FOR WAVE 1 FOR ADOLESCENT REPORT FOR THE OLDER ADOLESCENT

	Nonstep		Simple		Complex		Significant Main Effects and Interactions	Significant Contrasts
	Boys	Girls	Boys	Girls	Boys	Girls		
Cognitive Agency	.22	.21	-.31	.17	-.05	-.02		
	(.81)	(.82)	(.32)	(.92)	(.87)	(.84)		
Sociability	.18	.18	.20	.51	.13	.34		
	(.74)	(.93)	(.87)	(.83)	(.78)	(.82)		
Autonomy	-.09	.33	.03	.32	.02	.54	gender:	girls > boys
	(.74)	(.72)	(.95)	(.86)	(.89)	(.81)		
Self-Worth	-.16	-.03	.25	-.14	-.01	-.11		
	(.91)	(.77)	(.72)	(.66)	(.78)	(.81)		
Externalizing	.16	-.27	.00	-.11	.38	-.05	gender:	boys > girls
	(.94)	(.74)	(.83)	(.90)	(1.07)	(.96)		
Depressive Symptoms	.16	.26	-.03	.48	.17	.54	gender:	girls > boys
	(.87)	(.74)	(.70)	(.79)	(.85)	(.94)		

NOTE. NS = nonstepfamily; SS = simple stepfamily; CS = complex stepfamily.

TABLE 39

Means (Standard Deviations) for Adolescent Adjustment for Wave 1 for Mother and Father Reports for the Older Adolescent

	Nonstep		Simple		Complex/Own		Complex/Step		Significant Main Effects and Interactions	Significant Contrasts
	Boys	Girls	Boys	Girls	Boys	Girls	Boys	Girls		
Social Responsibility:										
Mother Report	.42 (1.04)	.64 (.92)	.37 (.95)	.34 (.92)	-.21 (1.02)	.27 (.91)	-.68 (1.32)	-.32 (1.05)	family: gender:	NS, SS, CO > CS; NS > CO girls > boys
Father Report	.34 (.92)	.37 (.84)	-.10 (.85)	-.05 (1.08)	-.16 (1.12)	.28 (.80)	-.32 (1.08)	.16 (1.00)	family: gender:	NS > CS girls > boys
Cognitive Agency:										
Mother Report	.26 (.85)	.52 (.86)	.13 (.97)	.36 (.85)	-.11 (.93)	.34 (.68)	-.28 (.84)	-.29 (.87)	family: gender:	NS, SS, CO > CS; NS > CO girls > boys
Father Report	.17 (.77)	.55 (.82)	-.26 (.97)	.09 (.92)	-.14 (.88)	-.12 (.66)	-.28 (.98)	.13 (.74)	family: gender:	NS > CO, CS girls > boys
Sociability:										
Mother Report	.05 (.83)	-.21 (.96)	-.03 (.90)	.23 (.84)	-.11 (.75)	.03 (.77)	-.67 (.69)	-.41 (.56)	family:	NS, SS, CO > CS
Father Report	-.25 (.79)	-.21 (.84)	-.40 (.80)	.01 (.69)	-.29 (.70)	-.29 (.75)	-.29 (.84)	-.24 (.85)		
Autonomy:										
Mother Report	.23 (.84)	.34 (.79)	.13 (.81)	.44 (.80)	.09 (.72)	.43 (.69)	-.06 (.63)	.21 (.76)	gender:	girls > boys
Father Report	-.11 (.82)	.14 (.75)	-.19 (.83)	.14 (.85)	.10 (.97)	.26 (.69)	-.20 (.79)	.05 (.81)	gender:	girls > boys

Externalizing:										
Mother Report	−.36 (.94)	−.43 (.80)	−.20 (.85)	−.29 (.82)	.25 (1.11)	−.17 (.91)	.44 (1.12)	.07 (.94)	family:	CO, CS > NS; CS > SS
Father Report	−.41 (.81)	−.49 (.57)	.34 (1.01)	.03 (1.10)	.04 (1.11)	−.30 (.82)	.30 (1.10)	−.20 (.86)	gender: family:	boys > girls CS, SS > NS
Depressive Symptoms:										
Mother Report	−.15 (.72)	.04 (.84)	−.26 (.80)	.06 (.83)	−.10 (.85)	.04 (.86)	.02 (.82)	.53 (1.12)	family:	CS > SS, CO
Father Report	−.17 (.91)	−.10 (.83)	−.14 (.70)	.15 (1.07)	−.02 (.90)	−.04 (.91)	−.23 (.81)	−.21 (.84)	gender:	girls > boys

NOTE. NS = nonstepfamily; SS = simple stepfamily; CO = target child is biologically related to (owned by) the reporter in a complex stepfamily; CS = target child is not biologically related to (not owned by) the reporter in a complex stepfamily.

TABLE 40

Means (Standard Deviations) for Adolescent Adjustment for Wave 1 for Adolescent Report for the Younger Adolescent

	Nonstep		Simple		Complex		Significant Main Effects and Interactions	Significant Contrasts
	Boys	Girls	Boys	Girls	Boys	Girls		
Cognitive Agency	.26	.14	-.16	.17	-.06	.16		
	(.74)	(.88)	(.94)	(.66)	(.86)	(.77)		
Sociability	-.21	-.17	-.06	.00	.02	.00		
	(.81)	(.79)	(.95)	(.79)	(.81)	(.79)		
Autonomy	-.42	-.06	-.39	.10	-.35	.10	gender:	girls > boys
	(.90)	(.81)	(.94)	(.92)	(.91)	(.83)		
Self-Worth	.06	.12	.04	-.08	.11	-.03		
	(.75)	(.63)	(.66)	(.64)	(.73)	(.70)		
Externalizing	.22	-.24	-.01	-.13	.29	-.09	gender:	boys > girls
	(1.07)	(.86)	(1.13)	(.89)	(.99)	(.93)		
Depressive Symptoms	.17	.21	.00	.23	.21	.38		
	(.86)	(.80)	(.56)	(.84)	(.86)	(.80)		

NOTE. NS = nonstepfamily; SS = simple stepfamily; CS = complex stepfamily.

The pattern of gender differences in adjustment suggests a paradoxical conclusion. On average, girls are perceived as more competent, despite the fact that they also are perceived as experiencing more depressive symptoms than boys experience. These findings may best be understood from a developmental perspective. Research has documented modest correlations between observer and self-reported competence (Tanaka & Westerman, 1988). It has been suggested that self-perceived competence and external reports may tap unrelated processes. Self-perceptions of competence may reflect feelings of self-efficacy and beliefs about abilities, whereas external reports may be related to actual behavior. Therefore, parents are reporting on competent behaviors exhibited by girls in areas such as autonomy and social responsibility. As supported by the lack of gender differences in adolescents' reports of competence, girls do not share their parents' views of being more competent compared to boys. Girls, however, are in agreement with parents that they experience more depressive symptoms than boys, possibly reflecting girls' lower level of self-esteem typically documented in adolescence (Block & Rubins, 1993).

Family type differences. It is in the eyes of parents and not in observers' ratings or adolescents' self-reports that family type differences are seen. No family type differences were noted by observers or adolescents, however, as hypothesized, parents perceived their own, biologically related offspring as better adjusted than their stepchildren. Furthermore, there are indications that being in a complex stepfamily is associated with more problems in adolescent adjustment.

Mothers of older children (see Table 39) from nonstepfamilies, simple stepfamilies, and complex stepfamilies rate their own children as more socially responsible, sociable, and higher in cognitive agency than stepmothers rate stepchildren in complex stepfamilies. Mothers in nonstepfamilies also rate their children as higher in social responsibility and cognitive agency than mothers' own children are rated in complex stepfamilies, suggesting an effect of being in a complex stepfamily in addition to biological relatedness. Stepchildren in complex stepfamilies also are seen by mothers as more depressed than mothers' own children in complex or simple stepfamilies. The maternal reports on externalizing behavior of older children (see Table 39) diverge somewhat from the pattern of other adjustment variables. Mothers see both their own children and their stepchildren in complex stepfamilies as more externalizing than those in nonstepfamilies, and their stepchildren in complex stepfamilies are viewed as more externalizing than their own children in simple stepfamilies. This finding for externalizing again underscores special difficulties in adjustment to complex stepfamilies.

139

TABLE 41

MEANS (STANDARD DEVIATIONS) FOR ADOLESCENT ADJUSTMENT FOR WAVE 1 FOR MOTHER AND FATHER REPORTS FOR THE YOUNGER ADOLESCENT

	Nonstep		Simple		Complex/Own		Complex/Step		Significant Main Effects and Interactions	Significant Contrasts
	Boys	Girls	Boys	Girls	Boys	Girls	Boys	Girls		
Social Responsibility:										
Mother Report	.23 (.81)	.66 (.75)	.04 (.99)	.13 (1.00)	-.17 (.94)	-.04 (.94)	-.47 (.93)	-.06 (.96)	family: gender:	NS > CS, CO girls > boys
Father Report	.26 (.96)	.30 (.96)	-.32 (.87)	-.22 (.93)	-.13 (.88)	.16 (.92)	-.50 (.95)	-.17 (.98)	family: gender:	NS, CO > CS; NS > SS girls > boys
Cognitive Agency:										
Mother Report	-.01 (.86)	.24 (.89)	-.07 (.88)	.20 (.79)	-.21 (.95)	.08 (.80)	-.36 (.83)	-.12 (.94)	gender:	girls > boys
Father Report	-.12 (.77)	.22 (.80)	-.36 (.77)	.02 (.77)	-.31 (.88)	.01 (.90)	-.33 (.96)	-.11 (.75)	gender:	girls > boys
Sociability:										
Mother Report	.20 (.80)	.22 (.74)	.38 (.89)	.36 (.75)	.09 (.73)	.08 (.78)	.00 (.63)	-.23 (.78)	family:	SS > CS, CO
Father Report	-.10 (.91)	.10 (.78)	.05 (.76)	.09 (.70)	-.02 (.81)	.00 (.88)	-.11 (.83)	-.05 (.70)		
Autonomy:										
Mother Report	-.01 (.81)	.17 (.78)	-.05 (.77)	.25 (.76)	-.18 (.65)	.12 (.74)	-.35 (.69)	-.13 (.74)	family: gender:	SS > CS girls > boys
Father Report	-.32 (.78)	-.04 (.74)	-.38 (.77)	-.02 (.81)	-.39 (.86)	-.13 (.92)	-.37 (.79)	-.08 (.67)	gender:	girls > boys

Externalizing:										
Mother Report	-.31	-.62	-.12	-.13	.17	-.13	.33	-.17	family:	CO, CS > NS
	(.89)	(.57)	(1.09)	(1.06)	(.99)	(.96)	(1.02)	(.83)	gender:	boys > girls
Father Report	-.24	-.39	.26	.13	.05	-.31	.27	-.12	family:	CS > NS
	(.85)	(.79)	(1.24)	(1.16)	(1.00)	(.73)	(1.05)	(1.00)	gender:	boys > girls
Depressive Symptoms:										
Mother Report	-.20	-.37	-.25	-.09	-.02	.14	.45	.32	family:	CS > NS, SS, CO
	(.82)	(.72)	(.78)	(.86)	(.93)	(.99)	(1.09)	(1.05)		
Father Report	-.37	-.36	-.13	.08	-.14	-.32	-.15	-.10	family:	cannot detect
	(.64)	(.85)	(.87)	(.88)	(.89)	(.67)	(.86)	(.81)		

NOTE. NS = nonstepfamily; SS = simple stepfamily; CO = target child is biologically related to (owned by) the reporter in a complex stepfamily; CS = target child is not biologically related to (not owned by) the reporter in a complex stepfamily.

With older adolescents (see Table 39), stepfathers in complex step-families report their stepchildren to be less socially responsible, lower in cognitive agency, and higher in externalizing than is reported by fathers in nonstepfamilies. Fathers also view, however, their own children in complex stepfamilies and their stepchildren in simple stepfamilies to be higher in externalizing behavior than those in nonstepfamilies.

It is interesting that with the younger adolescent (see Table 41), the effects of complexity in the stepfamily become stronger, especially in maternal reports. Mothers report both their own and their stepchild in complex stepfamilies to be less socially responsible and more antisocial than in nonstepfamilies. Mothers viewed children in complex stepfamilies as more depressed than any other group of children.

With the younger adolescent (see Table 41), stepfathers in complex stepfamilies again report their stepchildren as more externalizing than those in nonstepfamilies. Overall, fathers viewed their own children as being more socially responsible than their stepchildren. A univariate effect was found for family type on fathers' reports of depressive symptoms, but differences could not be detected on subsequent tests. The pattern suggests, however, that children in nonstepfamilies are perceived by fathers to be less depressed than those in stepfamilies. In summary, parents tend to perceive their stepchildren and children in complex stepfamilies as having more problems in adjustment.

Stability in Adolescent Adjustment Over Time

Pearson correlation coefficients were computed to examine the stability of adolescent adjustment over time. Correlations for the entire sample (not shown in the tables) indicated correlations between adjustment at Wave 1 and Wave 2 for the older adolescent ranged from .52 to .72. These correlations indicate that measures of adolescent competence, depressive symptoms, and externalizing behavior are extremely stable over time. It should be noted that the size of the correlation necessary to attain significance in different groups varies because of group differences in sample size. Correlations performed on boys and girls in each family type were large and significant with three exceptions (see Table 42). Correlations for self-worth were not significant for girls in nonstepfamilies (.35) and boys in simple stepfamilies (.46). Although these correlations did not reach significance, they are not significantly smaller than correlations for the other groups. In addition, the correlation for depressive symptoms for girls in simple stepfamilies (.29) was not significant, and is significantly smaller than that for girls in nonstepfamilies.

Correlations for the younger adolescent, as shown in Table 43, also revealed considerable stability in adjustment over time, ranging from .37 to .69. With the exception of self-worth, correlations between adjustment at

TABLE 42

Across-Wave Correlations for Multimethod, Multirespondent Composite Indices of Adolescent Adjustment for the Older Adolescent

	Autonomy	Social Responsibility	Self-Worth	Cognitive Agency	Sociability	Externalizing	Depressive Symptoms
Nonstep boys	.62**	.69**	.70**	.73**	.49**	.57**	.65**
Nonstep girls	.79**	.57**	.35	.79**	.43*	.68**	.76**
Simple step boys	.81**	.59*	.46	.64**	.73**	.64**	.57*
Simple step girls	.76**	.88**	.51*	.85**	.80**	.61**	.29
Complex step boys	.69**	.69**	.53**	.72**	.56**	.65**	.54**
Complex step girls	.64**	.67**	.52**	.57**	.62**	.51**	.60**

*p <.05; **p < .01.

TABLE 43

Across-Wave Correlations for Multimethod, Multirespondent Composite Indices of Adolescent Adjustment for the Younger Adolescent

	Autonomy	Social Responsibility	Self-Worth	Cognitive Agency	Sociability	Externalizing	Depressive Symptoms
Nonstep boys	.75**	.57**	.42*	.72**	.61**	.15	.53**
Nonstep girls	.55**	.32	.27	.68**	.45*	.39*	.70**
Simple step boys	.79**	.73**	.34	.61**	.82**	.62**	.66**
Simple step girls	.70**	.66**	.20	.31	.67**	.72**	.51*
Complex step boys	.65**	.68**	.47**	.76**	.63**	.75**	.61**
Complex step girls	.52**	.63**	.33*	.66**	.71**	.35**	.69**

*p <.05; **p < .01.

Wave 1 and Wave 2 were quite large. The correlation for externalizing in boys from nonstepfamilies is significantly smaller than the correlation for boys from complex stepfamilies and boys and girls from simple stepfamilies. The low and nonsignificant correlation for externalizing behavior in younger boys in nonstepfamilies is puzzling, since stability of externalizing behavior has been found to be remarkably higher in other studies (Loeber & Stouthamer- Loeber, 1998). It may be that late-starting boys who have not previously exhibited externalizing behavior are beginning to act out at this time (Loeber & Stouthamer-Loeber, 1998). More nonsignificant correlations were found for the younger than the older adolescents, with no consistent pattern. It appears that, although there is notable stability in adjustment for both groups of adolescents, younger adolescents experience more changes in adjustment than do older adolescents.

Analyses assessing changes in multimethod, multirespondent reports of adolescent adjustment over time. Repeated-measures MANOVAs were performed on the multimethod, multirespondent composite indices of adjustment as well as individual respondent composites of adjustment with the reduced sample size of 259 who were available and where both siblings remained in the home at Wave 2. Since family type and gender effects were consistent with those in the within-Wave 1 analyses, only wave and wave interactions will be discussed

As found in past research, adolescent adjustment changed as children grew older. Older, $F(1, 191) = 9.35$, $p < .01$, and younger, $F(1, 177) = 4.08$, $p < .05$, adolescents decreased in cognitive agency across waves. Contrary to the expectation that younger adolescents, but not older adolescents, would show marked declines in self-worth, however, this occurred for siblings in both age groups: older, $F(1, 191) = 9.89$, $p < .01$; younger, $F(1, 177) = 11.50$, $p < .01$. As expected, both older and younger adolescents increased in sociability: older, $F(1, 191) = 126.75$, $p < .001$; younger, $F(1, 177) = 67.24$, $p < .001$, and autonomy: older, $F(1, 191) = 131.57$, $p < .001$; younger, $F(1, 177) = 104.81$, $p < .001$, over time. Previous research (Skaggs, 1996) has shown that those in later stages of adolescence are more sociable and autonomous than those in earlier adolescence, thus increases in these areas over time appear to be attributable to age.

Two gender by wave interactions were found, Self-worth: younger, $F(1, 177) = 8.32$, $p < .01$; Depressive symptoms: younger, $F(1, 177) = 6.44$, $p < .05$. Consistent with past research (Block & Rubins, 1993), younger girls decreased in self-worth over time, whereas boys' self-worth remained relatively stable. In addition, boys demonstrated a significant decrease in depressive symptoms over time, whereas girls remained steady. Thus, at Wave 2, but not at Wave 1, significant gender differences in depressive symptoms were obtained. It is interesting that rather than gender differences in adolescence being attributable to the emergence and acceleration of depressive symptoms in girls, as was predicted, it was attributable to diminished depressive symptoms in boys.

Examining changes in individual respondents' assessments of adolescent adjustment over time. Although repeated-measures MANOVAs also were run for individual reporters, they will not be reported in detail here since family type and gender effects tended to be parallel to those found in the cross-sectional analysis of Wave 1.[4] Significant multivariate effects for wave were obtained for all reporters on both younger and older siblings and are similar to those found with the repeated-measures analyses of composites. There was considerable consensus that both older and younger adolescents increased in autonomy and sociability over time. Adolescents and fathers also concurred that older adolescents decreased in cognitive agency, and fathers reported that this decline also occurred for younger adolescents. Both older and younger adolescents reported declining self-worth, although this effect was significant in older adolescents only for boys. Although fathers noted decreases in depressive symptoms over time for both older and younger adolescents, observers reported increases for older adolescents and mothers reported increases for younger adolescents.

DISCUSSION

In this chapter, the adjustment of a younger and older adolescent in a male or female sibling pair living in a nonstepfamily, simple stepfamily or complex stepfamily was examined. Adolescents in stepfamilies demonstrated more difficulties in adjustment than did those in nonstepfamilies; however, these differences were largely confined to those involving complex stepfamilies. Differences between adolescents in nonstepfamilies and simple stepfamilies were rarely found in our composite measures and when they occurred the scores of children in simple stepfamilies tended to be intermediate between those in nonstepfamilies and complex stepfamilies. Our findings suggest that marital transitions, such as divorce and remarriage, pose adaptive challenges to children in both simple and complex stepfamilies. Difficulty coping with these challenges may be manifested in decreases in adaptive, competent behaviors and increases in maladaptive behaviors.

[4] Repeated-measures MANOVA results for individual reporters are available from the first author.

In complex stepfamilies, the challenge of dealing with the diverse bio-logical relationships between parents and children, shared and nonshared family histories, and varied alliances in complex stepfamilies may contribute to more problems in adolescent development. As discussed in Chapters III and IV, family relationships (i.e., parent-child, marital) in stepfamilies differ from those in nonstepfamilies. The effects of the differences in parent-child relationships with greater involvement and affection with their own children than with stepchildren so often reported in the literature (see Chapter IV, this volume; Bray & Berger, 1993; Henderson et al., 1996; Hetherington, 1993; Hetherington & Jodl, 1994) may be exacerbated in complex stepfamilies. Despite similarities in family relationships between simple stepfamilies and complex stepfamilies (i.e., less warmth, less mutual commit-ment), our findings demonstrate that adolescents in simple stepfamilies are, for the most part, as well adjusted as their peers in nonstepfamilies. These findings suggest complex linkages between family relationships and adoles-cent adjustment. Chapter VII will explore the linkages between family rela-tionships and adolescent adjustment and how these linkages vary depending on the complexity of the family structure and the biological relatedness of parents and children (i.e., ownness).

Some discrepancies in reports of informants occurred. Observers and adolescents seldom reported family type differences whereas mothers and fathers reported notable differences in the adjustment of children in stepfamilies and in nonstepfamilies. There was a marked proclivity for parents to view their stepchildren as more deviant than for parents to view their own children in either nonstepfamilies or stepfamilies. This "ownness" factor, how-ever, was sometimes overridden in complex stepfamilies where mothers per-ceived their own children as less responsible and lower in cognitive agency than adolescents were perceived to be by mothers in nonstepfamilies. In addi-tion, mothers in complex stepfamilies reported no difference between their own child and stepchild in externalizing behavior, but both were higher than those in nonstepfamilies.

Although the effect of complexity in stepfamilies was less marked for fathers than mothers, fathers did report differences in adjustment for their own children compared to their stepchildren. The areas in which differences between adolescents in stepfamilies and nonstepfamilies are most frequently reported (i.e., externalizing, social responsibility, cognitive agency, and, to a lesser extent, depressive symptoms) in other investigations (Amato & Keith, 1991a; Bray, 1988; Bray & Berger, 1993; Hetherington, 1993; Hetherington & Clingempeel, 1992; Hetherington & Jodl, 1994; Lee et al., 1994) were the ones in which family type differences emerged even in these long established re-married families.

Since the most notable differences in adjustment were found in parents' reports of their stepchildren being more poorly adjusted than their biologically related children, it would be easy to say that this is the eye of the beholder effect and that no real differences exist. Parents, however, may be reporting accurately their children's behavior in interactions with them. As was noted in the parent-child chapter, children are more negative, confrontational, noncompliant and conflictual and less affectionate and warm with their stepparents than with biological parents. Other studies have also reported greater resistant, noncooperative, contemptuous defiant behaviors and less cooperative, responsible, warm behavior in stepchildren (Hetherington & Jodl, 1994). Stepparents might appropriately label these behaviors as externalizing and lacking in social responsibility.

The greater adverse effects of being in a stepfamily on girls than on boys found in studies of younger children were not obtained in this study. As previously mentioned, this may be due to the length of remarriages in this study. Past studies have documented girls' difficulty forming relationships with stepfathers. It may take as long as 5 years for girls to establish a bond with a stepfather and accept his parental discipline (Bray & Berger, 1990). Remarried couples in our sample have been married an average of 9 years and may have surpassed this period of adjustment. In fact, investigations of the association between marital duration and adolescent adjustment in the present sample have not yielded significant results. Girls in stepfamilies may still have adjustment problems, but these problems do not appear to be any different from boys in stepfamilies.

Gender differences found in our study are consistent with past developmental research documenting the different ways in which boys and girls navigate through adolescence (Block & Rubins, 1993; Steinberg & Silverberg, 1986). As expected, girls were generally found more competent than boys. Girls were found to be more socially responsible, more autonomous, and higher in cognitive agency than boys. Steinberg and Silverberg (1986) found that girls become more peer-oriented, less dependent on their parents, and more self-reliant at an earlier age than do boys. They posit that researchers need to reconsider past findings that individuation and autonomy are mainly issues for identity development in boys. Findings from their study, as well as the present study, support the importance of increasing autonomy and self-reliance in adolescence in girls. Interestingly, only mothers and fathers reported significant gender differences in cognitive agency. It has been found in other studies that external reporters, such as teachers, fathers, and mothers, rate girls as more cognitively competent than boys, but that this difference is not found in self-reports (Granleese, Turner, & Trew, 1989; Hetherington & Clingempeel, 1992).

Although girls were found to be more competent than boys, they appear to be competent at a cost. A cluster analysis of patterns of adjustment in our sample of adolescents yielded a competence-at-a-cost cluster characterized by low externalizing and high social responsibility and cognitive agency, but also elevated depressive symptoms and low self-esteem.[5] This was more common in girls than in boys. It has been shown that, throughout adolescence, boys have higher self-esteem than girls, and that this discrepancy increases over time (Block & Rubins, 1993). This was supported in the present study. Adolescent girls reported lower self-worth than did boys, and boys increased in their self-worth over time, whereas girls remained at a steady, low level. In accord with past research (Cicchetti & Toth, 1998; Hetherington & Clingempeel, 1992), gender differences in depressive symptoms also were found. Girls exhibited more depressive symptoms than boys at both waves. Boys, however, decreased in their level of depressive symptoms over time, a decrease possibly related to their increasing self-worth. As girls progress through adolescence, they experience increasingly more challenges to their identity. The increased importance of physical attractiveness, the onset of puberty, and changes in relationships with parents pose challenges to girls' self-esteem and may cause disruptions in identity, school competence, and family and peer relationships.

As hypothesized and supported by past research, boys in this study exhibited more externalizing behavior than girls (Hetherington & Clingempeel, 1992; Loeber & Stouthamer-Loeber, 1998; Moffitt, 1993). Although past research has found increases in externalizing over time (Loeber & Stouthamer-Loeber, 1998; Moffitt, 1993), this was not consistently found in the present study. Our findings are consistent with the hypothesis that girls express distress through internalizing symptoms and boys are more prone to externalizing symptoms (e.g., Gjerde, Block, & Block, 1988).

The consistency of family type differences in mean level analyses of individual dimensions of adjustment suggests that adolescent adjustment does vary across nonstepfamilies and stepfamilies with complex stepfamilies especially likely to place children at risk for problems in adjustment. This chapter highlights that adolescents are affected by a number of contexts. Adolescents in simple and complex stepfamilies are faced with adaptive challenges of marital transitions (e.g., divorce and remarriage) and family transitions (e.g., birth of children to marriage, children moving in and out of the family home). Increases in depressive symptoms and externalizing behavior and difficulties engaging in competent behaviors may be the result for adolescents who are unable to cope with these challenges. It is important to remember, however, that adolescents also are affected by the social, emotional, and cognitive changes associated with

[5] A series of cluster analyses was conducted separately for boys and girls. Examination of family type differences across clusters yielded few significant differences (most likely due to small cell sizes). As a result, we chose not to report the findings in this chapter. Further information regarding these analyses can be obtained from the first author.

puberty, the challenge of transitioning into work, and forming close relationships. It is within the context of normative developmental challenges that one can appreciate the added stresses and challenges of divorce and remarriage faced by adolescents.

VII. RELATIONS AMONG RELATIONSHIPS: A FAMILY SYSTEMS PERSPECTIVE

Kathleen M. Jodl, Margaret Bridges, Jungmeen E. Kim,
Anne S. Mitchell, and Raymond W. Chan

The major objective of this chapter was to explore stress and coping from a family systems perspective. According to this viewpoint, the development of psychopathology at the individual level can only be fully understood by considering the larger network of interdependent relationships within the family (Minuchin, 1985). In this chapter, we examined linkages among various aspects of the marital relationship, parenting quality, the sibling relationship, and adolescent adjustment concurrently and over time using structural equation modeling.

A general theoretical model was developed based on past research findings (see Chapter I). This model explored four dimensions of adolescent competence and problematic adjustment in relation to the marital, parent-child, and sibling subsystems (see Figure 6). More specifically, marital distress, parental depressive symptoms, authoritative parenting, parent-child negativity/conflict, and sibling negativity and positivity were examined as predictors of adolescents' social responsibility and cognitive agency as well as their depressive symptoms and externalizing behaviors. Given the complexity of this omnibus model and a limited sample size, we were unable to include all variables in one model. Therefore, analyses were conducted on subportions of the larger conceptual model: (*a*) the marital subsystem in relation to the parent-child subsystem, and (*b*) the parent-child and sibling subsystems in relation to adolescent adjustment. Additionally, multiple group models were employed to investigate adolescent gender and family type differences in the criterion models by using a comparative model

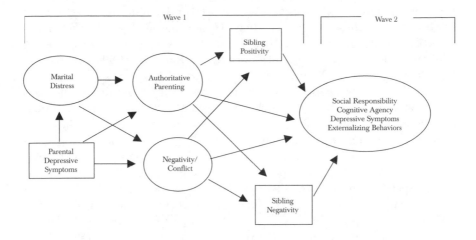

FIGURE 6. — A theoretical model for predicting adolescent adjustment.

testing approach. A final set of analyses explored the impact of differential parenting within the family on absolute levels of adolescent competence and psychopathology. The following hypotheses were derived from the theoretical perspectives and empirical findings reviewed in Chapter I.

The first set of hypotheses related to the role of parental depressive symptoms and marital distress as potential stressors affecting the quality of parenting at Wave 1. First, marital distress was hypothesized to be associated with disrupted authoritative parenting, and increased negativity and conflict in the parent-child relationship (see Davies & Cummings, 1994, for review; Forgatch, Patterson, & Skinner, 1988; Hetherington, 1989, 1999). Parental depressive symptomatology, in turn, was expected to predict marital distress, as well as disruptions in authoritative parenting and elevated levels of negativity in parent-child relationships (e.g., Radke-Yarrow, Richters, & Wilson, 1988; Simons, Lorenz, Wu, & Conger, 1993).

A second set of hypotheses explored linkages among the quality of parenting, sibling relationships, and adolescent adjustment concurrently and over time. First, authoritative parenting and parent-child negativity/ conflict were expected to have both direct effects and indirect effects mediated by the quality of the sibling relationship on adolescent adjustment. Authoritative parenting was expected to promote positive sibling relationships and positive adolescent adjustment, and to protect against the development of deviant developmental outcomes (e.g., Baumrind, 1991; Steinberg, Mounts, Lamborn, & Dornbusch, 1991). Hostile and coercive parent-child

151

relationships were predicted to increase negative sibling interactions and the development of psychopathology, and to undermine the development of competent, prosocial behaviors (e.g., Hetherington, 1988; Hetherington & Clingempeel, 1992; Miller, Cowan, Cowan, Hetherington, & Clingempeel, 1993; Patterson, DeBaryshe, & Ramsey, 1989; Patterson & Stouthamer-Loeber, 1984).

Furthermore, we hypothesized that the relations among these constructs would vary as a function of family composition and gender of the adolescent. Specifically, family subsystems were expected to be less closely linked in stepfamilies than in nonstepfamilies (Bray & Berger, 1993), and stepparents were predicted to exert less influence on the adjustment of stepchildren than their own children (Hetherington & Clingempeel, 1992). Marital distress, especially in fathers, was hypothesized to be more closely related to negativity/conflict with girls than with boys (Kerig, Cowan, & Cowan, 1993). And, finally, positive sibling relationships were expected to have a greater impact on the adjustment of girls than boys (Hetherington, 1989, 1993; Hetherington & Clingempeel, 1992).

A final set of within-family hypotheses was examined in this chapter using a difference score model (Rovine, 1994). Differential authoritative parenting and differential negativity/conflict were hypothesized to be associated with absolute levels of adolescent adjustment (e.g., Anderson, Hetherington, Reiss, & Plomin, 1994; Conger & Conger, 1994; Dunn & McGuire, 1994; Henderson, Hetherington, Mekos, & Reiss, 1996; Mekos, Hetherington, & Reiss, 1996). Specifically, we expected that the receipt of more authoritative parenting and less negative, coercive parenting relative to one's sibling would promote positive adjustment whereas the reverse would lead to increases in depressive symptoms and externalizing behaviors within Wave 1 and over time (Reiss et al., 1995).

METHOD

Analytic Strategy

Structural equation modeling (SEM; LISREL 8.12; Joreskog & Sorbom, 1993) was used to empirically validate the hypothesized relations detailed in our theoretical model (see Figure 6). Beyond simply building more reliable measures through latent factors (Bollen, 1990), this strategy differs from other statistical techniques (e.g., ANOVA) in that the focus is on *process* (i.e., structural relations) not mean differences. Unlike multiple regression, we can test complex models in which the interrelations among as well as between independent and dependent variables (i.e., variances, covariances, and regressions) are estimated simultaneously (Bank, Dishion, Skinner, &

Patterson, 1990). Moreover, SEM provides statistically legitimate ways for the systematic comparison of estimates across different samples using comprehensive models. To date, relatively few studies have investigated differences in associations among family process variables across diverse types of families or by gender. Of those studies that have examined such structural differences, most have analyzed the data from each sample independently, and then inferred group differences without directly testing for them. The multiple group modeling approach used in this chapter is clearly more rigorous.

Using criteria set forth by Loehlin (1992), the improvement in fit for a series of competing models was tested in order to establish criterion models for the full sample at Wave 1 ($N = 516$) and the adjusted sample ($n = 259$) over time. Next, a series of multiple group models were tested to examine differences in the parameter estimates across girls and boys, and across different family type/ownness groups in this sample. As noted in Chapter II, family type/ownness was defined using a four-group classification scheme that incorporated both family structure and biological relatedness (i.e., nonstep, simple step, complex step/own, and complex step/stepfamilies). All between-family analyses were conducted separately for younger and older siblings, and for mothers and fathers. A limited sample size did not permit the inclusion of both mothers and fathers in the same model. Finally, a series of within-family models were fit to the data using difference scores to test the hypotheses regarding differential treatment.

Several criteria were used to assess the overall fit including the associated chi-square and degrees of freedom (χ^2/df), the goodness-of-fit index (GFI), and the Root Mean Square Error of Approximation (RMSEA), an alternative fit index that is not affected by sample size. RMSEA can be considered an index of the percentage of "misfit" for the model. A RMSEA value less than .05 is considered indicative of a close model fit to the data, and a value less than .10 is considered adequate (Browne & Cudeck, 1993).

Both direct and indirect effects were examined in these models. A direct effect is delineated as a one-headed arrow connecting two variables. The effect of one variable on another is not transmitted through a third variable. For example, as shown in Figure 6, parental depressive symptoms have a direct effect on marital distress. In contrast, an indirect effect is observed when one variable affects another variable by way of a third variable. In Figure 6, marital distress is depicted as having an indirect effect on measures of adolescent adjustment via authoritative parenting and parent-child negativity/conflict.

Multiple group analyses were conducted using the criterion models obtained with the full sample at Wave 1. Parameters were estimated simultaneously using separate covariance matrices for each group. To preserve important information about group variability, covariance matrices rather

153

than correlation matrices were employed in these multiple group analyses (Raykov, Tomer, & Nesselroade, 1991). In a series of model comparisons, cross-group equality constraints were imposed to address the following general question: Are the groups equivalent with respect to the effects of family processes on adolescent adjustment? Thus, we were interested in examining group differences in the strength of the paths among the latent constructs.

Multiple group comparisons involved testing a series of theoretically related models in six steps. We used this six-step strategy in order to systematically test for differences among groups beginning with variance and covariances differences and ending with structural differences (i.e., regression weights, factor loadings). First, we fitted a model to the data in which all parameters were constrained to be equal across groups. This model represented the most restrictive model among those tested because it requires numeric invariance (versus pattern invariance) across groups (McArdle & Nesselroade, 1994). A second model was tested in which only the variances of the manifest and latent variables were allowed to vary across groups. If the change in chi-square ($\Delta\chi^2/\Delta df$) between these models was significant ($p < .05$), a third model was fit to the data in which both the variances and covariances among indicators were allowed to vary across groups. Otherwise, only the covariances were freed across groups in this third model. The fourth step involved freeing the regression weights along with any parameters tested previously (i.e., variances and covariances) and observed to be significantly different across groups. At the fifth step, the factor loadings were allowed to vary across groups along with all parameters (e.g., variances, covariances, regression weights) found to be significant in earlier steps. Finally, the least restrictive model tested was a model in which all equality constraints were relaxed across groups. In this case, only the pattern of structural relations among the variables remain the same rather than the actual numeric values (McArdle & Nesselroade, 1994).

Measures

Latent factors were constructed in order to create more reliable measures (Bollen, 1990). Indicators of the latent factor for *Marital Distress* included: (*a*) self-reports of the disagreement scale from the Locke-Wallace Marital Adjustment Test (MAT; Locke & Wallace, 1987); (*b*) an average score from mothers' and fathers' reports of symbolic aggression from the Conflict Tactics Scale (CTS; Straus, 1979); and (*c*) an observational measure of marital negativity that included anger, coercion, and transactional conflict (Hetherington, Hagan, & Eisenberg, 1992). A manifest variable for *Parental Depressive Symptoms* was created by computing an average score from two self-reports of the CES-D completed approximately one week apart at Wave 1.

An observational measure of authoritative parenting (Hetherington, Hagan, & Eisenberg, 1992) and the composites for monitoring/control and positivity/warmth described in Chapter II were used as indicators of the latent construct, *Authoritative Parenting*. In addition, three indicators of the latent factor, *Parent-Child Negativity/Conflict*, included: (a) parent reports of the Child Rearing Issues (CRI; Hetherington & Clingempeel, 1992) and Parent-Child Relationship (PCR; Hetherington & Clingempeel, 1992) questionnaires, and parent reports of the symbolic aggression subscale from the CTS; (b) youth reports of the CRI, PCR and the CTS symbolic aggression subscale; and (c) an observational rating of parent-child negativity, coercion, and transactional conflict (Hetherington, Hagan, & Eisenberg, 1992).

Finally, latent factors for adolescent *Depressive Symptoms*, *Externalizing Behaviors*, *Social Responsibility*, and *Cognitive Agency* were based on mother, father, adolescent, and observer reports (see Chapter II for complete description). Additionally, the quality of the sibling relationship was measured using two manifest composites for *Sibling Negativity* and *Sibling Positivity* (see Chapter II for more detail). Manifest composites rather than latent factors were used for sibling measures because the addition of two latent factors would have made the overall model unnecessarily complex given a limited sample size.

RESULTS

As noted previously, we divided the overall conceptual model into two parts—(a) the marital subsystem in relation to the parent-child subsystem, and (b) the parent-child and sibling subsystems in relation to adolescent adjustment—in order to test specific subsystems of interest and to ensure clarity in presentation. A first set of analyses examined associations among marital distress, parental depressive symptoms, and parenting quality at Wave 1 only. A second set of models explored linkages among authoritative parenting and parent-child negativity/conflict, the quality of the sibling relationship, and adolescent competence and psychopathology within Wave 1 and over time. For both sets of analyses, results will be presented separately for mothers and fathers. In addition, the best fitting models obtained with older adolescents were replicated using the younger sibling in the family as the target adolescent. Detailed findings will be presented for older adolescents only because comparable fit statistics were observed with younger adolescents.[6] For ease of interpretation, standardized parameter estimates will be presented rather than the raw coefficients. In addition,

---

[6] Detailed findings for younger siblings are available from the first author.

only significant parameters are included in the figures in order to preserve clarity in presentation. In some instances, these statistically significant parameter estimates are relatively small in magnitude. Of concern in these models is the possibility of multicollinearity and inflated R^2s stemming from the use of overlapping sources of information among latent factors. Despite our best efforts to minimize method variance by allowing same reporters to correlate within a model, this is an issue that should be kept in mind when interpreting the results.

Relations Among Marital Distress, Parental Depressive Symptoms, and Parenting Quality

Mothers and older siblings. Standardized parameter estimates for the most parsimonious model obtained at Wave 1 for older siblings and their mothers are shown in Figure 7. This criterion model accounted for 7% and 22% of the variance in authoritative parenting and mother-child negativity/conflict respectively. In this model, maternal depressive symptoms were associated positively with marital distress ($\beta = .48$, $t = 8.22$); however, mothers' self-reported depression was not associated directly with authoritative parenting or mother-child negativity/conflict. As expected, maternal marital distress was related to disruptions in authoritative parenting ($\beta = -.27$, $t = -3.24$), as well as to greater mother-child negativity/conflict ($\beta = .47$, $t = 5.67$). With respect to the measurement portion of this model, all factor

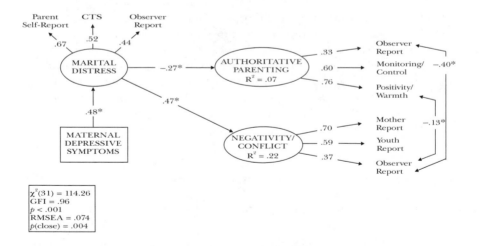

FIGURE 7.—Mothers' parenting of older siblings as a function of the marital relationship and maternal depressive symptoms within Wave 1 (*$p < .05$).

loadings were significant, ranging from .33 to .76. The chi-square value, $\chi^2(31) = 114.26$, and the goodness-of-fit indices for this model, GFI = .97, RMSEA = .074, p(close) = .004, suggest that the model provides an adequate fit to the data.

The modeling results depicted in Figure 7 were used as a baseline in multiple group analyses to test if the criterion model accurately described various subsamples simultaneously. Using this strategy, no gender differences were observed in multiple group analyses conducted with older adolescents and their mothers at Wave 1. The best fitting model was the model in which all parameters were constrained to be equal across girls and boys, $\chi^2(86) = 161.58$, GFI = .93, RMSEA = .042, p(close) = .900. These findings indicate that the structure of the relations between the marital and parenting subsystems is the same for girls and boys.

Multiple group analyses conducted by family type/ownness for older siblings and their mothers indicated that the best fitting model was one in which the variances and covariances among indicators were allowed to vary by family type/ownness, $\chi^2(151) = 264.91$, GFI = .87, RMSEA = .039, p(close) = .990. Despite differences in the variances and covariances across groups, it is important to note that the factor loadings and regression parameters in this model did not differ by family composition. Thus, the overall processes linking marital distress and maternal depressive symptoms to the parent-child subsystem are comparable across different family constellations.

Fathers and older siblings. A similar pattern of findings was observed for older adolescents and their fathers at Wave 1 with one notable exception (see Figure 8). As with mothers, marital distress among fathers was related significantly to disruptions in authoritative parenting ($\beta = -.30$, $t = -4.11$) and to greater father-child negativity/conflict ($\beta = .38$, $t = 4.99$). Moreover, paternal depressive symptoms were related significantly to higher levels of marital distress ($\beta = .37$, $t = 6.33$). Unlike the finding observed for mothers, however, fathers' self-reports of depressive symptoms were associated directly with greater father-child negativity/conflict ($\beta = .15$, $t = 2.71$). The fit indices for the model suggest a satisfactory fit to the data, $\chi^2(30) = 103.50$, GFI = .96, RMSEA = .070, p(close) = .012, and factor loadings ranged from .33 to .82. This criterion model explained 9% of the variance in authoritative parenting and 22% of the variance in father-child negativity/conflict at Wave 1.

Results from multiple group comparisons by gender indicated no significant differences across girls and boys in this sample—a finding consistent with the results observed for older adolescents and their mothers. Constraining all parameters to be equal across girls and boys provided the best fit to the data in this instance, $\chi^2(85) = 147.30$, GFI = .95, RMSEA = .039, p(close) = .970. For family type/ownness, in contrast, the best fitting model

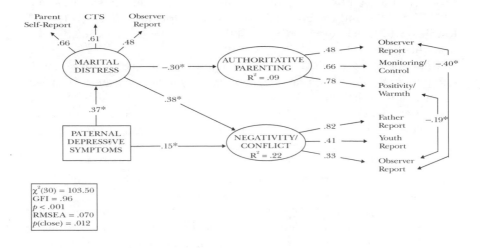

FIGURE 8.—Fathers' parenting of older siblings as a function of the marital relationship and paternal depressive symptoms within Wave 1 (*$p < .05$).

was one in which only the variance estimates were allowed to vary across groups, $\chi^2(156) = 252.08$, GFI = .95, RMSEA = .036, p(close) = 1.00. Allowing the regression paths and factor loadings to vary did not significantly improve the model fit. Therefore, no differences across family types were found in the processes underlying linkages among the manifest variables and latent factors in this model.

Summary. For both mothers and fathers, higher levels of marital distress were related to disruptions in authoritative parenting and to greater parent-child negativity/conflict. Although depressive symptomatology was associated with higher levels of marital distress for mothers and fathers, only depression in fathers was linked directly to greater negativity and conflict in their parent-adolescent relationships. The lack of group differences in these Wave 1 models suggests that the processes underlying interrelations among marital distress, parental depressive symptoms, and parenting operate similarly for girls and boys, and across nonstepfamilies and different types of stepfamilies.

Relations Among Parenting Quality, the Sibling Relationship, and Adolescent Adjustment

A second set of analyses was conducted to explore linkages among the quality of parenting, the sibling relationship, and measures of adolescent adjustment concurrently and over time. Models were fit separately for measures of positive adjustment (i.e., Social Responsibility and Cognitive Agency) and negative adjustment (i.e., Depressive Symptoms and Externalizing Behaviors). As before, results are presented for mothers and fathers separately, and the data from younger siblings were used to replicate findings obtained with older siblings in this sample. As in the previous models, detailed results are presented for older adolescents only because similar fits to the data were observed with younger siblings.[7]

Within-Wave Analyses

Mothers and older siblings. Figures 9 and 10 present the standardized parameter estimates for the best fitting models obtained for the full sample of older adolescents and their mothers at Wave 1. As shown, mother's authoritative parenting was associated with lower levels of depressive symptoms ($\beta = -.19$, $t = -3.28$) and externalizing behaviors ($\beta = -.31$, $t = -5.32$), as well as greater sibling positivity ($\beta = .45$, $t = 7.85$), but was unrelated to sibling negativity. Mother-child negativity/conflict was significantly related to both depressive symptoms and externalizing behaviors ($\beta = .57$, $t = 7.49$, and $\beta = .82$, $t = 9.05$, respectively). Moreover, mother-child negativity/conflict was associated with greater sibling negativity ($\beta = .49$, $t = 9.20$) and lower sibling positivity ($\beta = -.15$, $t = -3.12$). Interestingly, no direct effects of sibling

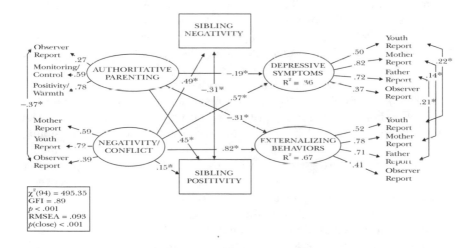

FIGURE 9.—Predicting negative adjustment in older siblings from mothers' parenting and the sibling relationship within Wave 1 (*$p < .05$).

[7] Contact first author for detailed findings for younger sibling.

159

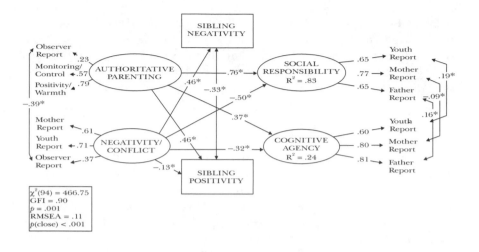

FIGURE 10.—Predicting positive adjustment in older siblings from mothers' parenting and the sibling relationship within Wave 1 (*p < .05).

negativity or positivity were observed for either depressive symptoms or externalizing behaviors among older adolescents in this sample. In terms of the measurement model, all factor loadings were significant, ranging from .27 to .82, and overall, this criterion model accounted for 36% of the variance in depressive symptoms and 67% of the variance in externalizing behaviors at Wave 1. An adequate fit to the data was indicated by the chi-square value, $\chi^2(94)$ = 495.35, and goodness-of-fit indices, GFI = .89, RMSEA = .093, p(close) < .001, for this model.

As depicted in Figure 10, maternal authoritative parenting was related positively to both latent indicators of competence (β = .76, t = 10.46, for social responsibility and β = .37, t = 6.61, for cognitive agency), and to sibling positivity (β = .46, t = 9.44) within Wave 1. Higher levels of mother-child negativity/conflict were associated with lower levels of social responsibility and cognitive agency (β = −.50, t = −7.84, and β = −.32, t = −5.54, respectively), and with more sibling negativity (β = .46, t = 7.76) and less sibling positivity (β = −.13, t = −2.59). As with the negative adjustment factors, sibling negativity and positivity were not related directly to social responsibility or cognitive agency. All factor loadings were significant ranging from .23 to .89, and the model fit was satisfactory, $\chi^2(67)$ = 466.75, GFI = .90, RMSEA = .11, p(close) < .001. This criterion model explained 83% and 24% of the variance in social responsibility and cognitive agency respectively. The high R^2 observed in this model may be inflated on account of multicollinearity among overlapping sources of information among latent factors.

Results from multiple group comparisons indicated significant differences across girls and boys when predicting depressive symptoms and externalizing behaviors within Wave 1. The best fitting model in this case was the model in which all parameter estimates were allowed to vary across groups, $\chi^2(188) = 617.81$, GFI = .89, RMSEA = .068, p(close) < .001. Significant differences in the measurement portion of the model suggest that the latent factors are not equivalent for girls and boys. Thus, the regression estimates across groups cannot be compared directly because the latent factors reflect different constructs for girls and boys in this sample. In contrast, only variance differences were found across girls and boys when predicting social responsibility and cognitive agency at Wave 1, $\chi^2(154) = 390.15$, GFI = .91, RMSEA = .055, p(close) = .091. Despite these variances differences, the processes underlying relations among mothers' parenting, the sibling relationship, and social and cognitive competence are comparable for girls and boys.

A series of multiple group models fit to the data for depressive symptoms and externalizing behaviors indicated that only the variances differed as a function of family type/ownness, $\chi^2(442) = 903.37$, GFI = .76, RMSEA = .046, p(close) = .940. Nonetheless, no differences were observed across family types in the effects of maternal authoritative parenting and mother-child negativity/conflict on depressive symptoms and externalizing behaviors. Significant family type differences were found, however, in the variances and regression weights linking the mother-child relationship to positive adolescent adjustment, $\chi^2(307) = 545.36$, GFI = .78, RMSEA = .040, p(close) = 1.00. Higher levels of maternal authoritative parenting were significantly associated with higher levels of social responsibility across all family types (βs ranged from .54 to .93), and with higher levels of cognitive agency in all families (βs ranged from .35 to .49) except for stepmothers and stepchildren in complex stepfamilies. Mother-child negativity/conflict was related negatively to social responsibility across all family types (βs ranged −.36 to −.64), and to cognitive agency in all families (βs ranged −.29 to −.93) except nonstepfamilies. Interestingly, mother-child negativity/conflict was significantly related to lower levels of sibling positivity with mothers and their biological children in complex stepfamilies only ($\beta = -.14$, $t = -2.08$).

Fathers and older siblings. Standardized parameter estimates for the criterion models obtained with older adolescents and their fathers at Wave 1 are depicted in Figures 11 and 12. With few exceptions, a similar pattern of findings was observed for fathers as was found for mothers in this sample. As shown in Figure 11, authoritative parenting on the part of fathers was associated with lower levels of adolescent depressive symptoms and externalizing behaviors ($\beta = -.12$, $t = -2.40$, and $\beta = -.27$, $t = -5.25$, respectively), and with greater sibling positivity ($\beta = .41$, $t = 7.83$). Higher levels of father-child negativity/conflict were related to higher levels of depressive

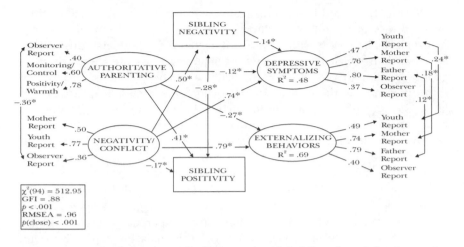

FIGURE 11.—Predicting negative adjustment in older siblings from fathers' parenting and the sibling relationship within Wave 1 (*p < .05).

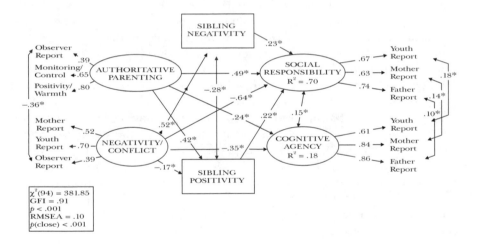

FIGURE 12.—Predicting positive adjustment in older siblings from fathers' parenting and the sibling relationship within Wave 1 (*p < .05).

symptoms (β = .74, t = 9.59) and externalizing behaviors (β = .79, t = 11.78), as well as to more sibling negativity (β = .50, t = 9.48) and to less sibling positivity (β = −.17, t = −3.53) at Wave 1. In contrast to results observed with mothers, a significant effect of sibling negativity was found for depressive symptoms (β = −.14, t = −2.62). Contrary to expectations, lower levels of sibling negativity were associated with higher levels of depressive symptoms. This finding differs from the original correlation matrix that indicated a *positive* relation between sibling negativity and depressive symptoms. Although an adequate fit to the data was indicated for this model, $\chi^2(93)$ = 512.95, GFI = .88, RMSEA = .096, p(close) < .001, the beta weights may not represent stable estimates, and therefore, these findings should be interpreted with caution. With factor loadings ranging from .36 to .80, this criterion model explained 48% of the variance in depressive symptoms and 69% of the variance in externalizing behaviors.

As with mothers, fathers' authoritative parenting and father-child negativity/conflict significantly predicted both social and cognitive competence at Wave 1 (see Figure 12). Fathers' authoritative parenting was positively related to greater social responsibility (β = .49, t = 7.01) and cognitive agency (β = .24, t = 4.29), as well as to greater sibling positivity (β = .42, t = 8.06). Likewise, higher levels of father-child negativity/conflict were associated with lower levels of social responsibility (β = −.64, t = −6.73) and cognitive agency (β = −.35, t = −5.30). Greater father-child negativity/conflict also was associated with greater sibling negativity (β = .52, t = 7.88) and less sibling positivity (β = −.17, t = −3.10) within wave. In contrast to results obtained with mothers, sibling positivity was associated with greater social responsibility (β = .22, t = 3.96). Surprisingly, higher levels of sibling negativity were related to higher levels of social responsibility (β = .23, t = 3.72). However, an examination of the original correlations indicated that sibling negativity was associated *negatively* with the indicators of social competence. As before, despite an adequate model fit, $\chi^2(64)$ = 381.85, GFI = .91, RMSEA = .10, p(close) < .001, the beta weights may not be stable estimates and should be interpreted cautiously. With factor loadings ranging from .36 to .87, the criterion model explained 70% and 18% of the variance in social responsibility and cognitive agency respectively.

As with the multiple group models obtained with mothers, few gender differences emerged for either negative or positive adjustment at Wave 1. No significant differences were observed in the regression paths linking the latent indicators of the father-child relationship and adolescent adjustment despite variance differences across girls and boys. In both instances, the model that provided the best fit to the data was one in which only the variances were allowed to vary across girls and boys, $\chi^2(208)$ = 664.45, GFI = .88, RMSEA = .067, p(close) < .001, for depressive symptoms and externalizing behaviors; $\chi^2(151)$ = 365.80, GFI = .90, RMSEA = .054, p(close) = .180, for social responsibility and cognitive agency. Thus, girls and boys did not differ with respect to the mechanisms underlying linkages among indicators of the parent-child relationship and adolescent adjustment.

Nonetheless, some differences were observed across family type/ownness for older siblings and their fathers at Wave 1. The best fitting model for predicting depressive symptoms and externalizing behaviors was the model in which all parameters were allowed to vary across groups, $\chi^2(386)$ = 824.94, GFI = .85, RMSEA = .050, p(close) = .430. In this case, the latent factors were not the same for different family types, and thus the regression estimates across groups cannot be compared directly. For social responsibility and cognitive agency, in contrast, only the covariances were found to differ by family type/ownness, $\chi^2(361)$ = 605.27, GFI = .91, RMSEA = .037, p(close) = 1.00. Despite these covariance differences, however, the processes underlying linkages among fathers' parenting, the sibling relationship, and social and cognitive competence are comparable across family constellations.

Summary. Overall, a similar pattern of relations was observed across mothers and fathers within Wave 1. Higher levels of mothers' and fathers' authoritative parenting were associated with lower levels of depressive symptoms and externalizing behaviors, and with higher levels of social responsibility and cognitive agency. Higher levels of parent-child negativity/conflict were related to higher levels of depressive symptoms and externalizing behaviors, and to lower levels of social and cognitive competence. In addition, authoritative parenting was linked to greater sibling positivity only, whereas parent-child negativity/conflict was associated with more sibling negativity as well as with less sibling positivity. Of note, sibling negativity and positivity were related to adolescent adjustment in the father models only. Sibling positivity was associated with greater social responsibility, and contrary to expectations, higher levels of sibling negativity were related to lower levels of depressive symptoms and to higher levels of social responsibility. These results for the quality of the sibling relationship should be interpreted with caution given the possibility of unstable parameter estimates and the fact that similar results were not obtained with mothers. Of note, the same measures were used in each model for mothers and fathers. One reason why a variable might seem important in one model and not in another is that SEM creates optimal weightings given all latent factors included in the model.

In general, few gender or family type differences were observed with respect to the mechanisms underlying concurrent relations among parenting, the sibling relationship, and adolescent adjustment. There was some suggestion that parenting may function somewhat differently in complex stepfamilies. For example, in complex stepfamilies, stepmothers' authoritative parenting did not influence levels of cognitive competence among their stepchildren. Such a finding is congruent with previous research that has shown stepparents exert less influence and control over their stepchildren's behavior than that found with biological parents and their children (Hetherington, 1993; Hetherington & Clingempeel, 1992; Hetherington & Jodl,

1994). Nonetheless, these results should be interpreted cautiously in light of small cell sizes for certain subsamples (e.g., complex stepfamilies).

Across-Wave Analyses

Although we recognize that influences among members of family dyads and among family subsystems are likely to be bidirectional, an assumption inherent to our theoretical model (see Figure 6) is that parenting influences changes in children's behavior over time rather than vice versa. Our latent variable models do not contain reciprocal influences or multiple feedback loops in part because it is extremely difficult to obtain proper solutions for models with such specifications. Moreover, a set of preliminary cross-lag analyses yielded little support for child-to-parent effects. These preliminary longitudinal analyses involved two sets of child-driven models that tested older siblings with their mothers and fathers separately. First, four cross-lag models were constructed using the latent factors for parenting (i.e., Authoritative Parenting, Negativity/Conflict) at Waves 1 and 2, and each latent adjustment factor (i.e., Depressive Symptoms, Externalizing Behaviors, Social Responsibility, Cognitive Agency). These models were run using the full sample of older adolescents. A second set of multiple group analyses examined family type/ownness differences using a simplified version of the larger cross-lag models described above. In this instance, cross-lag regression analyses were performed using manifest variables (as opposed to latent factors) for parenting and adolescent adjustment in order to maximize statistical power. Results from both sets of analyses provided little or no evidence that adolescents' behaviors influenced changes in their parents' behaviors over time. Although some significant parent-to-child effects were obtained in these analyses, only one significant child-to-parent effect was found for social responsibility. In this case, higher levels of social responsibility at Wave 1 predicted lower levels of mother-child negativity/conflict at Wave 2 in nonstep-families only ($\beta = -.40$, $t = -4.15$).[8] Therefore, in the longitudinal models presented here, parenting behaviors at Wave 1 were examined as predictors of adolescent adjustment at Wave 2. In these models, we controlled for the stabilities of the targeted adolescent behaviors over time by residualizing out the effects of these variables at Wave 1. The predictors in these models thus can be interpreted as predictors of change rather than final status. The stability coefficients for older siblings were .60 for depressive symptoms, .62 for externalizing behaviors, .72 for social responsibility, and .72 for cognitive agency.

[8] Detailed results from preliminary cross-lag analyses can be obtained from the first author.

Mothers and older siblings. Figures 13 and 14 display the standardized parameter estimates and fit statistics for the criterion models for predicting negative and positive adjustment over time. As shown in Figure 13, mothers' authoritative parenting only was associated with greater sibling positivity within Wave 1 (β = .45, *t* = 4.74). Although no direct effect of authoritative parenting was observed for either depressive symptoms or externalizing behaviors, authoritative parenting did appear to be related indirectly to externalizing behaviors via sibling positivity (β = −.22, *t* = −2.89). In contrast,

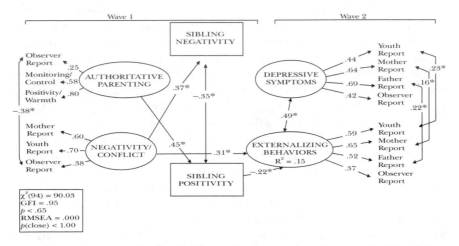

FIGURE 13.—Longitudinal model for predicting negative adjustment in older siblings from mothers' parenting and the sibling relationship (**p* < .05).

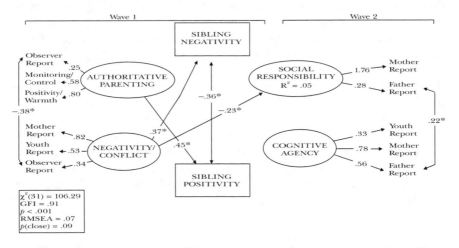

FIGURE 14.—Longitudinal model for predicting positive adjustment in older siblings from mothers' parenting and the sibling relationship (**p* < .05).

mother-child negativity/conflict was associated with increases in sibling nega-tivity (β = .37, t = 4.20) within Wave 1, and with increases in externalizing be-haviors (β = .31, t = 2.97) at Wave 2. Of interest is that authoritative parenting, mother-child negativity/conflict, and the quality of the sibling relationship did not predict depressive symptoms longitudinally. Although unable to predict depressive symptoms over time, this model explained 15% of the variance in externalizing behaviors at Wave 2. An excellent fit to the data was obtained for this model, $\chi^2(96)$ = 90.03, GFI = .95, RMSEA = .000, p(close) = 1.00.

As shown in Figure 14, only mother-child negativity/conflict at Wave 1 predicted social responsibility over time. Higher levels of mother-child negativity/conflict at Wave 1 were associated with lower levels of social re-sponsibility at Wave 2 (β = −.23, t = −3.84). No significant predictors, how-ever, were found for cognitive agency over time. Although this model provided a satisfactory fit to the data for older siblings and their mothers, $\chi^2(61)$ = 106.29, GFI = .91, RMSEA = .067, p(close) = .093, it accounted for only 5% of the variance in social responsibility at Wave 2.

In order to examine gender and family type/ownness differences, a series of multiple group models were fit to the longitudinal data for older siblings and their mothers. Few gender differences emerged for either negative or positive adjustment over time. For example, only significant variance and covariance differences were observed across girls and boys when predicting to depressive symptoms and externalizing behaviors at Wave 2, $\chi^2(203)$ = 203.28, GFI = .91, RMSEA = .000, p(close) = 1.00. Alternatively, for social responsibil-ity and cognitive agency, constraining all parameters to be equal across groups yielded an excellent fit to the data for older siblings and their moth-ers, $\chi^2(147)$ = 139.33, GFI = .90, RMSEA = .000, p(close) = 1.00. These find-ings thus indicate that the processes linking mothers' parenting and the sibling relationship to adolescent adjustment over time are similar for girls and boys in this sample.

Some differences were observed across family types when predicting to negative and positive adjustment at Wave 2. The model in which all parame-ters were constrained to be equal across groups provided the best fit to the data for depressive symptoms and externalizing behaviors at Wave 2, $\chi^2(498)$ = 537.96, GFI = .63, RMSEA = .019, p(close) = 1.00. In contrast, for predicting social responsibility and cognitive agency at Wave 2, significant group differ-ences were found in the regression weights and factor loadings, $\chi^2(287)$ = 357.40, GFI = .62, RMSEA = .036, p(close) = .980. The fact that the factor loadings varied across groups suggests that the measurement model is not equivalent for different family constellations. Therefore, the parameter estimates across groups cannot be compared directly because it is unclear whether the latent factors are measuring the same constructs for different family types.

Fathers and older siblings. Longitudinal results for the criterion models predicting negative and positive adjustment are shown in Figures 15 and 16. With few exceptions, the pattern for predicting depressive symptoms and externalizing behaviors at Wave 2 paralleled cross-wave findings observed with mothers and older siblings. First, no direct effect of fathers' authoritative parenting was observed for either depressive symptoms or externalizing behaviors over time (see Figure 15). Fathers' authoritative parenting was associated with greater sibling positivity ($\beta = .48$, $t = 4.78$) within wave; sibling positivity, in turn, was related to decreases in externalizing behaviors ($\beta = -.26$, $t = -3.30$) at Wave 2. Unlike the findings obtained with mothers in this sample, father-child negativity/conflict did not predict directly adolescents' externalizing behaviors over time. Father-child negativity/conflict, however, was linked indirectly to externalizing behaviors at Wave 2 via sibling positivity ($\beta = -.18$, $t = -2.06$). This model accounted for only 7% of the variance in externalizing behaviors over time despite a good fit to the data, $\chi^2(94) = 112.17$, GFI = .94, RMSEA = .028, p(close) = .970.

Contrary to results observed with mothers, father-child negativity/conflict at Wave 1 was not significantly related to social responsibility at Wave 2 (see Figure 16). In this model, neither fathers' authoritative parenting nor father-child negativity/conflict predicted social responsibility and cognitive

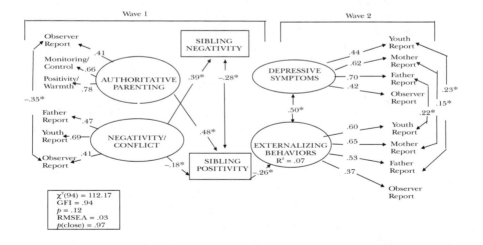

FIGURE 15.—Longitudinal model for predicting negative adjustment in older siblings from fathers' parenting and the sibling relationship (*$p < .05$).

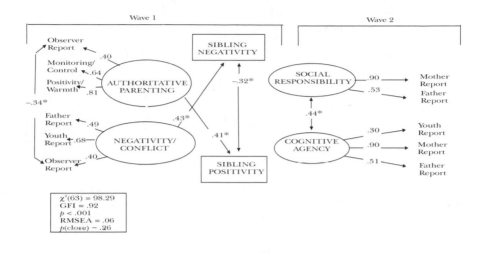

FIGURE 16.—Longitudinal model for predicting positive adjustment in older siblings from fathers' parenting and the sibling relationship (*p < .05).

agency over time. Although this model provided an adequate fit to the data, $\chi^2(63) = 98.29$, GFI = .92, RMSEA = .058, p(close) = .260, it was unable to account for any of the variance in social responsibility and cognitive agency at Wave 2.

Few differences by gender or family type/ownness were observed longitudinally for older siblings and their fathers. When examining gender differences, the model that best fit the data for depressive symptoms and externalizing behaviors at Wave 2 was one in which all parameters were constrained to be equal across groups, $\chi^2(228) = 278.54$, GFI = .87, RMSEA = .032, p(close) = .780. In comparison, only the variance estimates differed across girls and boys when predicting to social responsibility and cognitive agency at Wave 2, $\chi^2(130) = 167.59$, GFI = .85, RMSEA = .042, p(close) = .750. These results indicate that the mechanisms underlying associations between fathers' parenting and adolescents' long-term adjustment operate similarly for girls and boys—a finding consistent with the pattern observed with mothers in this sample.

Similarly, no significant differences by family type emerged over time. Constraining all parameters to be equal across groups provided the best fit to the data for predicting both negative and positive adjustment at Wave 2, $\chi^2(500) = 550.28$, GFI = .89, RMSEA = .021, p(close) = 1.00, for depressive symptoms and externalizing behaviors; $\chi^2(322) = 307.35$, GFI = .89, RMSEA

= .000, p(close) = 1.00, for social responsibility and cognitive agency. Thus, for older siblings and their fathers, similar processes appear to operate across different family types.

Summary. Although we found substantial associations between parenting and adolescent adjustment in the cross-sectional models, mothers' and fathers' authoritative parenting failed to predict either negative or positive adjustment over time. Only higher levels of mother-child negativity/conflict at Wave 1 were related directly to higher levels of externalizing behaviors and lower levels of social responsibility at Wave 2. No direct effects of father-child negativity/conflict were found for adolescents' long-term adjustment. Overall, few gender differences were observed longitudinally in model comparisons conducted with either mothers or fathers. Some differences did emerge by family type/ownness for older siblings and their mothers. For older adolescents and their fathers, however, the processes linking parenting, the sibling relationship and adolescent adjustment over time appear to be comparable across different family constellations.

Relations Between Differential Parenting and Absolute Levels of Adolescent Adjustment

A difference score model was used to test the hypothesis that differential parenting within families contributes to absolute levels of adolescent adjustment. In the tradition of others who have explored nonshared hypotheses (e.g., Daniels, Dunn, Furstenberg, & Plomin, 1985; Rovine, 1994; Tejerina-Allen, Wagner, & Cohen, 1994), difference scores were used as a measure of within-family environments. Differential authoritative parenting and differential parent-child negativity at Wave 1 were quantified by computing relative difference scores (i.e., older sibling – younger sibling). A positive sign indicates that the older child tends to score higher relative to his or her sibling, whereas a negative sign suggests that the younger sibling is scoring higher. This difference score method was chosen because it offers a straightforward and conceptually appealing approach to the measurement of differential experiences. Although often criticized as being inherently unreliable, difference scores are no less reliable than the original scores from which they are computed provided there is adequate variability and the correlation between constituent scores is low to moderate (Rovine, 1994). The data used in this study met these criteria, and thus pose no threat to reliability. Results will be presented for older adolescents only because a similar set of fit statistics was observed within wave and over time with younger siblings.[9]

---

[9] Detailed findings for younger siblings are available from the first author.

Within-Wave Nonshared Analyses

Mothers and older siblings. Figures 17 and 18 present the standardized parameter estimates for the nonshared models predicting absolute levels of older adolescents' negative and positive adjustment at Wave 1. First, mothers' differential authoritative parenting and mother-child differential negativity/conflict were related significantly to absolute levels of depressive symptoms and externalizing behaviors within wave (see Figure 17). Specifically, higher levels of maternal authoritative parenting directed toward the older sibling relative to the younger sibling were associated with lower levels of depressive symptoms ($\beta = -.23$, $t = -2.94$) and externalizing behaviors ($\beta = -.18$, $t = -2.40$) in older siblings. Greater maternal negativity and conflict directed toward the older sibling relative to the younger sibling were related to higher levels of depressive symptoms ($\beta = .37$, $t = 5.41$) and externalizing behaviors ($\beta = .39$, $t = 5.63$). That is, older siblings were less likely to be depressed and to act out when they were the recipients of more authoritative parenting and less maternal negativity relative to their younger sibling. This criterion model explained 19% and 18% of the variance in depressive symptoms and externalizing behaviors respectively. The chi-square value, $\chi^2(68) = 263.65$, and goodness-of fit statistics, GFI = .94, RMSEA = .070, p(close) < .001, suggest a satisfactory fit to the data.

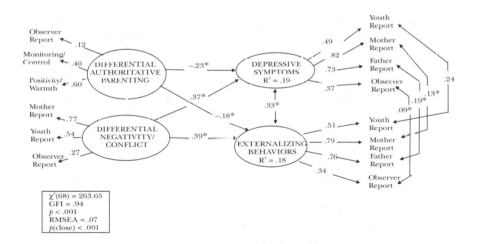

FIGURE 17.—Predicting negative adjustment in older siblings from mothers' differential parenting within Wave 1 (*p < .05).

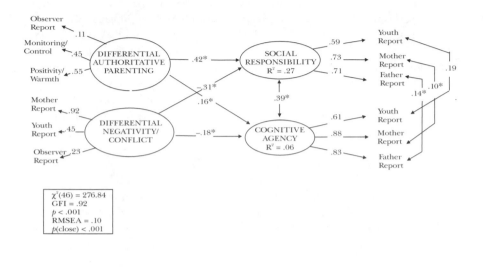

FIGURE 18.—Predicting positive adjustment in older siblings from mothers' differential parenting within Wave 1 (*p < .05).

As displayed in Figure 18, mothers' differential authoritative parenting as well as mother-child differential negativity/conflict significantly predicted absolute levels of social responsibility and cognitive agency in older siblings. Higher levels of maternal authoritative parenting directed toward the older adolescent relative to the younger sibling in the family were associated with greater social responsibility (β = .42, t = 4.95) and cognitive agency (β = .16, t = 2.10) in older siblings. Moreover, when older siblings were the recipients of greater maternal negativity and conflict, they exhibited lower levels of social responsibility (β = −.31, t = −4.67) and cognitive agency (β = −.18, t = −3.25). As indicated by the fit statistics, an adequate fit to the data was obtained with this criterion model, χ^2(46) = 276.84, GFI = .92, RMSEA = .100, p(close) < .001, which explained 27% and 6% of the variance in social responsibility and cognitive agency respectively.

Results from multiple group comparisons indicated few gender differences for mothers and older siblings in this sample. Despite significant variance differences across girls and boys, no differences were observed in the processes linking mothers' differential parenting to either negative or positive adjustment within Wave 1. For depressive symptoms and externalizing behaviors, the best fitting model was one in which only the variances were allowed to vary across girls and boys, χ^2(157) = 346.81, GFI = .91, RMSEA =

.049, p(close) = .630. Similarly, freeing the variances provided the best fit to the data for predicting absolute levels of social responsibility and cognitive agency, $\chi^2(110)$ = 351.09, GFI = .90, RMSEA = .065, p(close) < .001. These results suggest that the mechanisms underlying associations between maternal differential parenting and absolute levels of adolescent adjustment operate similarly for girls and boys.

In contrast, significant differences were observed by family type/ownness in the processes linking maternal differential parenting to both negative and positive adjustment within Wave 1. Allowing the variances and regression weights to vary across groups provided the best fit to the data for depressive symptoms and externalizing behaviors, $\chi^2(317)$ = 581.25, GFI = .80, RMSEA = .040, p(close) = .999. Mother-child differential negativity/conflict was associated positively with depressive symptoms and externalizing behaviors across all family types (βs ranged from .43 to .96 for depressive symptoms and βs ranged from .45 to .95 for externalizing behaviors) except stepmothers and their stepchildren in complex stepfamilies. When predicting absolute levels of positive adjustment, the model that afforded the best fit to the data was one in which the variances, covariances, and regression weights were allowed to vary across groups, $\chi^2(211)$ = 500.96, GFI = .77, RMSEA = .052, p(close) = .308. In this instance, mother-child differential negativity/conflict was significantly related to social responsibility and cognitive agency in simple stepfamilies (β = −.87, t = −3.36, and β = −.57, t = −2.67, respectively) and complex stepfamilies with mothers and their biological children only (β = −.36, t = 3.45, and β = −.21, t = −2.56, respectively). Thus, the processes underlying relations among mothers' differential parenting and absolute levels of adolescent adjustment appear to differ somewhat across family types.

Fathers and older siblings. With few exceptions, a similar pattern of findings was observed with fathers in this sample. Results from the nonshared analyses conducted using the full sample of fathers and older siblings at Wave 1 are depicted in Figures 19 and 20. As with mothers, fathers' differential authoritative parenting and father-child differential negativity/ conflict were related significantly to absolute levels of depressive symptoms and externalizing behaviors in older siblings. Lower levels of paternal authoritative parenting directed toward the older adolescent relative to the younger sibling were associated with higher levels of depressive symptoms (β = −.13, t = −2.19) and externalizing behaviors (β = −.16, t = −2.51) among older siblings. In addition, older siblings were more likely to exhibit depressive symptoms (β = .49, t = 5.26) and to act out (β = .52, t = 5.47) when they were the recipients of more paternal negativity and conflict than their younger sibling. An adequate fit to the data was observed, $\chi^2(68)$ = 269.42, GFI = .93, RMSEA = .080, p(close)

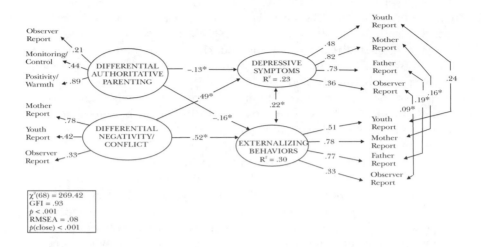

FIGURE 19.—Predicting negative adjustment in older siblings from fathers' differential parenting within Wave 1 (*$p < .05$).

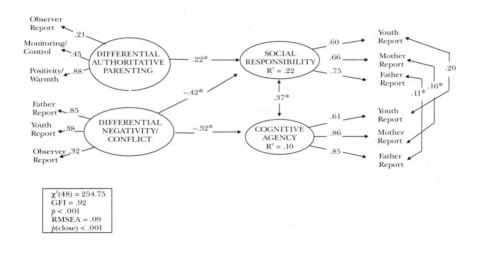

FIGURE 20.—Predicting positive adjustment in older siblings from fathers' differential parenting within Wave 1 (*$p < .05$).

< .001, and the model explained 23% of the variance in depressive symptoms and 30% of the variance in externalizing behaviors at Wave 1.

Contrary to results obtained with mothers, fathers' differential author-itative parenting did not significantly predict absolute levels of cognitive agency within Wave 1 (see Figure 20). Nonetheless, differential authorita-tive parenting on the part of fathers was related to social responsibility, and father-child differential negativity/conflict was associated with social re-sponsibility and cognitive agency within wave. Older siblings exhibited greater social responsibility when they received more paternal authorita-tive parenting than their younger brother or sister ($\beta = .22, t = 3.00$). Addi-tionally, when fathers directed more negativity toward the older adolescent versus their younger sibling, older adolescents demonstrated less social responsibility ($\beta = -.42, t = -4.36$) and less cognitive agency ($\beta = -.32, t = -4.02$) at Wave 1. This model provided a satisfactory fit to the data, $\chi^2(48) = 254.75$, GFI = .92, RMSEA = .09, p(close) < .001, and it accounted for 22% and 10% of the variance in social responsibility and cognitive agency respectively.

Multiple group comparisons indicated few gender differences for older siblings and their fathers at Wave 1—a pattern consistent with findings observed with mothers in this sample. Allowing the variances to be free across girls and boys afforded the best fit to the data for both negative and positive outcomes in older adolescents, $\chi^2(155) = 356.08$, GFI = .91, RMSEA = .050, p(close) = .466, for depressive symptoms and externalizing behaviors; $\chi^2(109) = 316.03$, GFI = .89, RMSEA = .061, p(close) = .012, for social responsibility and cognitive agency. Of note is the lack of significant group differences in the regression weights which indicates that the effects of fathers' differential parenting on absolute levels of negative and positive adjustment are similar for girls and boys.

In model comparisons conducted by family type/ownness, only the co-variances were found to differ across groups when predicting absolute levels of social responsibility and cognitive agency within Wave 1, $\chi^2(268) = 534.01$, GFI = .91, RMSEA = .044, p(close) = .967. In contrast, the model that yielded the best fit to the data for depressive symptoms and externalizing behaviors was one in which the covariances, regression weights, and factor loadings var-ied across groups, $\chi^2(325) = 594.87$, GFI = .91, RMSEA = .040, p(close) = .999. In this instance, the measurement portion of the model differed across fam-ily types indicating that the latent factors are not equivalent for different fam-ily constellations. Therefore, the regression estimates across groups cannot be compared directly. These results suggest that the processes linking fathers' differential parenting to adolescent depressive symptoms and externalizing behaviors differ by family composition.

Summary. At Wave 1, both mothers' and fathers' differential parenting were associated with absolute levels of adjustment among older adolescents in this sample. Older adolescents who experienced greater parent-child negativity relative to their sibling were more likely to exhibit depressive symptoms and act out, and to display less social responsibility and cognitive agency. Moreover, being the recipient of more authoritative parenting relative to one's sibling was linked to fewer depressive symptoms and externalizing behaviors, and to more social responsibility. Only mothers' differential authoritative parenting was related to cognitive agency in older adolescents.

Multiple group comparisons indicated that the processes linking parents' differential parenting to adolescent adjustment differed somewhat across various family constellations. For example, mother-child differential negativity/conflict was related to depressive symptoms and externalizing behaviors in all family types except complex stepfamilies with stepmothers and their stepchildren. Such a finding indicates an effect of biological relatedness rather than family type per se. In this instance, stepmothers' differential treatment appears to influence the behavior of biologically owned children, but not stepchildren's behavior. Although some gender differences were found with respect to the variances, the effects of differential parenting on adolescent adjustment within wave appear to be similar for girls and boys.

Unfortunately, both absolute levels of parenting and differential parenting could not be included in the same latent variable models because of sample size. A series of multiple regression analyses was performed, however, in which both absolute levels of parenting and differential parenting were entered into the equations. Results from these cross-sectional analyses indicated that differential parenting added little to the prediction of adolescent adjustment beyond that of absolute levels of parenting (ΔR^2 ranged from 0 to 3% at most).[10] This is reflected in the separate analyses presented in this *Monograph*, where differential parenting predicted a small part of the variance in adjustment relative to the substantial R^2s found in models involving absolute levels of authoritative or negative, conflicted parenting. In addition, no significant interactions between absolute levels of parenting and differential parenting were found in these analyses. Similar results were obtained in behavior genetic analyses conducted as part of the larger NEAD study, which included identical and fraternal twins as well as siblings in nonstepfamilies and stepfamilies. A covariance analysis (as opposed to difference scores) was used to estimate contributions of the nonshared environment, shared environment, and heritability to adolescent adjustment. Of the measures of adjustment examined in this chapter, a significant contribution of nonshared environment to adolescent adjustment was indicated for depressive symptoms at Wave 2 only (see Reiss, Neiderhiser, Hetherington, & Plomin, in press). This naturally was a disappointment in a study originally designed to explore contributions of the nonshared environment to adolescent development.

---

[10] Results from multiple regression analyses are available from the first author.

Across-Wave Nonshared Analyses

As before, we conducted a series of cross-lag analyses to explore the possibility that adolescent behaviors influence differences in parenting over time. In these preliminary longitudinal analyses, child influences were examined using models parallel to those previously tested using absolute levels of (as opposed to differences in) parenting. Results from these analyses indicated a stronger pattern for parent-to-child than child-to-parent effects. There was little evidence to suggest that adolescents' behaviors influenced changes in their parents' differential treatment over time. For social responsibility, a rather weak effect of adolescent behaviors was found among older adolescents and their mothers. Across all family types, older siblings who displayed greater social responsibility at Wave 1 experienced less maternal negativity at Wave 2 than their younger sibling ($\beta = -.12$, $t = -2.05$). A child-to-parent effect also was observed for externalizing behaviors among older adolescents growing up in nonstepfamilies only. In this instance, older adolescents who acted out more tended to be the recipients of greater maternal negativity over time relative to their younger sibling ($\beta = .38$, $t = 3.63$).[11] Therefore, in light of the (lack of) findings, we chose to examine models in which differences in parenting at Wave 1 predict absolute levels of adolescent adjustment at Wave 2. Adolescent adjustment at Wave 1 was controlled for in these longitudinal analyses, and thus we examined changes in adolescent adjustment over time.

Results from these longitudinal analyses indicated that neither mothers' nor fathers' differential authoritative parenting and differential negativity/conflict predicted absolute levels of adolescent adjustment over time. Across all models, we were unable to account for any of the variance in depressive symptoms and externalizing behaviors or social responsibility and cognitive agency at Wave 2. Multiple group comparisons revealed few gender or family type differences. Overall, the effects of mothers' and fathers' differential parenting on adolescents' long-term adjustment were comparable across girls and boys, and across different family types.[12]

An additional set of multiple regression analyses was performed in which both absolute levels of parenting and differential parenting were entered into the equations. Results from these longitudinal analyses indicated that neither differential nor absolute levels of parenting consistently added to the prediction of adolescent adjustment over time once the stability of the target behavior was accounted for in the equation. A notable exception to this general pattern was found for social responsibility. After accounting for

---

[11] Results from cross-lag analyses can be obtained from the first author.
[12] Contact the first author for detailed findings from nonshared longitudinal analyses.

social responsibility and absolute levels of parenting at Wave 1, fathers' differential negativity/conflict predicted social responsibility at Wave 2 among both older and younger siblings ($\Delta R^2 = .02$). Mothers' differential negativity/conflict explained 3% of the variance in social responsibility at Wave 2 among younger adolescents only.[13]

DISCUSSION

In this chapter, we examined dimensions of adolescent adjustment as a function of the marital, parent-child, and sibling subsystems concurrently and over time. Structural equation modeling techniques were employed to explore: (a) the marital subsystem in relation to the parent-child subsystem, and (b) the parent-child and sibling subsystems in relation to adolescent adjustment. A final set of analyses investigated the impact of differential parenting on absolute levels of adolescent competence and psychopathology. Overall, results from this study highlight the need to examine the larger network of relationships within the family in order to fully understand outcomes of risk and resilience at the individual level (Minuchin, 1985).

Consistent with past research (e.g., Brody & Forehand, 1988; Conger & Elder, 1994; Conger et al., 1992; Simons & Johnson, 1996), marital distress and parental depressive symptoms were associated with disruptions in parenting and the quality of parent-child relationships. Results were remarkably consistent across mothers and fathers with few exceptions. Mothers and fathers in distressed marriages were less likely to use an authoritative style of parenting, and they were more likely to engage in hostile, coercive interactions with their adolescents. Somewhat surprisingly, however, only among fathers were depressive symptoms associated directly with more negative, coercive, and conflicted parental relationships. The lack of a significant direct relationship between mother's depressive symptoms and her parenting behaviors is remarkable in light of other studies linking maternal depression and inept parenting practices (e.g., Brody & Forehand, 1988; Radke-Yarrow et al., 1988). It should be remembered that we refer to depressive symptoms rather than clinical depression in this study. Nonetheless, our findings confirm that for both mothers and fathers, the marital relationship may serve as a common pathway by which parental depression impinges upon the parent-child relationship (Cowan, Cowan, & Kerig, 1993; Miller et al., 1993).

---

[13] Results from multiple regression analyses are available from the first author.

Cross-sectional analyses revealed strong and consistent associations between both conflictual and authoritative parenting, and adolescent adjustment. Within Wave 1, authoritative parenting on the part of both mothers and fathers was related to lower levels of depressive symptoms and externalizing behaviors, and to higher levels of social responsibility and cognitive agency. In addition, adolescents who experienced higher levels of negativity in their parent-child relationships tended to be more depressed and act out, and to exhibit less social and cognitive competence. Similar results have been reported elsewhere such that family environments characterized by aversive or stressful relationships contribute to difficulties in adjustment for children and adolescents alike (e.g., Barrera & Garrison-Jones, 1992; Harold & Conger, 1997; Patterson et al., 1989; Patterson, Reid, & Dishion, 1992).

Also, as hypothesized, mothers' and fathers' authoritative parenting and parent-child negativity were associated concurrently with the quality of the sibling relationship. Specifically, authoritative parenting predicted greater sibling positivity only; however, hostile and coercive parent-child relationships were related to less sibling positivity and to more sibling negativity. These findings are consistent with the bulk of the empirical evidence that indicates congruence between the quality of the parent-child relationship and the quality of sibling relationships (e.g., Brody, Stoneman, & McCoy, 1994; Conger, Conger, & Elder, 1994). Of interest is that the quality of the sibling relationship was linked to adolescent adjustment in the father models only. Sibling positivity was associated with greater social responsibility only, and contrary to expectations, sibling negativity was related to lower levels of depressive symptoms and to higher levels of social competence. Nonetheless, these results should be interpreted cautiously, given similar findings were not observed with mothers in this sample, and the possibility of unstable parameter estimates.

Overall, few significant findings were observed longitudinally for either negative or positive indicators of adolescent adjustment at Wave 2. Only hostile, coercive mother-child relationships at Wave 1 predicted directly increases in externalizing behaviors and decreases in social responsibility over time. Neither authoritative parenting nor father-child negativity appeared to influence adolescents' long-term adjustment. There are several possible explanations as to why so few significant paths were observed longitudinally in these models. The substantial stability across time in family relationships and in adolescent behaviors combined with high within-wave correlations between these variables may have made the prediction of certain adolescent outcomes difficult at best. With so little change taking place, it is not surprising that identifying family relationship factors that contribute to change over time was such an arduous task. The patterns of relations observed in the cross-sectional analyses may have built up over an extended period of time—indeed, over the entire life course of family members interacting with one

179

another. The factors associated with patterns of concurrent relationships and adolescent adjustment may not necessarily be the same as those associated with changes in adjustment over time. Another possibility is that extrafamilial contexts not specified in these models begin to play a larger role in adjustment by middle to late adolescence. Parents' influence in determining adolescents' well-being may diminish as the peer group and/or the school assume greater importance (Hetherington, 1999).

An important caveat to the interpretation of these longitudinal data is that the processes identified in these models specified the direction of effects such that parenting at Wave 1 predicted adolescent adjustment at Wave 2. As with any correlational analysis, causal influences cannot be disentangled and may well be in directions opposite to those proposed. Several researchers have commented that the linkages between parenting and adolescents' short- and long-term adjustment probably reflect reciprocal rather than unidirectional processes (see Hetherington & Clingempeel, 1992, for further discussion). Preliminary analyses, however, revealed little or no evidence of any child-driven effects in this sample.[14] This was somewhat surprising, given earlier findings indicating that in the early years of remarriage stepchildren's externalizing and socially competent behaviors predict changes in their mothers' and stepfathers' parenting over time (Hetherington & Clingempeel, 1992). This discrepancy may reflect the fact that stepfamilies in the current study are stabilized (not newly constituted) stepfamilies that have been remarried an average of 9 years. Long past the tumultuous first years of a remarriage, adolescents—especially those who are stepchildren—may not elicit the same reactions from parents and stepparents as they did early on. Another possibility is that a selection effect has occurred among these long-term remarried families. Parents who experienced difficulties controlling an unruly child may have divorced long ago because of the stress, and thus are not a part of the sample.

In general, results from multiple group comparisons revealed few gender differences either within or across waves. These findings suggest that the processes linking the marital, parent-child, and sibling subsystems to adolescent adjustment are comparable for girls and boys. Although several investigators have noted few gender differences with respect to the parent-child relationship especially among adolescents (e.g., Hetherington & Clingempeel, 1992), some studies have reported that fathers under high levels of stress or those experiencing conflicted marital relations tend to be more negative and less positive toward daughters (e.g., Elder & Caspi, 1988; Hetherington, 1999; Kerig, Cowan, & Cowan, 1993). In addition, some research findings have indicated that fathers may be more salient for the

---

[14] Detailed findings from cross-lag analyses are availbale from the first author.

adjustment of boys and that mothers are more salient for girls' adjustment in certain domains and contexts (e.g., Gunnoe, Hetherington, & Reiss, in press). For example, Phares and Compas (1992), in their review of the literature, assert that fathers may be more influential than mothers in the development of externalizing problems especially among boys. Moreover, boys have been found to benefit more than girls from the presence of a supportive, authoritative stepfather (Amato & Keith, 1991; Hetherington, 1993; Hetherington & Jodl, 1994). Our findings, however, do not address this issue because gender and family type were examined separately. In short, the present study found no evidence of a different set of family processes operating for girls and boys in this sample.

Relatively few differences by family type/ownness were observed in multiple group analyses either within or across waves. Behavior geneticists might expect stronger associations between the behavior of parents and the adjustment of children in biologically related pairs than in nonbiologically related pairs. No support for this position was found for fathers in this sample. However, at Wave 1, there was some suggestion that mother-child relationships in stepfamilies may be somewhat unique especially among stepmothers and their stepchildren. For example, authoritative parenting on the part of stepmothers was not associated with higher levels of cognitive agency among their stepchildren. Similarly, stepmothers' differential negativity was related to indicators of both positive and negative adjustment for their biologically owned children, but not for their stepchildren. Such findings are indicative of an effect of biological relatedness rather than family type per se. Despite parenting in what might be considered an optimal manner, stepmothers appear unable to promote desirable behaviors in their stepchildren—a finding consistent with past research (Hetherington, 1993; Hetherington & Clingempeel, 1992; Hetherington & Jodl, 1994). Being an effective stepparent may not be enough to compensate for other vulnerabilities associated with the establishment of stepfamilies.

Over time, few differences emerged by family type. Taken together, the pattern of findings from within- and cross-wave analyses suggests that the processes underlying relations among the marital, parent-child, and sibling subsystems, and adolescent adjustment are comparable across nonstepfamilies and different types of stepfamilies. Unhappy marriages disrupt parenting and conflicted, negative parent-child interactions are associated with more negative and less positive sibling relationships. Parent-child relationships are more closely associated with adolescent adjustment than is the quality of the sibling relationship. As suggested by results reported in the sibling chapter, siblings' impact on the adjustment of younger children may have been greater if sibling adjustment (e.g., externalizing behaviors) had been substituted in lieu of sibling positivity or negativity in these models.

The lack of significant differences by family type/ownness is somewhat surprising particularly in light of the mean level differences that were reported by family type in earlier chapters (see Chapters IV and VI for further detail). Nonetheless, it is important to emphasize that the goal of this set of analyses was the examination of differences in family *process* and patterns of relationships. Functional relationships in different types of families are similar despite any mean differences in level attributable to family structure or composition.

An important question addressed by this research was whether or not differential parenting contributes to the development of competence and psychopathology among adolescents. Previous research has found differential parenting to be an important predictor of adolescent well-being (e.g., Anderson et al., 1994; Conger & Conger, 1994; Dunn & McGuire, 1994; Henderson et al., 1996; Mekos et al., 1996). Consistent with this body of literature, differential authoritative parenting and differential parent-child negativity were associated with absolute levels of adolescent adjustment within wave in the present study; however, the magnitude of these effects was small relative to absolute levels of parenting. Within-wave, adolescents who experienced more parent-child negativity and less authoritative parenting relative to their sibling were more likely to be depressed and to act out, and to exhibit less social responsibility and cognitive agency. Differential authoritative parenting on the part of mothers only was associated with lower levels of cognitive agency among adolescents at Wave 1. These cross-sectional data are consistent with results from other nonshared environment studies that have examined similar dimensions of parenting (e.g., Anderson et al., 1994; Reiss et al., 1995). For example, Reiss and his colleagues (Reiss et al., 1995) reported a socialization phenomenon for parent-child conflict and negativity which they termed the *sibling barricade* effect. Simply put, adolescents are least likely to show difficulties in adjustment if they are the recipients of less conflict and negativity from their parents and their siblings are the target of more parental negativity.

Over time, however, differences in parenting were not shown to predict absolute levels of adolescent competence and psychopathology in this sample. As in longitudinal analyses that examined absolute levels of parenting, the high cross-time stabilities and within-wave correlations may have contributed to difficulties in predicting change over time. Interestingly, neither absolute levels of parenting nor differences in parenting seemed to predict changes in adolescent adjustment over time.

In summary, our data support the notion that subsystems within families are interactive and dynamic (Minuchin, 1985). As reported here, linkages were observed between the marital and parent-child subsystems, as well as among the parent-child and sibling subsystems in relation to adolescents' short- and long-term adjustment. Unlike the ANOVAs presented in earlier chapters, the SEM approach adopted here contributes to our understanding of the family by delineating the *processes* (as opposed to mean level differences) by which diverse types of families influence adolescent development. Despite certain limitations, these findings highlight the importance of considering relations among multiple family subsystems in order to better understand change over time in adolescents' risks, resilience, and development.

VIII. FAMILY FUNCTIONING IN NONSTEPFAMILIES AND DIFFERENT KINDS OF STEPFAMILIES: AN INTEGRATION

E. Mavis Hetherington

Our findings suggest that even in these long-established stepfamilies, some differences in family relationships and in child adjustment from those in nonstepfamilies are found. These differences, however, do not seem to be based simply on having gone through marital dissolution, a remarriage, and the experience of living in a stepfamily; few differences between simple stepfamilies and nonstepfamilies were found. The differences obtained were associated with differences in biological relatedness between family members and with living in a complex stepfamily household.

THE MARITAL RELATIONSHIP

Both the couples in our stepfamilies and nonstepfamilies are past the early years of remarriage when marital dissolution is highest. These are marital survivors. Even these marital survivors, however, are showing declines in marital satisfaction and increased conflict over childrearing over the course of the study as they are dealing with the challenges of middle age and of at least two children in the household moving through adolescence. Adolescents' externalizing behavior was associated with declines in marital positivity and increases in marital negativity in nondivorced couples, but especially in remarried couples. Having a noncompliant, acting out, anti-social adolescent in the household takes its toll on the marital relationship and these behaviors, especially in girls in stepfamilies, are associated with declines in marital quality. Conflict over childrearing, although higher in both simple and complex stepfamilies than in nondivorced families, was not reflected in less positive or more negative marital relations. The interactive qualities in the relationship, such as warmth, supportiveness, positivity, and the general contentious, aversive behaviors in spouses, were more likely to influence the quality of the marital relationship than were the personality characteristics of the spouse. This suggests that personality characteristics that make an individual divorce prone, such as antisocial behavior, do not play the major role in marital dissatisfaction and instability.

The great similarity in marital relations in stepfamilies and first marriages is notable. As has been previously reported when differences in marital quality have emerged, it was with observational ratings, not self-reports (Bray & Berger, 1993; Hetherington, 1993; Hetherington & Clingempeel, 1992). More negative and less positive behavior was observed in spousal interactions in complex stepfamilies than in nonstepfamilies, but only in Wave 1. This suggests, however, that the challenges in dealing with the more diverse combinations of biological relatedness in siblings in complex stepfamilies disrupt conjugal functioning.

Findings associated with biological relatedness or what we have called owness are more interesting than those related to family type. With the older adolescents, conflicts about childrearing were greater if the child was the mother's biological child and the father's stepchild than if the adolescent was the biological child of both parents. Moreover, although mothers in all families assumed more responsibility for household tasks and childcare than did fathers, fathers participated more actively in the care of their own children than their stepchildren. In addition, fathers in all family types and biological relationships were more involved in the care of boys than of girls. The owness effects for childcare were less marked and consistent for mothers, occurring only with the older child.

In summary, in these long-established stepfamilies, there were more similarities than differences in marital relations between nondivorced and remarried couples. Parents were more involved, however, in the care of their own children than of stepchildren. In addition, there was an association between negativity in the marital relationship and externalizing in adolescents, especially with stepdaughters. Although no clear direction of effects could be established with cross-lagged analyses, in part because of the high stability across time in these measures, the markedly higher divorce rates found in remarriages with stepchildren (Tzeng & Mare, 1995) suggests that children may contribute to marital instability.

185

PARENT-CHILD RELATIONSHIPS

Marked differences in parenting between mothers and fathers were found. Mothers not only spent more time in childcare but also were more warm, more negative, more controlling, and more monitoring with their children's behaviors.

However, ownness and being in a complex stepfamily household influence parent-child relationships. Both mothers and fathers are warmer, more supportive, and more involved with their biological children than their stepchildren. Stepfathers also are less likely to monitor and exert control over stepchildren than over their own children in nonstepfamilies. The effects of ownness on conflict and negativity differ for mothers and fathers. Mothers are more likely than fathers to get into acrimonious coercive relationships with their own child than with their stepchild in complex stepfamilies. Being in a complex stepfamily household exacerbates problems in parenting. Within-family analyses indicated that differential parental treatment of siblings was most marked when one child was the parent's own child and one a stepchild. Differences are rarely found between parenting in nonstepfamilies and simple stepfamilies.

It is interesting to compare the results of this study with those of Hetherington and Clingempeel (1992), which used similar measures and included a comparison of parenting of adolescents in nondivorced and simple stepfather families over the course of the first 26 months of a remarriage. In these early years of a remarriage, biological mothers in simple stepfamilies, even 26 months after the remarriage, were monitoring and controlling their children's behavior less than those in nondivorced families. In addition, stepfathers were less positively involved, and less positive, controlling, and monitoring with their adolescent stepchildren than were fathers in nondivorced families. These results contrast with those found in the current study, with no differences found in mothers' parenting between those in nondivorced and simple stepfamilies. Differences found only in warmth for fathers could be attributable to the shorter time spent in a stepfather family in the Hetherington and Clingempeel (1992) study or to the fact that early adolescence is a particularly difficult age period in which to have a remarriage occur (Hetherington & Jodl, 1994). Although in this study stepparents have had a long period of time in which to become attached to their stepchildren, they remain more distant, are less warm and involved, and have less rapport with their stepchildren than parents with their biological children in nonstep- or in stepfamilies. These differences in warmth and involvement are stable across the two waves of the study and on the basis of past research, it is suspected that they are of long duration and will continue (Hetherington, 1999; Hetherington & Clingempeel, 1992; Hetherington & Jodl, 1994). In addition, children show more distant, less affectionate relationships with stepparents than with biological parents even in these long-established stepfamilies.

These results suggest that although many stepparents and stepchildren are able to establish close, constructive relationships, bonding is more difficult to establish in nonrelated parents and children. Both evolutionary theory and attachment theory would suggest that parents might have a greater investment and be more attached to their own children than to stepchildren. Biological relatedness, however, also implies greater genetic similarity between parents and children. It may be that parents and children who have similar attributes become more involved and attached—"a chip off the old block" hypothesis.

Another possible aspect, however, underlying differences in relationships between biological kin and stepkin needs to be considered. Most stepparents were not seeking stepchildren, they came as an adjunct, sometimes an unwelcome adjunct, to the marriage. In contrast, most married couples desired their children. It may be the involuntary nature of the addition of a child to the family rather than the biological ties that perturb stepparent-stepchildren relations. An informative comparison would be with adoptive families where there are nonbiological relationships between parents and children but the relationship was actively sought by the parents. We could find no studies comparing adoptive families to stepfamilies. Furthermore, studies comparing adoptive families to nondivorced first married families were usually poorly designed, often relying on a single reporter, and had inadequate measures of parenting often confined to communication about the adoptive status of the child (see Brodzinsky, Lang, & Smith, 1995, for a review). A study by Levy-Shiff, Goldschmidt, and Har-Even (1991) reports that adoptive Israeli parents, in comparison to biological parents, are equally attached to their infants and are more satisfied with the transition to parenthood than are nonadoptive parents, but cautions that these effects may not hold later in the adoptive process or when children are older. Adoption studies examining more frequently used dimensions of parenting and discipline or parenting typologies and utilizing multiple informants and observations are not available.

SIBLING RELATIONSHIPS

Again in the sibling relationship, the importance of biological relatedness was revealed. Biologically related siblings, whether in nondivorced families or in stepfamilies, were more likely than stepsiblings to be both more intensely positively and negatively engaged.

The quality of the sibling relationship was more strongly related to the adjustment of the biologically related siblings than to stepsiblings, and to boys' than to girls' adjustment. More similarity in siblings' adjustment also occurred with boys and for biologically related siblings in comparison with stepsiblings. Longitudinal analyses suggested that the influence of siblings' adjustment rather than the quality of the relationship is important in predicting long-term adjustment. Moreover, in agreement with a substantial body of research findings, cross-lagged models suggest that the similarity between siblings' inadjustment is attributable to younger siblings being influenced their older siblings' behavior.

ADOLESCENT ADJUSTMENT

Girls were found to be more autonomous, socially responsible, higher in cognitive agency, and lower in antisocial behavior than boys. They also, however, were higher in depression and lower in self-esteem. In contrast to the findings of studies that with young children (Hetherington, 1989), girls were not more disadvantaged by being in a stepfamily. Few gender by family type interactions occurred.

More problems in the adjustment of children in complex stepfamilies than in nonstepfamilies occurred. Differences that emerged were in domains that have frequently been reported in earlier studies — in antisocial behavior, social responsibility, and cognitive agency.

This contrasts with the findings in the newly remarried stepfamilies in the Hetherington and Clingempeel (1992) study where simple stepfamilies, in comparison to nondivorced families, were showing more problems not only in child adjustment but also in parent-child and sibling relationships. This suggests that if the remarriage has not occurred when children were adolescents, over time, the family relationships and the adjustment of children in simple stepfamilies show notable improvement. It should be remembered, however, that the most dysfunctional families would have divorced and not be included in our sample of stabilized stepfamilies, but this would be true for both remarried and first married families. Problems in complex stepfamilies remain in family functioning and in child adjustment even after an average of almost 9 years in a stepfamily. The unique challenges and complex array of family relationships in these families make adaptation difficult.

RELATIONS AMONG RELATIONSHIPS AND ADOLESCENT ADJUSTMENT

One of the main goals of this study was to examine whether patterns of relationships and associations among family relationships and child adjustment differed for boys and girls and for different types of families. After a horrendous amount of modeling, we had little to show for our efforts.

Multiple group comparisons revealed few gender or family type differences. The processes underlying relationships among parental depression, the marital relationship and parenting, and among parenting, sibling relations and child adjustment were for the most part similar for boys and girls and for different types of families. We have little evidence to support the position that different patterns of relationships are associated with positive or negative adolescent adjustment in stepfamilies and nonstepfamilies. Parental depression is associated with disrupted marital functioning, which in turn is related to less authoritative, more conflictual/coercive parenting in all families. Discordant, unsatisfying marital relations make effective authoritative parenting more difficult, and hostile, conflictual parent-child relations more likely. Similarly, competent, authoritative parenting and conflictual parenting are, for the most part, related to sibling relations and child adjustment similarly in nonstepfamilies and in stepfamilies. Authoritative parenting serves a protective role and negative conflictual parenting is a risk factor in the development of problems in sibling relations and child adjustment in all types of families.

Although absolute levels of parenting were associated with current adolescent adjustment, differential parenting had only a minor association with current adolescent adjustment and none with later adjustment. The results of the longitudinal models were disappointing. The high stability of our family process measures and of our adolescent and adult adjustment measures made it difficult to measure factors associated with change when little change was occurring. It seems likely that the patterns of family dynamics and child adjustment obtained in this study have formed over a long interactive history and are unlikely to be greatly affected by minor changes that occur in a 3-year period in adolescence. Moreover, although our models were unidirectional, because of the difficulty in dealing with multiple feedback loops in such models, it seems probable that many of the relationships were bidirectional.

CLINICAL IMPLICATIONS

This study suggests that even in long-established stepfamilies problems in family relations and adolescent adjustment may persist. These problems center around biological relatedness in stepfamilies and to a lesser extent in the complexity of stepfamily relationships. It is more difficult for nonbiologically related family members to develop rapport and to build strong affectionate relationships. In spite of the less close, more troubled relationships found between parents and children, husbands and wives in these long-established stepfamilies view their marital relationships as reasonably happy and similar but more egalitarian than that in first marriages.

With these survivors the quality of the marriage has been protected from the problems in parent-child relationships.

Although some clinicians argue that if stepfamilies aspire to be like nondivorced families, they are destined for difficulties, our findings suggest that the associations among the functioning of family subsystems and the pattern of the family relationships related to positive or negative adjustment in children are similar in stepfamilies and in nondivorced families. It has been recommended that stepparents attempt to exert control over their stepchildren's behavior only gradually and begin by trying to establish a friendly relationship with stepchildren and by supporting the biological parent's discipline. In these long-term and probably more successful stepfamilies, however, authoritative parenting characterized by higher warmth and control and monitoring was associated with better child adjustment just as was found in nonstepfamilies. This also has been found with stepfamilies in the earlier stages of remarriage (e.g., Hetherington & Clingempeel, 1992). Promoting authoritative parenting may be an important clinical goal in both nondivorced and remarried families.

Relations among stepsiblings although somewhat detached are not exceptionally agonistic and successful satellite relations can be formed with stepsiblings. Girls have more positive relations that do boys with their same-sexed siblings and as has been found in other studies (Hetherington 1988, 1989, 1991a) are better able to protect their siblings from adversity in times of stress. Strengthening sibling ties may help to counter some of the adverse consequences of disrupted parent-child relations and the stresses and changes in family life associated with a remarriage.

The models of family relations and adolescent adjustment show that in these longer established stepfamilies the associations seem to be parent-driven rather than child-driven. The results also suggest that older siblings' behavior influences that of younger siblings. Thus, therapeutic efforts should be directed toward the entire family. Interventions should include parents and siblings and not just the identified adolescent patient.

Family researchers have developed a battery of self-report and observational techniques that identify individuals, marriages, parent-child, and sibling relationships at-risk. Some of these, especially the self-report instruments, could be used by clinicians to identify at-risk families and children if efforts to establish norms for these instruments were made.

Furthermore, early intervention for the at-risk children seems imperative if therapeutic manipulations of family relationships are to be the central mechanism of change. With increasing age, adolescents become more autonomous and influenced by peers and experiences and groups external to the family who are more difficult to include in therapeutic interventions.

A CAUTIONARY NOTE

This study dealt with stabilized stepfamilies with adolescent offspring. The sample is predominantly White and middle-class. It is unknown if the findings can be generalized to stepfamilies of shorter duration with younger children, to other ethnic groups or to less educated, more impoverished populations.

In addition, this *Monograph* has focused on relationships within the primary household. Some of our adolescents, however, spent considerable time outside of the household with noncustodial parents, other kin, stepkin, and peers. Furthermore, as is appropriate for this age group, our adolescents were involved in activities and relationships in other settings—in school, the neighborhood, workplace, and peer group. These factors are all important in adolescent adjustment. A broader ecological perspective that involves both familial and extrafamilial factors will be explored in future work.

REFERENCES

Achenbach, T. M., & Edelbrock, E. (1983). *Manual for the Child Behavior Checklist and Revised Child Behavior Profile*. Burlington, VT: University of Vermont.

Ahrons, C. R., & Wallisch, L. (1987). Parenting in the binuclear family: Relationships between biological and stepparents. In K. Pasley & M. Ihinger-Tallman (Eds.), *Remarriage and stepparenting today: Current research and theory*. New York: Guilford.

Aiken, L. S., & West, S. G. (1991). *Multiple regression: Testing and interpreting interactions*. Newbury Park, CA: Sage.

Allison, P. D., & Furstenberg, Jr., F. F. (1989). How marital dissolution affects children: Variations by age and sex. *Developmental Psychology, 25*, 540–549.

Almeida, D. M., & Galambos, N. L. (1991). Examining father involvement and the quality of father-adolescent relations. *Journal of Research on Adolescence, 1*, 155–172.

Amato, P. R. (1991). Parental absence during childhood and depression in later life. *Sociological Quarterly, 32*, 543–556.

Amato, P. R. (1993). Children's adjustment to divorce: Theories, hypotheses, and empirical support. *Journal of Marriage and the Family, 55*, 23–38.

Amato, P. R. (1994). The implications of research findings on children in stepfamilies. In A. Booth & J. Dunn (Eds.), *Stepfamilies: Who benefits? Who does not?* Hillsdale, NJ: Lawrence Erlbaum.

Amato, P. R. (1996). Explaining the intergenerational transmission of divorce. *Journal of Marriage and the Family, 58*, 628–640.

Amato, P. R. (1999). Children of divorced parents as young adults. In E. M. Hetherington (Ed.), *Coping with divorce, single parenting and remarriage: A risk and resiliency perspective*. Hillsdale, NJ: Lawrence Erlbaum.

Amato, P. R., & Keith, B. (1991a). Parental divorce and the well-being of children: A meta analysis. *Psychological Bulletin, 110,* 26–46.

Amato, P. R., & Keith, B. (1991b). Parental divorce and adult well-being of children: A meta analysis. *Journal of Marriage and the Family, 53,* 43–58.

Anderson, E. R., Greene, S. M., Hetherington, E. M., & Clingempeel, W. G. (1999). The dynamics of parental remarriage: Adolescent parent and sibling influences. In E. M. Hetherington (Ed.), *Coping with divorce, single parenting, and remarriage: A risk and resiliency perspective*. Hillsdale, NJ: Lawrence Erlbaum.

Anderson, E. R., Hetherington, E. M., Reiss, D., & Plomin, R. (1994). Parents' nonshared treatment of siblings and the development of social competence during adolescence. *Journal of Family Psychology, 8*, 303–320.

Anderson, E. R., Lindner, M. S., & Bennion, L. D. (1992). The effect of family relationships on adolescent development during family reorganization. In E. M. Hetherington &

W. G. Clingempeel (Eds.), Coping with marital transitions: A family systems perspective. *Monographs of the Society for Research in Child Development*, **57** *(2–3, Serial No. 227)*.

Anderson, E. R., & Rice, A. M. (1992). Sibling relationships during remarriage. In E. M. Hetherington & W. G. Clingempeel (Eds.), *Coping with marital transitions: A family systems perspective. Monographs of the Society for Research in Child Development*, **57** *(2–3, Serial No. 227)*.

Avenevoli, S., Sessa, F. M., & Steinberg, L. (1999). Family structure, parenting practices and adolescent adjustment: An ecological examination. In E. M. Hetherington (Ed.), *Coping with divorce, single parenting and remarriage: A risk and resiliency perspective.* Hillsdale, NJ: Lawrence Erlbaum.

Bandura, A. (1969). Social-learning theory of identificatory processes. In D. A. Goslin (Ed.), *Handbook of socialization theory and research.* Chicago: McNally & Co.

Bank, L., Dishion, R., Skinner, M., & Patterson, G. R. (1990). Method variance in structural equation modeling: Living with "glop." In G. R. Patterson (Ed.), *Depression and aggression in family interaction.* Hillsdale, NJ: Lawrence Erlbaum.

Bank, S., & Kahn, N. (1982). *The sibling bond.* New York: Basic Books.

Barnett, R. C., & Baruch, G. K. (1987). Determinants of fathers' participation in family work. *Journal of Marriage and the Family*, **49**, 29–40.

Barrera, M., & Garrison-Jones, C. (1992). Family and peer social support as specific correlates of adolescent depressive symptoms. *Journal of Abnormal Child Psychiatry*, **140**, 825–832.

Baruch, G. K., & Barnett, R. C. (1987). Role quality and psychological well-being. In F. Crosby (Ed.), *Spouse, parent, worker.* New Haven, CT: Yale University Press.

Baucom, D. H., & Epstein, N. (1990). *Cognitive-behavioral marital therapy.* New York: Brunner/Mazel.

Baumrind, D. (1973). The development of instrumental competence through socialization. In A. D. Pick (Ed.), *Minnesota symposium on child psychology* (Vol. 7). Minneapolis: University of Minnesota Press.

Baumrind, D. (1991a). Effective parenting during the early adolescent transition. In P. Cowan & E. M. Hetherington (Eds.), *Advances in family research: Vol. 2 — Family Transitions.* Hillsdale, NJ: Erlbaum.

Baumrind, D. (1991b). The influence of parenting style on adolescent competence and substance use. *Journal of Early Adolescence*, **11**, 56–95.

Beer, W. R. (1992). *American stepfamilies.* New Brunswick, NJ: Transaction.

Belsky, J. (1984). The determinants of parenting: A process model. *Child Development*, **55**, 83–96.

Bernstein, A. C. (1989). *Yours, mine and ours: How families change when remarried parents have a child together.* New York: Scribner.

Block, J. H., Block, J., & Morisson, A. (1981). Parental agreement-disagreement on child-rearing orientations and gender-related personality correlates in children. *Child Development*, **52**, 965–974.

Block, J. H., & Rubins, R. W. (1993). A longitudinal study of consistency and change in self-esteem from early adolescence to early adulthood. *Child Development*, **64**, 909–923.

Boer, F., & Dunn, J. (Eds.). (1992). *Children's sibling relationships: Developmental and clinical issues.* Hillsdale, NJ: Erlbaum.

Bohannon, P. (1984). Stepparenthood: A new and old experience. In R. S. Cohen, B. J. Cohler, & S. H. Weissman (Eds.), *Parenthood: A psychodepmanic interpretation.* New York: Guilford.

Bollen, K. A. (1990). *Structural equations with latent variables.* New York: Wiley & Sons.

Booth, A., & Edwards, J. N. (1992). Starting over: Why remarriages are more unstable. *Journal of Family Issues*, **13**, 179–194.

Booth, A., Johnson, D., & Edwards, J. N. (1983). Measuring marital instability. *Journal of Marriage and the Family,* **45,** 387–393.

Bowlby, J. (1969). *Attachment and loss. I: Attachment.* London: Hogarth.

Boyd, J., & Weissman, M. M. (1982). The epidemiology of affective disorders: Depressive symptoms, nonbipolar depression, and bipolar disorder. In E. S. Paykel (Ed.), *Handbook of affective disorders.* New York: Churchill Livingstone.

Brand, E., & Clingempeel, W. G. (1987). Interdependency of marital and stepparent-stepchild relationships and children's psychological adjustment: Research findings and clinical implication. *Family Relations,* **36,** 140–145.

Brand, E., Clingempeel, W. G., & Bowen-Woodward, K. (1988). Family relationships and children's psychological adjustment in stepmother and stepfather families. Findings and conclusions from the Philadelphia Stepfamily Research Project. In E. M. Hetherington & J. D. Arasteh (Eds.), *Impact of divorce, single parenting and stepparenting on children.* Hillsdale, NJ: Lawrence Erlbaum.

Bray, J. H. (1988). Children's development during early remarriage. In E. M. Hetherington & J. D. Arasteh (Eds.) *Impact of divorce, single parenting, and stepparenting on children.* Hillsdale, NJ: Lawrence Erlbaum.

Bray, J. H. (1990a). *Developmental Issues in Stepfamilies Research Project: Final report.* Unpublished manuscript, Texas Woman's University, Houston.

Bray, J. H. (1990b, August). *The developing stepfamily II: Overview and previous findings.* Paper presented at the 98th Annual Conference of the American Psychological Association, Boston.

Bray, J. H. (1991). Psychosocial factors affecting custodial and visitation arrangements. *Behavioral Sciences and the Law,* **9,** 419–437.

Bray, J. H. (1999). From marriage to remarriage and beyond: Findings from the Developmental Issues in Stepfamilies Research Project. In E. M. Hetherington (Ed.), *Coping with divorce, single parenting and remarriage: A risk and resiliency perspective.* Hillsdale, NJ: Lawrence Erlbaum.

Bray, J. H., & Berger, S. H. (1993). Developmental Issues in Stepfamilies Research Project: Family relationships and parent-child interactions. *Journal of Family Psychology,* **7,** 1–17, 76–90.

Bray, J. H., Berger, S. H., Silverblatt, A. H., & Hollier, A. (1987). Family process and organization during early remarriage: A preliminary analysis. In J. Vincent (Ed.), *Advance in family intervention assessment, and theory.* Greenwich, CT: JAI.

Bray, J. H., & Hetherington, E. M. (1993). Families in transition: Introduction and overview. Special Section: Families in transition. *Journal of Family Psychology,* **7,** 3–8.

Brody, G. H., & Forehand, R. (1988). Multiple determinants of parenting: Research findings and implications for the divorce process. In E. M. Hetherington & J. D. Arasteh (Eds.), *Impact of divorce, single parenting, and stepparenting on children.* Hillsdale, NJ: Erlbaum.

Brody, G. H., Stoneman, Z., & McCoy, J. K. (1994). Contributions of family relationships and child temperaments to longitudinal variations in sibling relationship quality and sibling relationship styles. *Journal of Family Psychology,* **8,** 274–286.

Brodzinsky, D. M., Lang, R., & Smith, D. W. (1995). Parenting adopted children. In M. H. Bonrstein (Ed.), *Handbook of parenting, Vol. 3: Status and social conditions of parenting.* Mahwah, NJ: Lawrence Erlbaum.

Brook, J. S., Whiteman, M., Gordon, A. S., & Brook, D. W. (1989). The role of older brothers in younger brothers' drug use viewed in the context of parent and peer influences. *The Journal of Genetic Psychology,* **15,** 59–75.

Brown, A. C., Green, R. J., & Druckman, J. (1990). A comparison of stepfamilies with and without child-focused problems. *American Journal of Orthopsychiatry,* **60,** 556–579.

Browne, M. W., & Cudeck, R. (1993). Alternative ways of assessing model fit. In K. Bollen & S. Long (Eds.), *Testing structural equation models*. Beverly Hills, CA: Sage.

Buhrmester, D. (1992). The developmental course of sibling and peer relationships. In F. Boer & J. Dunn (Eds.), *Children's sibling relationships*. Hillsdale, NJ: Lawrence Erlbaum.

Bumpass, L. L. (1984a). Children and marital disruption: A replication and update. *Demography*, **21**, 71–82.

Bumpass, L. L. (1984b). Some characteristics of children's second families. *American Journal of Sociology*, **90**, 608–623.

Bumpass, L. L., Martin, T. C., & Sweet, J. A. (1991). The impact of family background and early marital factors on marital disruption. *Journal of Family Issues*, **12**, 22–42.

Bumpass, L. L., & Raley, R. K. (1995). Redefining single-parent families: Cohabitation and changing family reality. *Demography*, **32**, 97–109.

Bumpass, L. L., & Sweet, J. A. (1989). *Children's experience in single-parent families: Implications of cohabitation and marital transitions* (NSFH Working Paper No. 3). Madison: University of Wisconsin, Center for Demography and Ecology.

Bumpass, L. L., Sweet, J. A., & Castro-Martin, T. (1990). Changing patterns of remarriage. *Journal of Marriage and the Family*, **52**, 747–756.

Capaldi, D. M., & Patterson, G. R. (1991). Relations of parental transitions to boys' adjustment problems: I. A linear hypothesis. II. Mothers at risk for transitions and unskilled parenting. *Developmental Psychology*, **27**, 489–504.

Chase-Lansdale, P. L., Cherlin, A. J., & Kiernan, K. E. (1995). The long-term effects of parental divorce on the mental health of young adults: A developmental perspective. *Child Development*, **66**, 1614–1634.

Cherlin, A. J., & Furstenberg, F. F., Jr. (1994). Stepfamilies in the United States: A reconsideration. In J. Blake & J. Hagen (Eds.), *Annual review of sociology*. Palo Alto, CA: Annual Reviews.

Cherlin, A. J., & McCarthy, J. (1985). Remarried couple households: Data from the June 1980 current population survey. *Journal of Marriage and the Family*, **47**, 23–30.

Cicchetti, D., Rogosch, F. A., & Toth, S. L. (1997). Ontogenesis, depressotypic organization, and the depressive spectrum. In S. S. Luthar, J. A. Burack, D. Cicchetti, & J. R. Weisz (Eds.), *Developmental psychopathology: Perspectives on adjustment, risk, and disorder*. New York: Cambridge University Press.

Cicchetti, D., & Toth, S. L. (1998). The development of depression in children and adolescents. *American Psychologist*, **53**, 221–241.

Clarke, S. C., & Wilson, B. F. (1994). The relative stability of remarriages. *Family Relations*, **43**, 305–310.

Clingempeel, W. G. (1981). Quasi-kin relationships and marital quality. *Journal of Personality and Social Psychology*, **41**, 890–901.

Clingempeel, W. G., Brand, E., & Ievoli, R. (1984). Stepparent-stepchild relations in stepmother and stepfather families. *Child Development*, **57**, 474–484.

Clingempeel, W. G., Brand, E., & Segal, S. (1987). A multilevel-multivariable-developmental perspective for future research on stepfamilies. In K. Pasley & M. Ihinger-Tallman (Eds.), *Remarriage and stepparenting today: Current research and theory*. New York: Guilford.

Clingempeel, W. G., Ievoli, R., & Brand, E. (1984). Structural complexity and the quality of stepfather-stepchild relationships. *Family Process*, **23**, 547–556.

Cohn, D. A., Cowan, P. A., Cowan, C. P., & Pearson, J. (1992). Working models of childhood attachment and couple relationships. *Journal of Family Issues*, **13**, 432–449.

Cohen, J. (1968). Weighted kappa: Nominal scale agreement with provisions for scale disagreement or partial credit. *Psychological Bulletin*, **70**, 213–220.

195

Coleman, M. (1994). Stepfamilies in the United States: Challenging biased assumptions. In A. Booth & J. Dunn (Eds.), *Stepfamilies: Who benefits? Who does not?* Hillsdale, NJ: Lawrence Erlbaum.

Conger, K. L., & Conger, R. D. (1994). Differential parenting and change in sibling differences in delinquency. *Journal of Family Psychology, 8,* 287–303.

Conger, K. L., Conger, R. D., & Elder, G. H., Jr. (1994). Sibling relations during hard times. In R. D. Conger & G. H. Elder, Jr. (Eds.), *Families in troubled times: Adapting to change in rural America.* New York: Aldine.

Conger, R. D., & Chao, W. (1996). Adolescent depressed mood. In R. Simons & Associates (Eds.), *Understanding differences between divorced and intact families: Stress, interaction, and child outcome.* Thousand Oaks, CA: Sage.

Conger, R. D., Conger, K. J., Elder, G. H., Jr., Lorenz, F. O., Simons, R. L., & Whitbeck, L. B. (1992). A family process model of economic hardship and adjustment of early adolescent boys. *Child Development, 63,* 526–541.

Conger, R. D., & Elder, G. H., Jr. (1994). *Families in troubled times: Adapting to change in rural America.* New York: Aldine.

Cowan, C. P. (1988). Working with men becoming fathers: The impact of a couples group intervention. In P. Bronstein & C. P. Cowan (Eds.), *Fatherhood today: Men's changing role in the family.* New York: Wiley.

Cowan, P. A., & Cowan, C. P. (1990). Becoming a family: Research and intervention. In I. Sigel & G. A. Brody (Eds.), *Family research.* Hillsdale, NJ: Lawrence Erlbaum.

Cowan, P. A., Cowan, C. P., & Kerig, P. K. (1993). Mothers, fathers, sons & daughters: Gender differences in family formation and parenting style. In P. A. Cowan (Ed.), *Family, self & society: Toward a new agenda for family research.* Hillsdale, NJ: Erlbaum.

Cowan, P. A., Cowan, C. P., & Schulz, M. S. (1996). Thinking about risk and resilience in families. In E. M. Hetherington & E. A. Blechman (Eds.), *Stress, coping, and resiliency in children and families. Family research consortium: Advances in family research.* Hillsdale, NJ: Lawrence Erlbaum.

Crockett, L., Losoff, M., & Petersen, A. C. (1984). Perceptions of the Peer Group and Friendship in Early Adolescence. *Journal of Early Adolescence, 4,* 155–181.

Crosbie-Burnett, M. (1984). The centrality of the step relationship: A challenge to family theory and practice. *Family Relations, 33,* 459–464.

Crosbie-Burnett, M. (1989). Impact of custody arrangement and family structure on remarriage. *Journal of Divorce, 13,* 1–16.

Crouter, A. C., Perry-Jenkins, M., Huston, T. L., & McHale, S. M. (1987). Processes underlying father involvement in dual-earner and single-earner families. *Developmental Psychology, 23,* 431–440.

Daly, M., & Wilson, M. I. (1987). The Darwinian psychology of discriminative parental solicitude. *Nebraska Symposium on Motivation, 35,* 91–144.

Daly, M., & Wilson, M. I. (1996). Violence against stepchildren. *Current Directions in Psychological Science, 5,* 77–81.

Daniels, D., Dunn, J., Furstenberg, F., & Plomin, R. (1985). Environmental differences within family and adjustment differences within pairs of adolescent siblings. *Child Development, 56,* 764–774.

Davies, P. T., & Cummings, E. M. (1994). Marital conflict and child adjustment: An emotional security hypothesis. *Psychological Bulletin, 116,* 387–411.

Deater-Deckard, K., & Dunn J. (1999). Multiple risks and adjustment in young children growing up in different family settings: A British Community study of stepparent, single mothers and nondivorced families. In E. M. Hetherington (Ed.), *Coping with divorce, single parenting and remarriage: A risk and resiliency perspective.* Hillsdale, NJ: Lawrence Erlbaum.

Demo, D. H., & Acock, A. C. (1993). Family diversity and the division of domestic labor: How much have things really changed? *Family Relations,* **42,** 323–331.

Demo, D. H., & Acock, A. C. (1996). Family structure, family process, and adolescent well-being. *Journal of Research on Adolescence,* **6,** 457–488.

Dindia, K., & Cavary, D. J. (1993). Definitions and theoretical perspectives on maintaining relationships. *Journal of Social and Personal Relationships,* **10,** 163–174.

Dornbusch, S. M., Carlsmith, J. M., Bushwall, S. J., Ritter, P. L., Liederman, H., Hastrof, A. H., & Gross, R. T. (1985). Single parents, extended households, and the context of adolescents. *Child Development,* **56,** 326–341.

Duberman, L. (1973). Step-kin relations. *Journal of Marriage and the Family,* **35,** 283–292.

Duberman, L. (1975). *The reconstituted family: A study of remarried couples and their children.* Chicago: Nelson Hall.

Duncan, T. E., Duncan, S. C., & Hops, H. (1996). The role of parents and older siblings in predicting adolescent substance use: Modeling development via structural equation latent growth methodology. *Journal of Family Psychology,* **10,** 158–172.

Dunn, J., & Kendrick, C. (1982). Social behavior of young siblings in the family context: Differences between same-sex and different-sex dyads. *Annual Progress in Child Psychiatry & Child Development,* **21,** 166–181.

Dunn, J., & McGuire, S. (1994). Young children's nonshared experiences: A summary of studies in Cambridge and Colorado. In E. M. Hetherington, D. Reiss, & R. Plomin (Eds.), *Separate social worlds of siblings: The impact of nonshared environment on development.* Hillsdale, NJ: Lawrence Erlbaum.

Dunn, J., Stocker, C., & Plomin, R. (1990). Nonshared experiences within the family: Correlates of behavioral problems in middle childhood. *Development and Psychopathology,* **2,** 113–126.

East, P. L. (1996). The younger sisters of childbearing adolescents: Their attitudes, expectations, and behaviors. *Child Development,* **67,** 267–282.

East, P. L., Felice, M. E., & Morgan, M. C. (1993). Sisters' and girlfriends' sexual and childbearing behavior: Effects on early adolescent girls' sexual outcomes. *Journal of Marriage and the Family,* **55,** 953–963.

East, P. L., & Shi, C. R. (1997). Pregnant and parenting adolescents and their younger sisters: The influence of relationship qualities for younger sister outcomes. *Developmental and Behavioral Pediatrics,* **18,** 84–90.

Eccles, J., Wigfield, A., Hareold, R. D., & Blumenfield, P. (1993). Age and gender differences in children's self- and task performance during elementary school. *Child Development,* **64,** 830–847.

Elder, G. H. Jr., & Caspi, A. (1988). Economic stress in lives: Developmental perspectives. *Journal of Social Issues,* **44,** 25–45.

Elder, G. H. Jr., & Russell, S. T. (1996). Academic performance and future aspirations. In R. Simons & Associates (Eds.), *Understanding differences between divorced and intact families: Stress, interaction, and child outcome.* Thousand Oaks, CA: Sage.

Emery, R. E., & Forehand, R. (1994). Parental divorce and children's well-being: A focus on resilience. In R. J. Haggerty, L. R. Sherrod, N. Garmezy, & M. Rutter (Eds.), *Stress, risk, and resilience in children and adolescents.* Cambridge, England: Cambridge University Press.

Erickson, R. J. (1993). Reconceptualizing family work: The effect of emotion work on perceptions of marital quality. *Journal of Marriage and the Family,* **55,** 888–900.

Farrell, J., & Markman, H. (1986). Individual and interpersonal factors in the etiology of marital distress: The example of remarital couples. In R. Gilmour & S. Duck (Eds.), *The emerging field of personal relationships.* Hillsdale, NJ: Lawrence Erlbaum.

197

Fauber, R., Forehand, R., Long, N., & Burke, M. (1987). The relationship of young adolescent Children's Depression Inventory (CDI) scores to their social and cognitive functioning. *Journal of Psychopathology and Behavior Assessment, 9,* 161–172.

Fine, M. A., & Kurdek, L. A. (1992). The adjustment of adolescents in stepfather and stepmother families. *Journal of Marriage and the Family, 54,* 725–736.

Fine, M. A., & Kurdek, L. A. (1994a). Parenting cognitions in stepfamilies: Differences between parents and stepparents and relations to parenting satisfaction. *Journal of Social and Personal Relationships, 11,* 95–112.

Fine, M. A., & Kurdek, L. A. (1994b). A multidimensional cognitive-developmental model of stepfamily adjustment. In K. Pasley & M. Ihinger-Tallman (Eds.), *Stepparenting: Issues in theory, research and practice.* Westport, CT: Greenwood Press.

Fine, M. A., & Kurdek, L. A. (1995). Relation between marital quality and (step)parent-child relationships quality for parents and stepparents in stepfamilies. *Journal of Family Psychology, 9,* 216–223.

Fine, M. A., Kurdek, L. A., & Hennigen, L. (1992). Perceived self competence, stepfamily myths, and (step)parent role ambiguity in adolescents from stepfather and stepmother families. *Journal of Family Psychology, 6,* 69–76.

Fine, M. A., Voydanoff, P., & Donnelly, B. W. (1993). Relations between parental control and warmth and child well-being in stepfamilies. *Journal of Family Psychology, 7,* 222–232.

Finkelhor, D. (1987). The sexual abuse of children: Current research reviewed. *Psychiatric Annals, 17,* 233–241.

Forehand, R., & Nousiainen, S. (1993). Maternal and paternal parenting: Critical dimensions in adolescent functioning. *Journal of Family Psychology, 7,* 213–221.

Forgatch, M. S., Patterson, G. R., & Ray, J. A. (1995). Divorce and boys' adjustment problems: Two paths with a single model. In E. M. Hetherington & E. A. Blechman (Eds.), *Stress, coping, and resiliency in children and families.* Hillsdale, NJ: Lawrence Erlbaum.

Forgatch, M. S., Patterson, G. R., & Skinner, M. L. (1988). A mediational model for the effect of divorce on antisocial boys. In E. M. Hetherington & J. D. Arasteh (Eds.), *Impact of divorce, single parenting, and stepparenting on children.* Hillsdale, NJ: Lawrence Erlbaum.

Furstenberg, F. F., Jr. (1987). The new extended family: The experiences of parents and children after remarriage. In K. Pasley & M. Ihinger-Tallman (Eds.), *Remarriage and stepparenting: Current research and theory.* New York: Guilford Press.

Furstenberg, F. F., Jr. (1988). Child care after divorce and remarriage. In E. M. Hetherington & J. Arasteh (Eds.), *Impact of divorce, single parenting, and stepparenting on children.* Hillsdale, NJ: Lawrence Erlbaum.

Furstenberg, F. F., Jr. (1990). Divorce and the American family. *Annual Review of Sociology, 16,* 379–403.

Furstenberg, F. F., Jr., & Cherlin, A. J. (1991). *Divided families: What happens to children when parents part.* Cambridge, MA: Harvard University Press.

Furstenberg, F. F., Jr., & Nord, C. W. (1987). Parenting apart: Patterns of childrearing after marital disruption. *Journal of Marriage and the Family, 47,* 893–905.

Furstenberg, F. F., Jr., & Spanier, G. B. (1984). The risk of dissolution in remarriage: An examination of incomplete institutionalization. *Family Relations, 33,* 433–441.

Ganong, L., & Coleman, M. (1987). Effects of parental remarriage on children: An updated comparison of theories, methods and findings from clinical and empirical research. In K. Pasley & M. Ihinger-Tallman (Eds.), *Remarriage and stepparenting today: Current research and theory.* New York: Guilford.

Ganong, L., & Coleman, M. (1988). Do mutual children cement bonds in stepfamilies? *Journal of Marriage and the Family, 50,* 687–698.

Ganong, L., & Coleman, M. (1989). Preparing for remarriage: Anticipating the issues, seeking solutions. *Family Relations, 38,* 28–33.

Ganong, L., & Coleman, M. (1994). *Remarried family relationships*. Newbury Park, CA: Sage.

Giles-Sims, J. (1987). Social exchange in remarried families. In K. Pasley & M. Ihinger-Tallman (Eds.), *Remarriage and stepparenting: Current research and theory*. New York: Guilford.

Gjerde, P. F., Block, J., & Block, J. H. (1988). Depressive symptoms and personality during late adolescence: Gender differences in the internalization of symptom expression. *Journal of Abnormal Psychology, 97,* 475–486.

Glenn, N. D. (1994). Biology, evolutionary theory, and family social science. In A. Booth & J. Dunn (Eds.), *Stepfamilies: Who benefits? Who does not?* Hillsdale, NJ: Lawrence Erlbaum.

Glenn, N. D., & Kramer, K. B. (1985). The psychological well-being of adult children of divorce. *Journal of Marriage and the Family, 47,* 905–912.

Gotlib, I. H., & Hooley, J. M. (1998). Depression and marital distress: Current status and future directions. In S. Duck, D. F. Hay, S. E. Hobfoll, W. Ickes, & B. M. Montgomery (Eds.), *Handbook of personal relationships: Theory, research and interventions*. Chichester, England: Wiley.

Gotlib, I. H., & McCabe, S. B. (1990). Marriage and psychopathology. In F. D. Fincham & T. N. Bradbury (Eds.), *The psychology of marriage*. New York: Guilford.

Gotlib, I. H., & Meltzer, S. J. (1987). Depression and the perception of social skill in dyadic interaction. *Cognitive Therapy and Research, 11,* 41–53.

Gotlib, I. H., & Whiffen, V. E. (1989). Depression and marital functioning: An examination of specificity and gender differences. *Journal of Abnormal Psychology, 98,* 23–30.

Gottman, J. M. (1993). A theory of marital dissolution and stability. *Journal of Family Psychology, 7,* 57–75.

Gottman, J. M. (1994). *What predicts divorce?* Hillsdale, NJ: Erlbaum.

Granleese, J., Turner, I., & Trew, K. (1989). Teachers' and boys' and girls' perceptions of competence in the primary school: The importance of physical competence. *British Journal of Education Psychology, 59,* 31–37.

Greenberger, E., & O'Neil, R. (1993). Spouse, parent, worker: Role commitments and role-related experiences in the construction of adults' well-being. *Developmental Psychology, 29,* 181–197.

Greene, S. M., & Anderson, E. R. (1999). Observed negativity in large family systems: Incidents and reactions. *Journal of Family Psychology, 13,* 372–392.

Guisinger, S., Cowan, P., & Schuldberg, D. (1989). Changing parent and spouse relations in the first years of remarriage of divorced fathers. *Journal of Marriage and the Family, 51,* 445–456.

Gunnoe, M. L., Hetherington, E. M., & Reiss, D. (in press). Parental religiosity, parenting style, and adolescent competence. *Journal of Early Adolescence*.

Harold, G. T., & Conger, R. D. (1997). Marital conflict and adolescent distress: The role of adolescent awareness. *Child Development, 68,* 333–350.

Harter, S. (1982). The perceived competence scale for children. *Child Development, 53,* 87–97.

Harter, S. (1990). Self and identity development. In S. Feldman & G. R. Elliot (Eds.), *At the threshold: The developing adolescent*. Cambridge, MA: Harvard University Press.

Heaton, T. B., & Albrecht, S. L. (1991). Stable unhappy marriages. *Journal of Marriage and the Family, 53,* 747–758.

Helsel, W. J., & Matson, J. C. (1984). The assessment of depression in children: The internal structure of the Children's Depression Inventory (CDI). *Behavior Research and Therapy, 22,* 289–298.

Henderson, S. H., Hetherington, E. M., Mekos, D., & Reiss, D. (1996). Stress, parenting, and adolescent psychopathology in nondivorced and stepfamilies: A within-family perspective. In E. M. Hetherington & E. A. Blechman (Eds.), *Advances in family research: Stress, coping and resiliency in children and families*. Hillsdale, NJ: Lawrence Erlbaum.

Hetherington, E. M. (1988). Parents, children, and siblings six years after divorce. In R. Hinde & J. Stevenson-Hinde (Eds.), *Relationships within families*. New York: Oxford University Press.

Hetherington, E. M. (1989). Coping with family transitions: Winners, losers, and survivors. *Child Development, 60,* 1–14.

Hetherington, E. M. (1990). Social capital and the development of youth from nondivorced, divorced, and remarried families. In A. Collins (Ed.), *Relationships as developmental contexts: The 29th Minnesota Symposium on Child Psychology*. Hillsdale, NJ: Lawrence Erlbaum.

Hetherington, E. M. (1991a). Families, lies and videotapes. *Journal of Research on Adolescence,* **1,** 323–348.

Hetherington, E. M. (1991b). The role of individual differences in family relations in coping with divorce and remarriage. In P. Cowan & E. M. Hetherington (Eds.), *Advances in family research: Vol. 2, Family transitions*. Hillsdale, NJ: Lawrence Erlbaum.

Hetherington, E. M. (1993). An overview of the Virginia longitudinal study of divorce and remarriage with a focus on early adolescence. *Journal of Family Psychology, 7,* 39–56.

Hetherington, E. M. (1994). Siblings, family relationships and child development: Introduction: Special Section: Sibling, family relationships and child development. *Journal of Family Psychology,* **8,** 251–253.

Hetherington, E. M. (1999). Should we stay together for the sake of the children? In E. M. Hetherington (Ed.), *Coping with divorce, single parenting and remarriage: A risk and resiliency perspective*. Mahwah, NJ: Erlbaum.

Hetherington, E. M., Bridges, M., & Insabella, G. M. (1998). What matters? What does not? Five perspectives on the association between marital transitions and children's adjustment. *American Psychologist, 53,* 167–184.

Hetherington, E. M., & Clingempeel, W. G. (1992). Coping with marital transitions: A family systems perspective. *Monographs of the Society for Research in Child Development,* **57** *(2–3, Serial No. 227)*.

Hetherington, E. M., Cox, M., & Cox, R. (1982). Effects of divorce on parents and children. In M. E. Lamb (Ed.), *Nontraditional families*. Hillsdale, NJ: Erlbaum.

Hetherington, E. M., Cox, M., & Cox, R. (1985). Long-term effects of divorce and remarriage on the adjustment of children. *Journal of the American Academy of Child Psychology and Psychiatry,* **24,** 518–539.

Hetherington, E. M., Hagan, M. S., & Eisenberg, M. M. (1992). *Family Interaction Global Coding System*. Unpublished manuscript, University of Virginia.

Hetherington, E. M., & Henderson, S. H. (1997). Fathers in stepfamilies. The role of the father in child development. In M. E. Lamb (Ed.), *The role of the father in child development*. New York: John Wiley & Sons.

Hetherington, E. M., & Jodl, K. M. (1994). Stepfamilies as settings for child development. In A. Booth & J. Dunn (Eds.), *Stepfamilies: Who benefits? Who does not?* Hillsdale, NJ: Lawrence Erlbaum.

Hetherington, E. M., & Stanley-Hagan, M. S. (1995). Parenting in divorced and remarried families. In M. Bornstein (Ed.), *Handbook of parenting*. Hillsdale, NJ: Lawrence Erlbaum.

Hetherington, E. M., & Stanley-Hagan, M. S. (1997). The effects of divorce on fathers and their children. In M. Bornstein (Ed.), *The role of the father in child development*. New York: John Wiley.

Hobart, C. (1988). The family system in remarriage: An exploratory study. *Journal of Family Issues,* **8,** 259–277.

Hoffman, L. W. (1989). Effects of maternal employment in the two-parent family. *American Psychologist,* **44,** 283–292.

Hops, H., Biglan, A., Sherman, L., Arthur, J., Friedman, L., & Osteen, V. (1987). Home observations of family interactions of depressed women. *Journal of Consulting and Clinical Psychology,* **55,** 341–346.

Ihinger-Tallman, M. (1987). Sibling and step sibling bonding in stepfamilies. In K. Pasley & M. Ihinger-Tallman (Eds.), *Remarriage and stepparenting today: Current research and theory.* New York: Guilford.

Jacobson, D. S. (1987). Family type, visiting and children's behavior in the stepfamily: A linked family system. In K. Pasley & M. Ihinger-Tallman (Eds.), *Remarriage and stepparenting today: Current research and theory.* New York: Guilford.

Jessor, R., & Jessor, S. L. (1977). *Problem behavior and psycho-social development.* New York: Academic Press.

Johnson, D. R., Amoloza, T. O., & Booth, A. (1992). Stability and developmental change in marital quality: A three-wave panel analysis. *Journal of Marriage and the Family,* **54,** 582–594.

Johnson, S. L., & Jacob, T. (1997). Marital interactions of depressed men and women. *Journal of Consulting and Clinical Psychology,* **65,** 15–23.

Joreskog, K. G., & Sorbom, S. D. (1993). *LISREL 8.12* [Computer software]. Chicago, IL: Scientific Software International, Inc.

Karney, B. R., & Bradbury, T. N. (1995). The longitudinal course of marital quality and stability: A review of theory, methods and research. *Psychological Bulletin,* **118,** 3–34.

Kazdin, A. E. (1997). Conduct disorder across the life-span. In S. S. Luthar, J. A. Burack, D. Cicchetti, & J. R. Weisz (Eds.), *Developmental psychopathology: Perspectives on adjustment, risk and disorder.* Cambridge, UK: Cambridge University Press.

Kelly, E. L., & Conley, J. J. (1987). Personality and compatibility: A prospective analysis of marital stability and marital satisfaction. *Journal of Personality and Social Psychology,* **52,** 27–40.

Kelly, P. (1992). Healthy stepfamily functioning. *Journal of Contemporary Human Services,* **73,** 579–587.

Kerig, P. K., Cowan, P. A., & Cowan, C. P. (1993). Marital quality and gender differences in parent-child interactions. *Developmental Psychology,* **29,** 931–939.

Kovacs, M. (1985). The Children's Depression Inventory (CDI). *Psychopharmacology Bulletin,* **4,** 995–998.

Kurdek, L. A. (1991). Predictors of increases in marital distress in newlywed couples: A 3-year prospective longitudinal study. *Developmental Psychology,* **27,** 627–636.

Kurdek, L. A. (1994). Remarriages and stepfamilies are not inherently problematic. In A. Booth & J. Dunn (Eds.), *Stepfamilies: Who benefits? Who does not?* Hillsdale, NJ: Erlbaum.

Kurdek, L. A. (1995a). Developmental changes in marital satisfaction: A 6-year prospective longitudinal study of newlywed couples. In T. N. Bradbury (Ed.), *The developmental course of marital dysfunction.* New York: Cambridge University Press.

Kurdek, L. A. (1995b). Predicting change in marital satisfaction from husbands' and wives' conflict resolution styles. *Journal of Marriage and the Family,* **57,** 1–112.

Kurdek, L. A. (1996). Parenting satisfaction in mothers and fathers with young children. *Journal of Family Psychology,* **10,** 331–342.

Kurdek, L. A. (1998). The nature and predictors of the trajectory of change in marital quality over the first 4 years of marriage for first-married husbands and wives. *Journal of Family Psychology,* **12,** 494–510.

Kurdek, L. A., & Fine, M. A. (1993a). Parent and nonparent residential family members as providers of warmth, support and supervision to young adolescents. *Journal of Family Psychology, 7,* 245–249.

Kurdek, L. A., & Fine, M. A. (1993b). The relation between family structure and young adolescents' appraisals of family climate and parenting behavior. *Journal of Family Issues,* **14,** 279–290.

Kurdek, L. A., Fine, M. A., & Sinclair, R. J. (1994). The relation between parenting transitions and adjustment in young adolescents: A multisample investigation. *Journal of Early Adolescence,* **14,** 412–431.

Kurdek, L. A., Fine, M. A., & Sinclair, R. J. (1995). School adjustment in sixth graders: Parenting transitions, family climate, and peer norm effects. *Child Development,* **66,** 430–445.

Lamb, M. E. (1977, June). *The relationships between mothers, fathers, infants, and siblings in the first two years of life.* Paper presented at the biennial conference of the International Society for the Study of Behavioural Development, Pavia, Italy.

Larson, J. H., & Allgood, S. M. (1987). A comparison of intimacy in first married and remarried couples. *Journal of Family Issues,* **8,** 319–331.

Lee, V. E., Burkham, D. T., Zimiles, H., & Ladewski, B. (1994). Family structure and its effect on behavioral and emotional problems in young adolescents. *Journal of Research on Adolescence,* **4,** 405–437.

Levy-Shiff, R., Goldschmidt, I., & Har-Even, D. (1991). Transition to parenthood in adoptive families. *Developmental Psychology,* **27,** 131–140.

Lewinsohn, P. M., Roberts, R. E., Seeley, J. R., Rohde, P., Gotlib, I., & Hops, H. (1994). Adolescent psychopathology: II. Psychosocial risk factors for depression. *Journal of Abnormal Psychology,* **103,** 302–315.

Lindner-Gunnoe, M. (1993). *Noncustodial mothers' and fathers' contributions to the adjustment of adolescent stepchildren.* Unpublished doctoral dissertation, University of Virginia.

Locke, H. J., & Wallace, K. M. (1987). Marital Adjustment Test. In N. Fredman and R. Sherman (Eds.), *Handbook of measurements for marriage and family therapy.* New York: Bunner/Mazel.

Loeber, R., & Stouthamer-Loeber, M. (1998). The development of juvenile aggression and violence: Some common misperceptions and controversies. *American Psychologist,* **53,** 242–259.

Loehlin, J. C. (1992). *Latent variable models: An introduction to factor, path, and structural analysis.* Hillsdale, NJ: Lawrence Erlbaum.

Lytton, H., Singh, J. K., & Gallagher, L. (1995). Parenting twins. In M. H. Bornstein (Ed.), *Handbook of parenting* (Vol. 3). Hillsdale, NJ: Lawrence Erlbaum.

Maccoby, E. E. & Mnookin, R. H. (1992). *Dividing the child: Social and legal dilemmas of custody.* Cambridge, MA: Harvard University Press.

MacDonald, W. L., & DeMaris, A. (1996). Parenting stepchildren and biological children: The effects of stepparents' gender and new biological children. *Journal of Family Issues,* **17,** 5–25.

Markman, H. J., & Hahlweg, K. (1993). The prediction and prevention of marital distress: An international perspective. *Clinical Psychology Review,* **13,** 29–43.

Masten, A. S. & Coatsworth, J. D. (1998). The development of competence in favorable and unfavorable environments: Lessons from research on successful children. *American Psychologist,* **53,** 205–220.

Mathjjisen, J. J., Koot, H. M., Verhulst, F. C., DeBryn, E. E., & Oud, J. H. (1998). The relationship between marital family relations and child psychopathology. *Journal of Child Psychology and Psychiatry and Allied Disciplines,* **39**(4), 477–487.

Matthews, L. S., Wickrama, K. A., & Conger, R. D. (1996). Predicting marital instability from spouse and observer reports of marital interaction. *Journal of Marriage and the Family,* **58,** 641–655.

McArdle, J. J., & Nesselroade, J. R. (1994). Using multivariate data to structure developmental change. In S. H. Cohen & H. W. Reese (Eds.), *Life-span developmental psychology: Methodological contributions.* Hillsdale, NJ: Lawrence Erlbaum.

McGoldrick, M., & Carter, E. A. (1989). Forming a remarried family. In E. A. Carter & M. McGoldrick (Eds.), *The family cycle: A framework for family therapy.* New York: Gardner.

McGue, M., & Lykken, D. T. (1992). Genetic influence on risk of divorce. *Psychological Science,* **6,** 368–373.

McLanahan, S. S. (1999). Father absence and the welfare of children. In E. M. Hetherington (Ed.), *Coping with divorce, single parenting and remarriage: A risk and resiliency perspective.* Hillsdale, NJ: Lawrence Erlbaum.

McLanahan, S. S., & Bumpass, L. (1988). Intergenerational consequences of family disruption. *American Journal of Sociology,* **94,** 130–152.

McLanahan, S. S., & Sandefur, G. (1994). *Growing up with a single parent: What hurts, what helps.* Cambridge, MA: Harvard University Press.

McLeod, J. D., & Eckberg, D. A., (1993). Concordance of depressive disorders and marital quality. *Journal of Marriage and the Family,* **55,** 733–746.

McLloyd, V. (1998). Socioeconomic disadvantage and child development. *American Psychologist,* **53,** 185–204.

Mekos, D., Hetherington, E. M., & Reiss, D. (1996). Sibling differences in problem behavior and parental treatment in nondivorced and remarried families. *Child Development,* **67,** 2148–2165.

Meyer, D. R., & Garasky, S. (1993). Custodial fathers: Myths, realities, and child support policy. *Journal of Marriage and the Family,* **55,** 73–89.

Miller, N., Cowan, P., Cowan, C., Hetherington, E. M., and Clingempeel, W. G. (1993). Externalizing in preschool and early adolescents: A cross-study replication of a family model. *Developmental Psychology,* **29,** 3–18.

Mills, D. (1984). A model for stepfamily development. *Family Relations,* **33,** 365–372.

Minuchin, P. (1985). Families and individual development: Provocations from the field of family therapy. *Child Development,* **56,** 289–302.

Mitchell, A. S. (1998). *The nature of sibling relationships in adolescence: A sequential analysis of verbal and nonverbal behaviors in twins and non-twins.* Unpublished master's thesis, University of Virginia, Charlottesville.

Moffitt, T. E. (1993). Adolescence-limited and life-course-persistent antisocial behavior: A developmental taxonomy. *Psychological Review,* **100,** 674–701.

Morrison, P., & Masten, A. (1991). Peer reputation in middle childhood as a predictor of adaptation in adolescence: A seven-year-follow-up. *Child Development,* **62,** 991–1007.

O'Connor, T. G., Hawkins, N., Dunn, J., Thorpe, K., & Golding, J. (1998). Family type and maternal depression in pregnancy: Factors mediating risk in a community sample. *Journal of Marriage and the Family,* **60,** 757–770.

O'Connor, T. G., Hetherington, E. M., & Reiss, D. (1998). Family systems and adolescent development. Shared and nonshared risk and protective factors in nondivorced and remarried families. *Development and Psychopathology,* **10,** 353–375.

O'Leary, K. D., Christian, J. L., & Mendell, N. R. (1994). A closer look at the link between marital discord and depressive symptomatology. *Journal of Social and Clinical Psychology,* **13,** 33–41.

Orme, J. G., Reis, J., & Herz, E. J. (1986). Factorial and discriminant validity of the Center for Epidemiological Studies Depression (CES-D) scale. *Journal of Clinical Psychology,* **42,** 28–33.

Papernow, P. (1993). *Becoming a stepfamily: Patterns of development in remarried families*. New York: Gardner.

Pasley, K., & Ihinger-Tallman, M. (1988). Remarriage and stepfamilies. In C. S. Chilman, E. W. Nunnally, & F. M. Cox (Eds.), *Variant family forms. Families in trouble series, 5*. Newbury Park, CA: Sage.

Patterson, G. R. (1982). *Coercive family process*. Eugene, OR: Castalia.

Patterson, G. R. (1984). Siblings: Fellow travelers in coercive family processes. In R. J. Blanchard & D. C. Blanchard (Eds.), *Advances in the study of aggression* (Vol. 1). Orlando, FL: Academic Press.

Patterson, G. R., DeBaryshe, B. D., & Ramsey, E. (1989). A developmental perspective on antisocial behavior. *American Psychologist, 44,* 329–335.

Patterson, G. R., Reid, J. B., & Dishion, T. J. (1992). *Antisocial boys*. Eugene, OR: Castalia.

Patterson, G. R., & Stouthamer-Loeber, M. (1984). The correlation of family management practices and delinquency. *Child Development, 55,* 1299–1307.

Perry-Jenkins, M., & Folk, F. (1994). Class, couples, and conflict: Effects of the division of labor on assessment of marriage in dual-earner families. *Journal of Marriage and the Family, 56,* 165–180.

Phares, V., & Compas, B. E. (1992). The role of fathers in child and adolescent psycho-pathology: Make room for daddy. *Psychological Bulletin, 111,* 387–412.

Pina, D. L., & Bengtson, V. L. (1993). The division of household labor and wives' happiness: Ideology, employment, and perceptions of support. *Journal of Marriage and the Family, 55,* 901–912.

Pleck, J. H. (1985). *Working wives, working husbands*. Beverly Hills, CA: Sage.

Plomin, R., Reiss, D., Hetherington, E. M., & Howe, G. (1994). Nature and nurture: Genetic influence on measures of the family environment. *Developmental Psychology, 30,* 32–43.

Powell, J. L. (1993). *Describing the "Twin Situation": A comparison of twin and nontwin sibling relationships*. Unpublished honors thesis, University of Virginia, Charlottesville.

Radke-Yarrow, M., Richters, J., & Wilson, W. E. (1988). Child development in a network of relationships. In R. A. Hinde & J. Stevenson-Hinde (Eds.), *Relationships within families: Mutual influences*. New York: Oxford University Press.

Radloff, L. S. (1977). The CES-D scale: A self-report depression scale for research in the general population. *Applied Psychological Measurement, 1,* 385–401.

Radloff, L. S., & Teri, L. (1986). Use of the Center for Epidemiological Studies–Depression scale with older adults. *Clinical Gerontologist, 5,* 119–136.

Raykov, T., Tomer, A., & Nesselroade, J. R. (1991). Reporting structural equation modeling results in psychology and aging: Some proposed guidelines. *Psychology and Aging, 6,* 499–503.

Reiss, D. (1997). Mechanisms linking genetic and social influences in adolescent development: Beginning a collaborative search. *Current Directions in Psychological Science, 6,* 100–105.

Reiss, D., Hetherington, E. M., Plomin, R., Howe, G. W., Simmens, S. J., Henderson, S. H., O'Connor, T. J., Bussell, D. A., Anderson, E. R., & Law, T. (1995). Genetic questions for environmental studies: Differential parenting and psychopathology in adolescence. *Archives of General Psychiatry, 52,* 925–936.

Reiss, D., Neiderheiser, J., Hetherington, E. M., & Plomin, R. (in press). *The relationship code: Deciphering genetic and social patterns in adolescent development*. Cambridge, MA: Harvard University Press.

Reiss, D., Plomin, R., Hetherington, E. M., Howe, G. W., Rovine, M. J., Tryon, A., & Hagan, M. S. (1994). The separate worlds of teenage siblings: An introduction to the study of the nonshared environment and adolescent development. In E. M. Hetherington &

D. Reiss (Eds.), *Separate social worlds of siblings: The impact of nonshared environment on development*. Hillsdale, NJ: Lawrence Erlbaum.

Rosenberg, E. B., & Hajfal, F. (1985). Step sibling relationships in remarried families. Social casework. *The Journal of Contemporary Social Work*, **661**, 287–292.

Ross, C., Mirowsky, J., & Huber, J. (1983). Dividing work, sharing work and in between. *American Sociological Review*, **48**, 809–823.

Rossi, A. S., & Rossi, P. H. (1990). *Of human bonding: Parent-child relations across the life course*. Hawthorne, NY: Aldine de Gruyter.

Rovine, M. J. (1994). Estimating nonshared environment using sibling discrepancy scores. In E. M. Hetherington, D. Reiss, & R. Plomin (Eds.), *Separate social worlds of siblings: The impact of nonshared environment on development*. Hillsdale, NJ: Lawrence Erlbaum.

Rowe, D. C., & Gulley, B. L. (1992). Sibling effects on substance use and delinquency. *Criminology*, **30**, 213–233.

Rowe, D. C., Rodgers, J. L., & Meseck-Bushey, S. (1992). Sibling delinquency and the family environment: Shared and unshared influences. *Child Development*, **63**, 59–67.

Rowe, D. C., Rodgers, J. L., Meseck-Bushey, S., & St. John, C. (1989). Sexual behavior and nonsexual deviance: A sibling study of their relationship. *Developmental Psychology*, **25**, 61–69.

Russell, D. E. (1984). The prevalence and seriousness of incestuous abuse: Stepfathers vs. biological fathers. *Child Abuse and Neglect*, **8**, 15–22.

Rutter, N., & Redshaw, J. (1991). Annotation: Growing up as a twin: Twin-singleton differences in psychological development. *Journal of Child Psychology and Psychiatry*, **32**, 885–895.

Samuels, H. R. (1977, March). *The role of the sibling in the infant's social environment*. Paper presented at the biennial meetings of the Society for Research in Child Development, New Orleans, LA.

Santrock, J. W., Sitterle, K. A., & Warshak, R. A. (1988). Parent-child relationships in stepfather families. In P. Bronson & C. P. Cowan (Eds.), *Contemporary fathers*. New York: Wiley.

Schacfei, E., & Edgerton, M. (1981). *The Sibling Inventory of Behavior*. Unpublished manuscript, University of North Carolina, Chapel Hill.

Schultz, N. C., Schultz, C. L., & Olson, D. H. (1991). Couple strengths and stressors in complex and simple stepfamilies in Australia. *Journal of Marriage and the Family*, **53**, 555–564.

Seltzer, J. A., & Bianchi, S. M. (1988). Children's contact with absent parents. *Journal of Marriage and the Family*, **50**, 663–677.

Sigafoos, A., Feinstein, C. B., Damond, M., & Reiss, D. (1988). The measurement of behavioral autonomy in adolescence: The Autonomous Functioning Checklist. *Adolescent Psychiatry*, **15**, 432–462.

Simons, R. L., & Associates. (1996). *Understanding differences between divorced and intact families: Stress, interaction, and child outcome*. Thousand Oaks, CA: Sage.

Simons, R. L., & Chao, W. (1996). Conduct problems. In R. Simons & Associates (Eds.), *Understanding differences between divorced and intact families: Stress, interaction, and child outcome*. Thousand Oaks, CA: Sage.

Simons, R. L., & Johnson, C. (1996). Mothers' parenting. In R. L. Simons & Associates (Eds.), *Understanding differences between divorced and intact families: Stress, interaction, and child outcome*. Thousand Oaks, CA: Sage.

Simons, R. L., Johnson, C., & Lorenz, F. O. (1996). Family structure differences in stress and behavioral predispositions. In R. Simons & Associates (Eds.), *Understanding differences between divorced and intact families: Stress, interaction, and child outcome*. Thousand Oaks, CA: Sage.

Simons, R. L., Lorenz, F. O., Wu, C., & Conger, R. D. (1993). Marital and spouse support as mediator and moderator of the impact of economic strain upon parenting. *Developmental Psychology, 29,* 368–381.

Skaggs, M. J. (1996). *Developmental change in competence perceptions of adolescents.* Unpublished master's thesis, University of Virginia, Charlottesville.

Smucker, M. R., Craighead, E. W., Craighead, L. W., & Green, B. J. (1986). Normative and reliability data for the Children's Depression Inventory. *Journal of Abnormal Child Psychology,* **14**(1), 25–39.

Spanier, G. B., & Furstenberg, Jr., F. F. (1982). Remarriage after divorce: A longitudinal analysis of well-being. *Journal of Marriage and the Family,* **44**(3), 709–720.

Steinberg, L. (1989). Pubertal maturation and family relations: Evidence for the distancing hypothesis. In G. R. Adams, R. Montemayor, & T. P. Gulotta (Eds.), *Advances in adolescent development.* Beverly Hills, CA: Sage.

Steinberg, L., Mounts, N., Lamborn, S., & Dornbusch, S. (1991). Authoritative parenting and adolescent adjustment across various ecological niches. *Journal of Research on Adolescence,* **1,** 19–36.

Steinberg, L., & Silverberg, S. B. (1986). The vicissitudes of autonomy in early adolescence. *Child Development,* **57,** 841–851.

Stipek, D., & Daniels, D. (1990). Children's use of dispositional attributes in predicting the performance and behavior of classmates. *Journal of Applied Developmental Psychology,* **11,** 13–28.

Stocker, C. M. (1995). Differences in mothers' and fathers' relationships with siblings: Links with children's behavior problems. *Development and Psychopathology,* **7,** 499–512.

Straus, M. A. (1979). Measuring intrafamily conflict and violence: The Conflict Tactics (CT) Scales. *Journal of Marriage and the Family,* **41,** 75–88.

Suitor, J. J. (1991). Marital quality and satisfaction with the division of household labor across the family cycle. *Journal of Marriage and the Family,* **53,** 221–230.

Sweet, I. A., & Bumpass, L. A. (1987). *American families and households.* New York: Russell Sage Foundation.

Tanaka, J. S., & Westerman, M. A. (1988). Common dimensions in the assessment of competence in school-aged girls. *Journal of Educational Psychology,* **80,** 579–584.

Tejerina-Allen, M., Wagner, B. M., & Cohen, P. (1994). A comparison of across-family and within-family parenting predictors of adolescent psychopathology and suicidal ideation. In E. M. Hetherington, D. Reiss, & R. Plomin (Eds.), *Separate social worlds of siblings: Impact of nonshared environment on development.* Hillsdale, NJ: Erlbaum.

Thoits, P. A. (1992). Identity structures and psychological well-being: Gender and marital status comparisons. *Social Psychology Quarterly,* **55,** 236–256.

Thomson, E., McLanahan, S. S., & Curtin, R. B. (1992). Family structure, gender and parent socialization. *Journal of Marriage and the Family,* **54,** 368–78.

Thompson, L. (1991). Family work: Women's sense of fairness. *Journal of Family Issues,* **12,** 181–196.

Thompson, L., & Walker, A. J. (1989). Gender in families: Women and men in marriage, work and parenthood. *Journal of Marriage and the Family,* **51,** 845–871.

Tzeng, J. M., & Mare, R. D. (1995). Labor market and socioeconomic effects on marital stability. *Social Science Research,* **24,** 329–351.

U.S. Bureau of the Census. (1995). Statistical abstract of the United States: 1995 (115th ed.). Washington, DC: U.S. Government Printing Office.

Visher, E. B., & Visher, J. S. (1978). Major areas of difficulty for stepparent couples. *American Journal of Family Therapy,* **6,** 70–80.

Visher, E. B., & Visher, J. S. (1988). *Old loyalties, new ties: Therapeutic strategies with stepfamilies.* New York: Brunner/Mazel.

Visher, E. B., & Visher, J. S. (1990). Dynamics of successful stepfamilies. *Journal of Divorce and Remarriage, 14*, 3–11.

Vuchinich, S., Hetherington, E. M., Vuchinich, R. A., & Clingempeel, W. G. (1991). Parent and child interaction and gender differences in early adolescents' adaptation to stepfamilies. *Developmental Psychology, 27*, 618–626.

Waldren, T. E. (1986). *A multivariate comparison of dimensions of family functioning for first married and remarried families.* Unpublished doctoral dissertation, Department of Home Economics, Texas Tech University.

Walker, K. N., & Messinger, L. (1979). Remarriage after divorce: Dissolution and reconstruction of family boundaries. *Family Process, 18*, 185–191.

Walsh, W. M. (1992). Twenty major issues in remarriage families. *Journal of Counseling and Development, 70*, 709–715.

Ward, R. A. (1993). Marital happiness and household equity in later life. *Journal of Marriage and the Family, 55*, 427–438.

Weiss, R. S. (1979). Growing up a little faster: The experience of growing up in a single-parent household. *Journal of Social Issues, 35*, 97–111.

Werner, E. E. (1993). Risk, resilience and recovery: Perspectives from the Kauai Longitudinal Study. *Development and Psychopathology, 54*, 503–515.

Whitbeck, L. B., Simons, R. L., & Goldberg, F. (1996). Adolescent sexual intercourse. In R. Simons & Associates (Eds.), *Understanding differences between divorced and intact families: Stress, interaction and child outcome.* Thousand Oaks, CA: Sage.

White, L. K. (1994). Stepfamilies over the life course: Social support. In A. Booth & J. Dunn (Eds.), *Stepfamilies: Who benefits? Who does not?* Hillsdale, NJ: Lawrence Erlbaum.

White, L. K., & Booth, A. (1985). The quality and stability of remarriages: The role of stepchildren. *American Sociological Review, 50*, 689–698.

White, L. K., & Reidmann, A. (1992). When the Brady Bunch grows up: Step, half and full sibling relationships in adulthood. *Journal of Marriage and the Family, 54*, 197–208.

Whitsett, D., & Land, H. (1992). The development of a role strain index for stepparents. *The Journal of Contemporary Human Services, 73*, 14–22.

Wierson, M., Armistead, L., Forehand, R., Thomas, A. M., & Fauber, R. (1990). Parent-adolescent conflict and stress as a parent: Are there differences between being a mother or a father? *Journal of Family Violence, 5*, 187–197.

Wierzbicki, M., & McCabe, M. (1988). Social skills and subsequent depressive symptomatology in children. *Journal of Clinical Child Psychology, 17*, 203–208.

Wilson, B. F., & Clarke, S. C. (1992). Remarriages: A demographic profile. *Journal of Family Issues, 13*, 123–141.

Wilson, M. I., Daly, M., & Weghorst, S. J. (1980). Household composition and the risk of child abuse and neglect. *Journal of Biosocial Science, 12*, 333–340.

Zill, N. (1985). *Behavior problems scales developed from the 1981 Child Health Supplement to the National Health Interview Survey.* Washington, DC: Child Trends, Inc.

Zill, N. (1988). Behavior, achievement, and health problems among children in stepfamilies. In E. M. Hetherington & J. D. Arasteh (Eds.), *Impact of divorce, single parenting, and stepparenting on children.* Hillsdale, NJ: Lawrence Erlbaum.

Zill, N. (1994). Understanding why children in stepfamilies have more learning and behavior problems than children in nuclear families. In A. Booth & J. Dunn (Eds.), *Stepfamilies: Who benefits? Who does not?* Hillsdale, NJ: Lawrence Erlbaum Associates.

Zill, N., Morrison, D. R., & Coiro, M. J. (1993). Long-term effects of parental divorce on parent-child relationships, adjustment, and achievement in young adulthood. *Journal of Family Psychology, 7*, 91–103.

Zill N., & Peterson, J. L. (1983, March). *Marital disruption, parent-child relationships, and behavior problems in children*. Paper presented at the meeting of the Society for Research in Child Development, Detroit.

Zimiles, H., & Lee, V. E. (1991). Adolescent family structure and educational progress. *Developmental Psychology, 27,* 314–320.

ACKNOWLEDGMENTS

This research was supported by grants from the National Institute of Mental Health and the Grant Foundation. The Nonshared Environment in Adolescent Development Project (NEAD), from which the data in this *Monograph* were drawn, was initiated by David Reiss, Mavis Hetherington, and Robert Plomin, with the encouragement and support of Joy Schulterbrandt, who was at that time the chief of the Behavioral Sciences Section at NIMH.

So many other individuals played critical and important roles in this endeavor that it is not possible to list them by name. The grant was a multisite grant and involved graduate students and support staff at Pennsylvania State University, George Washington University Medical School, and the University of Virginia. At the University of Virginia alone, where the observational coding was done, over 50 undergraduates and 18 graduate students were involved in the project. Special thanks are extended to the graduate students who labored through multiple revisions of this *Monograph* and to our reviewers, who provided thoughtful and constructive critiques. This research project was a group effort, in which graduate students, undergraduates, project coordinators, and senior investigators worked together as a collaborative team. It has been a privilege to have worked with and learned from such a gifted and dedicated group of young scholars.

Please address correspondence to E. Mavis Hetherington, Department of Psychology, Gilmer Hall, University of Virginia, Charlottesville, VA 22903-2477 or emh2f@virginia.edu.

STEPFAMILIES: THE INTERSECTION OF CULTURE, CONTEXT, AND BIOLOGY

James H. Bray

Stepfamilies are an old family structure that has undergone rapid change and increased in numbers during the past 25 years. Mavis Hetherington and her colleagues have set the standard for research on divorce and remarriage for the past 3 decades. Their current effort, "Adolescent Siblings in Stepfamilies," again raises the bar on research in this area and further enhances our understanding of the processes within stepfamilies and the impact they have on adolescents. This *Monograph* adds significantly to our understanding of mature, stable stepfamilies with adolescents. Their research confirms some of our long-standing clinical perspectives on stepfamilies (e.g., complex stepfamilies are more difficult) and challenges others (stepfamily processes are always different than nondivorced family processes). While this *Monograph* can stand on its own as an excellent contribution to our understanding of the effects of marital transitions on children, comparing and contrasting the results of this study with previous Hetherington studies and similarly designed research make this piece an invaluable link to understanding the processes and context of divorce and remarriage.

The richness of this work could easily yield several monographs of comment. This commentary will focus, however, on five areas: (1) nature and nurture issues, (2) deviance versus normative behavior in stepfamilies, (3) context and meaning in different types of families, (4) intersecting developmental trajectories, and (5) gender differences. I will draw upon work in the Developmental Issues in StepFamilies (DIS) Research Project (Bray, 1988a, 1988b; Bray & Berger, 1993; Bray & Kelly, 1998), which is a similarly designed longitudinal study of stepfamilies with children and adolescents.

Nature and Nuture Influences on Stepfamilies

A major contribution of this work is the authors' attempt to untangle the complex web of connections between family relations and biological influences. This study does this by including multiple kinds of stepfamilies with varying degrees of biological relatedness among family members. A conclusion drawn from this work is that the differences in (step)parent-(step)child relations are more a function of biological relatedness rather than family interactions or structure, with stepparents having less involved relations with stepchildren than parents with biological children. These findings give new meaning to the common occurrence in stepfamilies in which a stepchild says to a stepparent, "I don't have to do what you say because you are not my *real* dad (or mom)!" Furthermore, the findings indicate that stepparents may really be saying, "I don't have to deal with you because you are not my *real* child." It is difficult, however, to separate biology from family context and I argue that it is not necessarily possible to do so because of the implications for social policy that will be discussed later.

This study utilizes developmental and family systems theories to generate hypotheses about marital transitions. From systems perspectives, the issue of nature or biology versus nurture or social relations is an incorrect question, because a nondualistic (both/and), rather than a dualistic (either/or) viewpoint should be utilized. Most systems theorists, such as Bowen (1978), Minuchin (1984) and von Bertalanffy (1950), considered the entire range, from biological to cultural, in their systems theories. Many of our theories, research and clinical interventions have focused exclusively, however, on the psychosocial perspective and ignored or downplayed the role of biology. This is certainly the case when it comes to understanding and working with stepfamilies. As this *Monograph* points out, however, the realities of stepfamily life make it difficult to ignore one for the other, and clinicians and researchers alike need to consider both in future work.

The interpretation offered by the authors that biological relatedness is more important than family relations may have unintended social policy implications. Recent publications by Popenoe (1993, 1994) and others in biosocial bases of family life have once again brought to the fore the nature versus nurture controversy. The sociobiological argument (Daly & Wilson, 1983) indicates that animals are reproductive strategists who maximize the survival of their genes into the next generation by nurturing their biological offspring. As White (1994) stated, "there is no genetic predisposition to nurture another's children." In fact, nonbiological children may be seen as rivals who endanger one's own children's survival. Furthermore, a sociobiological perspective indicates that in addition to stepparent-stepchild conflict, when stepchildren become adolescents, they become sexual competitors to their parents. Thus, in stepfamilies with adolescents, stepfamilies with girls would

211

be the most problematic and unstable. This hypothesis was not supported by the present research.

Popenoe (1994) has taken a strong nature perspective and argues that biosocial theory dictates why certain types of families are more likely to have problems and other types to succeed. He concludes that social biology indicates that "a growing body of evidence suggests that the increase of step-families has created serious problems for child welfare" (p. 5) and therefore "we as a society should be doing much more to halt the growth of stepfamilies" (p. 21). Popenoe and others, however, ignore strong scientific evidence that less than 50% of behavior is explained by genetic and other biological factors and that the expression of such factors is always influenced by the social context of the person. This research, while examining biological relatedness, certainly points to the importance of both biological and psychosocial factors, and clearly indicates that *both* are critical factors in understanding adolescent adjustment and family relationships. Furthermore, it is clear from this and other research that stepfamilies can be a positive and safe place to raise children and adolescents.

Stepfamily Norms or Deviance?

Cherlin (1978) argues that stepfamilies are an incomplete institution because there are not clear social norms and expectations for them, and therefore stepfamilies are more likely to experience problems in relationships and have adverse outcomes. Many others who have argued the need for the development of stepfamily norms and understanding their unique developmental paths have echoed this viewpoint (Bray, 1994; Coleman & Ganong, 1990).

Two central questions arise from this perspective: (1) what is the appropriate comparison group for research on stepfamilies, and (2) are observed differences between stepfamilies and nonstepfamilies pathology/deviance or simply normative differences? Coleman and Ganong (1990) argue that the most appropriate comparison groups for research on stepfamilies *are not* nonstepfamilies (i.e., first-marriage nuclear families), but other types of stepfamilies or stepfamilies with and without identified problems. This really depends, however, on the question being asked. If the question concerns relative outcomes for children, then a comparison between children in different family structures is appropriate.

The question of whether observed differences in family relations between stepfamilies and nonstepfamlies are normative or deviant, however, still remains. It appears that the perspective taken in this *Monograph* is one of deviance. I argue that it should be one of normative difference and that one of the major contributions of this work is to help us understand and develop norms for stepfamilies. In order to make this argument, it is necessary to raise a methodological issue about interpreting the data from this study.

Most of the measures used in this study are based on nonclinical families and characteristics, such as warmth, parenting, and so on. This includes both the self-report measures and the behavioral ratings. While there are differences between family structure groups on various measures of family relations, they are relatively small and represent differences in a "normal range." There is no context provided to the reader, however, for interpreting the differences. There are several examples that illustrate this issue. Most of the studies using the Child Behavior Checklist (Achenbach & Edelbrock, 1983) find that children in stepfamilies have more externalizing problems and lower social competency than children in intact families (Bray & Berger, 1993; Hetherington & Clingempeel, 1992). The means for both groups of children, however, are in the "normal–nonclinical range." Thus, while stepchildren may act out a bit more, they are not suffering from a mental or behavioral disorder. In both the Bray and Hetherington studies, they found 70%–80% of children in stepfamilies functioned in the nonclinical range and only 20–30% were in the clinical range. This compares to about 85–90% of children in intact families functioning in the nonclinical range. Thus, the risk is double, but, again, most children in stepfamilies are functioning normally. A second example is the discussion about family process. Again, while there are often more negative and conflictual relationships in stepfamilies, as compared to nonstepfamilies, the means for *both* groups are in the positive range. Specifically, if you look at the behavioral ratings of the Hetherington and Bray studies, the scales are usually 1–5, with 5 being highly negative. Most of the means are in the 1 to 2 range for both types of families. Thus, it is not accurate to characterize stepfamilies as "negative, conflictual, and distant." If this is done, then the data will be misinterpreted by both scholars and social policy analysts.

The reliable differences found in this and other research do reflect normative characteristics of stepfamilies. While adults in stepfamilies develop satisfying and close marital relations, they tend to express their negative opinions with each other as rated on the videotapes of marital interactions. This may be a function of less effective communication skills, stress in the family, or based on their historical experience about what works in a marriage. Likewise, stepparents and stepchildren tend to have more distance and disagreements in their relationships. This may be a function of biological relatedness, less shared history with each other, or a psychological story that says that it should be that way. This research and, especially, the examination of relationships within the family help us understand that both biological relatedness and family psychosocial factors explain these normative differences. Furthermore, after stepfamilies have been together for 5 or more years, there are more similarities than differences in the ways in which families function and the processes that impact outcomes for adolescents. This further supports the clinical notion that many problems blamed on being in a stepfamily are simply common problems and issues faced by all families. In a clinical setting, this normative context often helps members of stepfamilies develop new solutions to problems.

Context and Meaning in Stepfamilies

The structural equation models (SEMs) that compared stepfamilies and nonstepfamilies provided useful but perplexing results. Most of the models indicated few family structure differences and suggest that marital relations, parenting, and sibling relationships operate similarly in nonstepfamilies and mature, stable stepfamilies. This suggests that, after a period of several years of initial adjustment, high quality parenting, good marital relations, and positive sibling relations are keys to positive outcomes for adolescents in all types of families. This was unexpected, since most research has indicated different relationship patterns in stepfamilies and nuclear families. It appears that in long-term stable stepfamilies, relationship patterns converge with those in nondivorced families (Bray & Kelly, 1998).

It is important to note that it takes *several years* and not several months, for these families to converge. One of the most problematic expectations in stepfamilies is the "nuclear family myth" (Bray & Kelly, 1998), in which members of stepfamilies use a first-marriage nuclear family model for their family. Comparing this research with other studies that examined stepfamilies in the initial years after remarriage (Bray & Berger, 1993; Hetherington & Clingempeel, 1992), it is clear that stepfamily relationships change over time and become more similar to family relationships in first-marriage families, although there are still some differences that were not examined in this study (such as nonresidential parent relationships).

The lack of fit for some of the measurement models for groups, however, raises perplexing questions and indicates that constructs may operate differently in different family groups. For example, in the DIS study, we found that, while there were few differences in levels of conflict in stepfamilies and first-marriage families, conflict was a much stronger predictor of child adjustment in stepfamilies. This may be due to members of stepfamilies interpreting questions differently than members of nonstepfamilies. Since the context is different, the meaning of interactions may be different, and additional work may be needed to insure that the measures are comparable across different groups (Baer & Bray, 1999). An argument in a stepfamily may raise the memory of an awful divorce and call into question the relationship or, alternatively, may not even be recognized as an argument (as in the difference between self-reports and behavioral observations), while in a first-marriage family it means something quite different. While Hetherington and colleagues are to be complimented on their attempts to model the data, perhaps they need to step back and examine possible differences in context and measurement. Such an examination would certainly yield valuable findings about how marital transitions impact the interpretation of family interactions and processes.

Intersecting Developmental Trajectories

Examining this research in light of previous work on newer stepfamilies with different-aged children points to the importance of considering the intersecting development and historical trajectories of individuals and families. Relationships in stepfamilies change over time and are affected by previous individual and family experiences, developmental issues within the stepfamily, and developmental issues for individual family members. Marital and family experiences during the first marriage, separation, and divorce may have a great impact on the functioning of the stepfamily (Bray & Berger, 1993; Hetherington, Cox, & Cox, 1982). Thus, the multiple developmental trajectories of family members and the stepfamily life cycle are important to consider in understanding the functioning of stepfamilies.

Forming a stepfamily with young children is likely to be different than forming a stepfamily with young adolescents, because of the differing developmental needs of children and adolescents (Bray, 1995). The stepfamily life cycle and individual developmental issues may be congruent, as in the case of a new stepfamily with young children, or may be quite divergent, as in the case of a new stepfamily with adolescents. The developmental issues are congruent in new stepfamilies with young children, because both the children and stepfamily need close, cohesive family relationships. The centripetal forces of stepfamily formation coincide with the need that young children have for affective involvement and structure. In the latter case, the stepfamily is moving to develop a cohesive unit, while the adolescents are moving to separate from the family. Adolescents want to be *less* cohesive and more separate from the family unit as they struggle with identity formation and separation from the family of origin. In this case, the developmental needs of the adolescent are at odds with the developmental push of the new stepfamily for closeness and bonding. Stepfamilies are usually less cohesive than first-marriage nuclear families, although their ideal levels of cohesion are usually similar to nuclear families (Bray & Berger, 1993; Pink & Wampler, 1985).

Where Have All the Gender Differences Gone?

Previous research on the effects of divorce and remarriage indicated that boys and girls had different experiences and outcomes through their parents' marital transitions. Boys seemed to have a more difficult time with parental divorce (Hetherington et al., 1982), while younger girls had a more difficult adjustment to parental remarriage (Hetherington, 1993). This study examined gender differences and found that, while boys and girls differ in their behavioral adjustment, it is quite similar in stepfamilies and nonstepfamilies. The lack of gender differences is on the one hand puzzling, but also confirms clinical experience that adolescents are converging in their expression of problem behavior. The potential for "stepdaughter wars" that was found for stepfamilies with younger children does not appear to happen for adolescents in stepfamilies.

The lack of differences may be due to the type of stepfamilies studied, namely mature, stable stepfamilies. These families have transitioned through the initial adjustment phase and have developed stable and workable patterns. in fact, the stability of the relationships across time far overshadowed any changes in relationships and outcomes. Furthermore, the SEM models indicate that marital and parenting factors have less direct effects on adolescent adjustment. Thus, the lack of differences may be due to other factors, such as peer and school influences, rather than within-family factors.

In addition, the lack of differences may indicate the focus on normative adjustment and development, rather than other areas of potential differences. Previous research has indicated that there are potential gender differences in several areas that were not examined in this study. These include a higher incidence of sexual abuse of girls in stepfamilies, a higher incidence of runaways or dropping out of school for boys in stepfamilies, and boys more likely to change custody from mothers to fathers during adolescence (Bray & Kelly, 1998).

From a prevention and clinical intervention standpoint, the lack of gender differences is a positive outcome. This suggests that similar prevention and intervention programs can be developed and the target of these programs needs to be both the parents *and siblings*. While family therapists usually include all members of the family, most prevention programs tend to focus on parenting skills or an identified adolescent, and ignore the possible influence of sibling relationships. This research clearly points to the importance of including both biological siblings and stepsiblings.

There are three final points to consider. First, Hetherington suggests that clinicians should consider using measures from this study in their work with families. I strongly concur. Normative research with clinical and nonclinical families with these instruments is essential, however, before they can be directly applied in clinical settings. Research on the Minnesota Multiphasic Personality Instrument (MMPI) is a good example of this. The basic scales of the MMPI have very different meanings when they are in the normative range versus when they are in the clinical range. At this point, we have very little data about the use of these measures and observation systems with clinical stepfamilies, although initial reports indicate that they may be useful (Bray, 1992).

Second, Hetherington and colleagues are correct to point out that this and most other research on stepfamilies has been conducted on White, middle-class families. While having similar samples makes it easier to compare across studies, the external validity and application of these findings to families from other ethnic and socioeconomic backgrounds is greatly limited. For example, in African American families, it is quite common to have biologically unrelated people be considered important family members. Thus, we can only speculate if the findings about biological relatedness would hold true in these types of families. Furthermore, one would wonder if the differences in stepfather-stepchild relationships would be even greater in Hispanic families, in which biological family relationships are emphasized. These and other potential ethnic differences remain for future research.

Finally, it is important to remember that the data used in this *Monograph* come from a larger project designed to examine the interrelations between family interactions, family environment, and sociobiological influences on adolescent adjustment and development. While the focus of this *Monograph* was on the within-family relationships of parenting, marriage, and siblings, this work reveals important questions about the extended stepfamily system. Many potential extended family and other outside influences exist and are important for adolescent adjustment. We eagerly await publications on these aspects of family relationships.

The field is again indebted to Dr. Hetherington and her team for studying a very difficult and complex developmental phenomenon and doing so in a rigorous and comprehensive manner. This research has increased our understanding of not only the dynamics and outcomes for adolescents in stepfamilies, but also enhanced our general understanding of intrafamilial relationships in all kinds of families.

REFERENCES

Achenbach, T. M., & Edelbrock, C. S. (1983). *Manual for the Behavior Checklist and Revised Child Behavior Profile.* Burlington, VT: University of Vermont, Child Psychiatry.

Baer, P. E., & Bray, J. H. (1999). Adolescent individuation and alcohol usage. *Journal of Studies on Alcohol,* **13,** 52–62.

Bowen, M. (1978). *Family therapy in clinical practice.* New York: Jason Aronson.

Bray, J. H. (1988a). Children's development during early remarriage. In E. M. Hetherington & J. Arasteh (Eds.), *The impact of divorce, single-parenting and step-parenting on children*. Hillsdale, NJ: Lawrence Erlbaum..

Bray, J. H. (1988b). *Developmental Issues in StepFamilies Research Project: Final Report (Grant Number RO1 HD18025)*. Bethesda, MD: National Institute of Child Health and Human Development.

Bray, J. H. (1992). Family relationships and children's adjustment in clinical and nonclinical stepfather families. *Journal of Family Psychology, 6,* 60–68.

Bray, J. H. (1994). What does a typical stepfamily look like? *The Family Journal, 2,* 66–69.

Bray, J. H. (1995). Family oriented treatment of stepfamilies. In R. Mikesell, D. D. Lusterman, & S. McDaniel (Eds.), *Integrating family therapy: Handbook of family psychology and systems therapy*. Washington, DC: American Psychological Association.

Bray, J. H., & Berger, S. H. (1993). Developmental issues in stepfamilies research project: Family relationships and parent-child interactions. *Journal of Family Psychology, 7,* 76–90.

Bray, J. H., & Kelly, J. (1998). *StepFamilies: Love, marriage, and parenting in the first decade*. New York: Broadway Books.

Cherlin, A. J. (1978). Remarriage as an incomplete institution. *American Journal of Sociology, 84,* 634–650.

Coleman, M., & Ganong, L. H. (1990). Remarriage and stepfamily research in the 1980s: Increased interest in an old family form. *Journal of Marriage and the Family, 52,* 925–940.

Daly, M., & Wilson, M. (1983). *Sex, evolution, and behavior* (2nd ed.). Belmont, CA: Wadsworth.

Hetherington, E. M. (1993). An overview of the Virginia longitudinal study of divorce and remarriage. *Journal of Family Psychology, 7,* 39–56.

Hetherington, E. M., & Clingempeel, W. G. (1992). Coping with marital transitions: A family systems perspective. *Monographs of the Society for Research in Child Development, 57*(2–3, Serial No. 227).

Hetherington, E. M., Cox, M., & Cox, R. (1982). Effects of divorce on parents and children. In M. E. Lamb (Ed.), *Nontraditional families: Parenting and child development*. Hillsdale, NJ: Lawrence Erlbaum.

Minuchin, S. (1984). *Family kaleidoscope*. Cambridge: Harvard University Press.

Pink, J. T., & Wampler, K. S. (1985). Problem areas in stepfamilies: Cohesion, adaptability, and the stepfather-adolescent relationship. *Family Relations, 34,* 327–335.

Popenoe, D. (1993). American family decline, 1960–1990: A review and appraisal. *Journal of Marriage and the Family, 55,* 527–542.

Popenoe, D. (1994). The evolution of marriage and the problem of stepfamilies: A biosocial perspective. In A. Booth and J. Dunn (Eds.), *Stepfamilies: Who benefits? who does not?* Hillsdale, NJ: Lawrence Erlbaum.

von Bertalanffy, L. (1950). An outline of General System Theory. *British Journal of Philosophy of Science, 1,* 134–165.

White, L. (1994). Stepfamilies over the life course: Social support. In A. Booth and J. Dunn (Eds.), *Stepfamilies: Who benefits? Who does not?* Hillsdale, NJ: Lawrence Erlbaum.

E. Mavis Hetherington (Ph.D. 1958, University of California, Berkeley) is the James M. Page Professor of Psychology at the University of Virginia. She has been president of the Society for Research in Child Development and the Society for Research on Adolescence and editor of *Child Development*. She has written over 200 papers and is author or editor of about a dozen books or monographs. Her main research interests are in vulnerability and resiliency in children and families coping with stressful life experiences, with a focus on divorce, single-parent families, and stepfamilies. Numerous professional organizations have recognized her research contributions by awarding her their Distinguished Scientist Award, including the American Psychological Society, the Society for Research in Child Development, the Society for Research in Adolescence, the American Association for Marriage and Family Therapy, and the Association on Family and Conciliation Courts.

Sandra H. Henderson (Ph.D. 1991, Catholic University) was the Project Director for the Nonshared Environment in Adolescent Development (NEAD) project at the University of Virginia. She is currently investigating coparenting and child adjustment in nontraditional families at Virginia Commonwealth University. Her research interests include child psychopathology, parent-child relationships, and family process.

David Reiss (M.D. 1962, Harvard University Medical School) is Professor of Psychiatry and Behavioral Sciences and of Psychology in the Department of Psychiatry and Behavioral Sciences at The George Washington University Medical Center. He completed the psychiatry residency program at Massachusetts Mental Health Center in Boston. Dr. Reiss is the current editor of the journal *Psychiatry: Interpersonal and Biological Processes*. He has received many distinguished research awards, including the coveted NIMH Merit Award. His publications are numerous, spanning the areas of family process and therapy, and, over the past decade, genetic and environmental influences in developing psychopathology.

Edward R. Anderson (Ph.D. 1989, University of Virginia) is an Assistant Professor in the Department of Human Ecology at University of Texas–Austin. He is currently a co–Principal Investigator of an NIMH-funded 6-year follow-up study of prevention efforts for children and families after divorce. His research interests include adjustment to nonnormative life transitions, sibling relationships, family process in remarried families, and longitudinal research methodology.

James H. Bray (Ph.D. 1980, University of Houston) is Director, Family Psychology Programs and Associate Professor in the Department of Family and Community Medicine, Baylor College of Medicine, in Houston, Texas. He has published and presented numerous works in the areas of divorce, remarriage, adolescent alcohol use, intergenerational family relationships, and collaboration between physicians and psychologists. He recently published a book on his research on stepfamilies with John Kelly, *StepFamilies: Love, Marriage, and Parenting in the First Decade* (Broadway Books, 1998). As a family and clinical psychologist he conducts research and teaches resident physicians, medical students, and psychology students. In addition to his research, he also maintains an active clinical practice focusing on children and families. He is active in the governance of the APA: APA Board of Educational Affairs, Past President of the Division of Family Psychology, past Chair of the APA Committee on Rural Health, and APA Primary Care Task Force. He has received numerous awards including election into the National Academies of Practice for Psychology, the Karl F. Heiser APA Presidential Award for Advocacy on Behalf of Professional Psychology, 1994 Psychologist of the Year from the Houston Psychological Association, and the 1992 Federal Advocacy Award from the APA Practice Directorate.

Margaret Bridges (Ph.D. 1998, University of Virginia) is a postdoctoral research fellow at the University of California, San Francisco. Her research interests include examining individual and family process influences on adolescent adjustment and sexuality.

Raymond W. Chan (Ph.D. 1999, University of Virginia) is an Associate Project Manager at National Analysts Marketing Research and Consulting. His research interests are in social and personality development across the life-span and the role of families in shaping development. Of special interest are issues surrounding close relationships, adolescent development, ethnic minority identities, and quantitative methods.

Glendessa Insabella (M.A. 1996, University of Virginia) is a doctoral candidate at the University of Virginia. Her research interests include marital relationships in nondivorced families and stepfamilies and the sexual behavior and romantic relationships of adolescents as studied from a family process perspective.

Kathleen M. Jodl (Ph.D. 1997, University of Virginia) is a postdoctoral research fellow at the University of Michigan. Her research interests include understanding family processes that contribute to adolescents' short- and long-term well-being. She is currently investigating parents' role in shaping early adolescents' educational and occupational aspirations; siblings' differential experiences within families as predictors of their adjustment; and the costs associated with competence and resilience in adolescence.

Jungmeen E. Kim (Ph. D. 1998, University of Virginia) is a postdoctoral associate in the Cornell Employment and Family Careers Institute, Department of Human Development, at Cornell University. Her research interests include life-span developmental research methodology, quantitative methods for studying variability and change, social and personality development, and family and peer relations in adolescents.

Anne S. Mitchell (M.A. 1998, University of Virginia) is a doctoral candidate at the University of Virginia. Her research interests include the influence of sibling relationships on child and adolescent development, and the moderating role of siblings' biological relationship on the associations between sibling relationship quality and child adjustment.

Thomas G. O'Connor (Ph.D. 1995, University of Virginia) is a lecturer in developmental psychology in the Departments of Psychology and Child and Adolescent Psychiatry at the Institute of Psychiatry, University of London. His research interests focus on family systems and family development and incorporate diverse perspectives, including behavioral genetic and attachment theory.

Monica J. Skaggs (M.A. 1996, University of Virginia) is a doctoral candidate at the University of Virginia. Her research interests include the impact of normative and nonnormative life experiences on adolescent adjustment, particularly within the contexts of family and peer relationships.

Lorraine C. Taylor (Ph.D. 1997, University of Virginia) is an Assistant Professor in the Department of Psychology at the University of South Carolina, Columbia. Her research interests include children and families in poverty, welfare reform, families in rural communities, parental and cultural influences on the transition to school, and academic achievement.

STATEMENT OF EDITORIAL POLICY

The *Monographs* series is intended as an outlet for major reports of developmental research that generate authoritative new findings and use these to foster a fresh and/or better-integrated perspective on some conceptually significant issue or controversy. Submissions from programmatic research projects are particularly welcome; these may consist of individually or group-authored reports of findings from some single large-scale investigation or of a sequence of experiments centering on some particular question. Multiauthored sets of independent studies that center on the same underlying question can also be appropriate; a critical requirement in such instances is that the various authors address common issues and that the contribution arising from the set as a whole be both unique and substantial. In essence, irrespective of how it may be framed, any work that contributes significant data and/or extends developmental thinking will be taken under editorial consideration.

Submissions should contain a minimum of 80 manuscript pages (including tables and references); the upper limit of 150–175 pages is much more flexible (please submit four copies; a copy of every submission and associated correspondence is deposited eventually in the archives of the SRCD). Neither membership in the Society for Research in Child Development nor affiliation with the academic discipline of psychology is relevant; the significance of the work in extending developmental theory and in contributing new empirical information is by far the most crucial consideration. Because the aim of the series is not only to advance knowledge on specialized topics but also to enhance cross-fertilization among disciplines or subfields, it is important that the links between the specific issues under study and larger questions relating to developmental processes emerge as clearly to the general reader as to specialists on the given topic.

The corresponding author for any manuscript must, in the submission letter, warrant that all coauthors are in agreement with the content of the manuscript. The corresponding author also is responsible for informing all coauthors, in a timely manner, of manuscript submission, editorial decisions, reviews received, and any revisions recommended. Before publication, the corresponding author also must warrant in the submission letter that the study has been conducted according to the ethical guidelines of the Society for Research in Child Development.

Potential authors who may be unsure whether the manuscript they are planning would make an appropriate submission are invited to draft an outline of what they propose and send it to the Editor for assessment. This mechanism, as well as a more detailed desctiption of all editorial policies, evaluation processes, and format requirements, is given in the "Guidelines for the Preparation of *Monographs* Submissions," which can be obtained by contacting the Editor-Elect, Willis Overton, Department of Psychology, 567 Weiss Hall, Temple University, Philadelphia, PA 19122 [e-mail: overton@vm.temple.edu].